GOA

AND THE

BLUE MOUNTAINS

OR

SIX MONTHS OF SICK LEAVE

GOA
AND THE
BLUE MOUNTAINS
OR
SIX MONTHS OF SICK LEAVE

RICHARD F. BURTON

GYAN

Published by

Gyan Publishing House
5, Ansari Road
Daryaganj, New Delhi-110002
Phone: 011-47034999, 9811692060
E-mail: books@gyanbooks.com

Distribution Network
gyanbooks.com
India, USA, Canada, UK, Australia, France

ISBN: 978-81-212-3439-9 (PB)
First Published, London, 1851

2nd Impression 2020

Printed at: Gyan Press, Delhi.

Goa and the Blue Mountains
Author: Richard F. Burton

S. Burton del.

Printed by Hullmandel & Walton.

VIEW OF OLD GOA FROM THE MANDOVA OR CREEK.

London: Richard Bentley, New Burlington Street 1851

TO

MISS ELIZABETH STISTED,

THIS LITTLE WORK,

WHICH OWES ITS EXISTENCE TO HER

FRIENDLY SUGGESTIONS,

IS DEDICATED,

IN TOKEN OF GRATITUDE AND AFFECTION,

BY

THE AUTHOR.

CONTENTS.

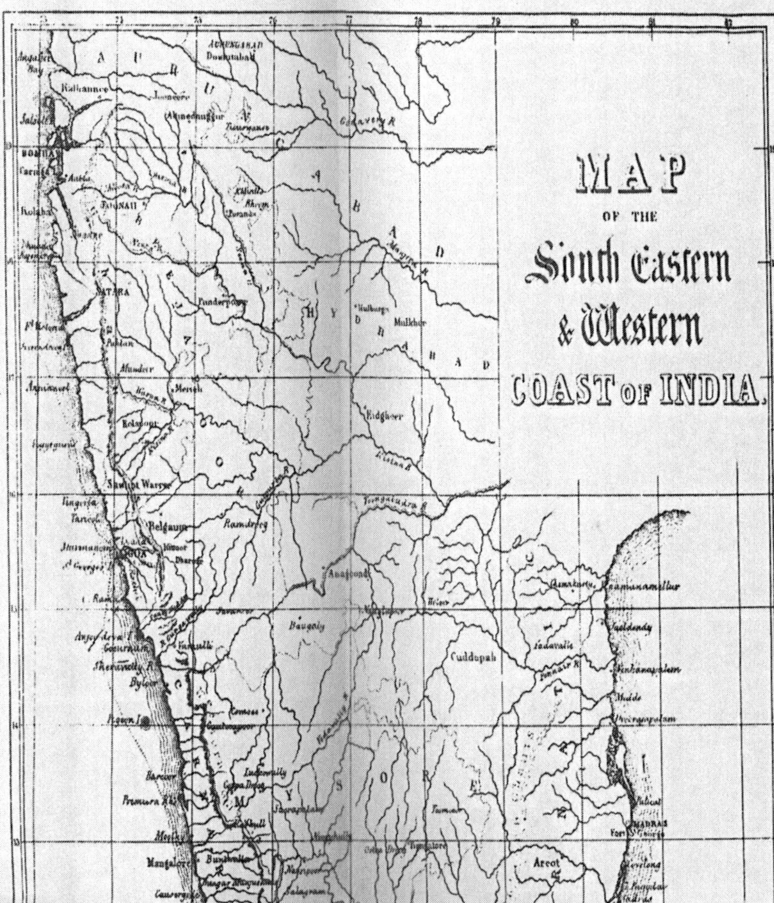

London Richard Bentley New Burlington Street

Printed by Dahmande & Walter

GOA,

AND THE BLUE MOUNTAINS;

OR,

SIX MONTHS OF SICK LEAVE.

CHAPTER I.

THE VOYAGE.

WHAT a glad moment it is, to be sure, when the sick and seedy, the tired and testy invalid from pestiferous Scinde or pestilential Guzerat, "leaves all behind him" and scrambles over the sides of his Pattimar.

His what?

Ah! we forget. The gondola and barque are household words in your English ears, the budgerow is beginning to own an old familiar sound, but you are right—the "Pattimar" requires a definition. Will you be satisfied with a pure landsman's description of the article in question. We have lost ou r edition of "The Ship," and to own humbling truth, though we have spent many a weary month on the world of waters, we never could master the intricacies of blocks and braces, skylights and deadlights, starboards and larboards. But if we are to believe the general voice of the amphibious race, we terrestrial animals never fail to mangle the science of seamanship most barbarously. So we will not expose ourselves by pretension to the animadversions of any small nautical critic, but boldly talk of going "up-stairs" instead of "on deck," and unblushingly allude to the "behind" for the "aft" and the "front" instead of the "fore" of our conveyance.

But the Pattimar—

De suite: you shall pourtray it from our description. Sketch a very long boat, very high behind, and very low before, composed of innumerable bits of wood tied together with coir, or cocoanut rope, fitted up with a dark and musty little cabin, and supplied with two or three long poles intended as masts, which lean forward as if about to sink under the weight of the huge lateen sail. Fill up the outline with a penthouse of cadjans (as the leaves of that eternal cocoanut tree are called) to protect the bit of deck outside the cabin from the rays of a broiling sun. People the square space in the middle of the boat with two nags tethered and tied with halters and heel ropes, which sadly curtail the poor animals' enjoyment of kicking and biting; and half-a-dozen black "tars" engaged in pounding rice, concocting bilious-looking masses of curry, and keeping up a fire of some unknown wood, whose pungent smoke is certain to find its way through the cabin, and to terminate its wanderings in your eyes and nostrils. Finally, throw in about the same number of black domestics courting a watery death by balancing themselves over the sides of the vessel, or a fever by sleeping in a mummy case of dirty cotton cloth—

And you have a pattimar in your mind's eye.

Every one that has ever sailed in a pattimar can oblige you with a long list of pleasures peculiar to it. All know how by day your eyes are blinded with glare and heat, and how by night mosquitos, a trifle smaller than jack snipes, assault your defenceless limbs; how the musk rat defiles your property and provender; how the common rat and the cockchafer appear to relish the terminating leather of your fingers and toes; and, finally, how the impolite animal which the transatlantics delicately designate a "chintz," and its companion, the lesser abomination, do contribute to your general discomfort. Still these are transient evils, at least compared with the permanent satisfaction of having "passed the Medical Board"—a committee of ancient gentlemen who never will think you sufficiently near death to meet your wishes—of having escaped the endless doses of the garrison surgeon, who has probably, for six weeks, been bent upon trying the effects of the whole Materia Medica upon your internal and external man—of enduring the diurnal visitation of desperate duns who threaten the bailiff without remorse; and to crown the climax of your happiness, the delightful prospect of two quiet years, during which you may call life your own, lie in bed half or the whole day if you prefer it, and forget the very existence of such things as pipeclay and parade, the Court Martial and the Commander-in-chief. So if you are human, your heart bounds, and whatever its habits of grumbling may be, your tongue involuntarily owns that it is a joyful moment when you scramble over the side of your pattimar. And now, having convinced you of that fact, we will request you to walk up stairs with us, and sit upon the deck by our side, there to take one parting look at the boasted

Bay of Bombay, before we bid adieu to it, with a free translation of the celebrated Frenchman's good bye, "*Canards, canaux, canaille,*"—adieu ducks, dingies, drabs, and duns.*

Gentlemen tourists, poetical authors, lady prosers, and, generally, all who late in life, visit the "palm tasselled strand of glowing Ind," as one of our European celebrities describes the country in prose run mad, certainly are gifted with wonderful optics for detecting the Sublime and Beautiful. Now this same bay has at divers and sundry times been subjected to much admiration; and as each succeeding traveller must improve upon his predecessors, the latest authorities have assigned to its charms a rank above the Bay of Naples—a bay which, in our humble opinion, places every other bay in a state of abeyance. At least so we understand Captain Von Orlich—the gentleman who concludes that the Belochees are of Jewish origin, *because* they divorce their wives. To extract Bombay from the Bay of Naples, proceed thus. Remove Capri, Procida, Ischia, and the other little pictu-

* "Ducks" are the Bombayites in general: "Dingies" is the name popularly given to the smaller specimens of native craft. The Dun and the Drab are probably familiar to the reader's ears.

resque localities around them. Secondly, level Vesuvius and the rocky heights of St. Angelo with the ground. Thirdly, convert bright Naples, with its rows of white palazzi, its romantic-looking forts, its beautiful promenade, and charming background into a low, black, dirty port, *et voici* the magnificent Bombahia.* You may, it is true, attempt to get up a little romance about the "fairy caves" of Salsette and Elephanta, the tepid seas, the spicy breeze, and the ancient and classical name of Momba-devi.

But you 'll fail.

Remember all we can see is a glowing vault of ultramarine-colour sky, paved with a glaring expanse of indigo-tinted water, with a few low hills lining the horizon, and a great many merchant ships anchored under the guns of what we said before, and now repeat, looks like a low, black, dirty port.

We know that you are taking a trip with us to the land flowing with rupees and gold mohurs—growing an eternal crop of Nabobs and Nawwábs †

* Bombahia, the Portuguese P. N. of the town: it was probably suggested by "Momba-devi," as the place was called by the Hindoos after the patron goddess of the spot.

† The Nabob is the European, the Nawwáb the Asiatic, grandee.

—showing a perpetual scene of beauty, pleasure and excitement.

But we can't allow you to hand your rose-coloured specs. over to us. We have long ago superseded our original "greens" by a pair duly mounted with sober French grey glasses, and through these we look out upon the world as cheerily as our ophthalmic optics will permit us to do.

Now the last "nigger," in a manifest state of full-blown inebriation, has rolled into, and the latest dun, in a fit of diabolical exasperation, has rolled out of, our pattimar. So we will persuade the Tindal, as our Captain is called, to pull up his mud-hook, and apply his crew to the task of inducing the half acre of canvas intended for a sail to assume its proper place. Observe if you please, the Tindal swears by all the skulls of the god Shiva's necklace, that the wind is foul—the tide don't serve—his crew is absent—and the water not yet on board.

Of course!

But as you are a "griff," and we wish to educate you in native peculiarities, just remark how that one small touch of our magic slipper upon the region of the head, and the use of that one little phrase "Suar ka Sala" (*Anglicè*, "O brother-in-law of a hog!) has made the wind fair, the tide serve, the crew muster, and the water pots abound in water. And, furthermore, when you have got over your horror of seeing a "fellow-creature" so treated—and a "fellow subject" subjected to such operation, kindly observe that the Tindal has improved palpably in manner towards us;—indeed, to interpret his thoughts, he now feels convinced that we are an "Assal Sahib"—a real gentleman.

Evening is coming on, the sea-breeze (may it be increased!) is freshening fast, and Dan Phœbus has at last vouchsafed to make himself scarce. After watching his departure with satisfaction—with heartfelt satisfaction, we order our hookah up, less for the pleasure of puffing it, than for the purpose of showing you how our servant delights to wander through heaps of hay and straw, canvas, and coir rope, with that mass of ignited rice ball, rolling about on the top of our pipe. You are looking curiously at our culinary arrangements. Yes, dear sir, or madam, as the case may be, that dreadful looking man, habited in a pair of the dingiest inexpressibles only, excepting the thick cap on his furzy head—that is our cook. And we dare say you have been watching his operations. If not, you must know that he prepared for our repast by inserting his black claw into that hencoop, where a dozen of the leanest possible chickens have been engaged for some time in pecking the polls of one another's heads, and after a rapid examination of breast-bone, withdrew his fist full of one of the aforementioned lean chickens, shrieking in dismay. He then slew it, dipped the corpse in boiling water to loosen the feathers, which he stripped off in masses, cut through its breast longitudinally, and with the aid of an iron plate, placed over a charcoal fire, proceeded to make a spatchcock, or as it is more popularly termed, a "sudden death." After this we can hardly expect the pleasure of your company at dinner to-day. But never mind! you will soon get over the feeling *nolens*, if not *volens*. Why, how many Scinde "Nabobs" have not eaten three hundred and sixty-five lean chickens in one year?

We will not be in any hurry to go to bed. In these latitudes, man lives only between the hours of seven P.M. and midnight. The breeze gives strength to smoke and converse; our languid minds almost feel disposed to admire the beauty of the moonlit sea, the serenity of the air, and the varying tints of the misty coast. Our lateen sail is doing its duty right well, as the splashing of the water and the broad stripe of phosphoric light eddying around and behind the rudder, prove. At this rate we shall make Goa in three days, if kindly fate only spare us the mortification of the morning calms which infest these regions. And we being "old hands" promise to keep a sharp look out upon the sable commander of the "Durrya Prashad" the "Joy of the Ocean," as his sweetheart of a pattimar is called. Something of the kind will be necessary to prevent his creeping along the shore for fear of squalls, or pulling down the sail to ensure an unbroken night's rest, or slackening speed so as not to get the voyage over too soon. As he is a Hindoo we will place him under the *surveillance* of that grim looking bushy-bearded Moslem, who spends half his days in praying for the extermination of the infidel, and never retires to rest without groaning over the degeneracy of the times, and sighing for the good old days of Islam, when the Faithful had nothing to do but to attack, thrash, rob, and murder, the Unfaithful.

Now the last hookah has gone out, and the most restless of our servants has turned in. The roof of the cabin is strewed with bodies anything but fragrant, indeed, we cannot help pitying the melancholy fate of poor Morpheus, who is traditionally supposed to encircle such sleepers with his soft arms. Could you believe it possible that through such a night as this they choose to sleep under those wadded cotton coverlets, and dread not instantaneous asphixiation? The only waker is that grisly old fellow with the long white mustachios flourishing over his copper coloured mouth like cotton in the jaws of a Moslem body. And even he nods as he sits perched at the helm with his half-closed eyes mechanically directed towards the binnacle, and its satire upon the mariner's compass, which has not shifted one degree these last two years. However there is little to fear here. The fellow knows every inch of shore, and can tell you to a foot what depth of water there is beneath us. So as this atmosphere of drowsiness begins to be infectious, we might as well retire below. Not into the cabin, if you please. The last trip the Durrya Prashad made was, we understand, for the purpose of conveying cotton to the Presidency. You may imagine the extent of dark population left to colonise her every corner. We are to sleep under the penthouse, as well as we may; our servants, you observe, have spread the mats of rushes—one of the much vaunted luxuries of the East—upon our humble couches, justly anticipating that we shall have a fair specimen of the night tropical. Before you "tumble in" pray recollect to see that the jars of cold water have been placed within reach, for we are certain to awake as soon after our first sleep as possible, suffering from the torments of Tantalus. And we should advise you to restore the socks you have just removed, that is to say, if you wish the mosquitos to leave you the use of your feet to-morrow.

"Good night!"

The wish is certainly a benevolent one, but it sounds queer as a long grace emphatically prefixed to a "spread" of cold mutton or tough beefsteak, for which nothing under a special miracle could possibly make one "truly thankful." However, good night!

From Bombay southwards as far as Goa, the coast,* viewed from the sea, merits little admira-

* Note for readers geographically disposed.

This region, the Ariake of the Greeks, Kemkem of the Arabs, Kukan of the Hindoos, Concan of the present possessors, and, as Vincent says, "the pirate coast of all," is well adapted for its ancient occupation by a multitude of small ports, uninterrupted view along the coast, high ground favour-

tion. It is an unbroken succession of gentle rises and slopes, and cannot evade the charge of dulness and uniformity. Every now and then some fort or rock juts out into the water breaking the line, but the distance we stand out from land prevents our distinguishing the features of its different

able to distant vision, and the alternate land and sea breezes that oblige vessels to hug the shore. Moreover, the ports, besides being shallow, are defended against large ships by bars; a defect from which even Goa is not exempt, although Tavernier calls it "one of the finest harbours in the world, rivalling those of Toulon and Constantinople." The pirates were protected by the strength of the inland country, and, like the Greeks, had only to lie secure in port until they discovered their prey. During the Monsoon they cultivated the ground, or lived peaceably at home: when the fine weather set in, they launched their boats, and set out in quest of adventure. Pliny notices the depredations they committed on the Roman East India trade, and our early travellers are full of horrible tales about them.

It is curious to observe that the whole line of coast between the mouth of the Euphrates and Cape Comorin, has been infamous for the piratical propensities of the many and various tribes that inhabit it. The Persian Gulf still requires the presence of our armed cruisers; the ancient annals of Scinde enlarge upon its celebrity for robbery; the Coolies of Kutch and Guzerat were known as pirates from Marco Polo's time till A. D. 1800; the Angria territory was a nest of thieves till we destroyed their fleet; and Tavernier testifies that the natives of Malabar were not inferior in enterprise to their northern brethren.

"lions," such as Severndroog "the Golden Fortress," Rutnageree "the Hill of Jewels," and the Burnt Islands,* or Vingorla Rocks. The voyage, therefore, will be an uninteresting one—though at this season of the year, early spring, it will not be tedious.

The ancient Hindoos have a curious tradition concerning the formation and population of this coast. They believe that Parasu Rama, one of their demigods, after filling the earth with the blood of the offending Kshatriya, or regal and military caste, wished to perform an expiatory sacrifice. As, however, no Brahmin would attend, his demigodship found himself in rather an awkward predicament. At length, when sitting on the mountains of Concan (*i.e.* the Sayhadree Range, or Western Ghauts), he espied on the shore below, the putrefied corpses of fourteen Mlenchhas (any people not Hindoos), which had floated there borne by the

* They lie in lat. 15° 52′ 30″, about thirty-five miles from Goa, and seven off the shore, from which they are separated by a deep channel. The group consists of more than twenty small rocks, amongst which are six or seven about as large as the Sirens Isles in the Gulf of Salerno. The Greeks called them Σησεκρειεναι, which Mr. Hamilton understands to signify "black rabbits;" and Vincent supposes them to have been so termed, because in form they may be fancied to resemble those animals crouching.

tides from distant lands to the westward. Rama restored them to life, taught them religious knowledge, and, after converting them into Brahmins, performed his sacrifice. He afterwards, by means of his fiery darts, compelled Samudra, the Indian Neptune, to retire several miles from the foot of the Ghauts, and allotted to his *protegés* the strip of land thus recovered from the sea. From these fourteen men sprang the Kukanastha, or Concanese tribe of Maharattas, and the pious Hindoo still discovers in their lineaments, traces of a corpse-like expression of countenance inherited from their forefathers.

We remarked that it was a glad moment when we entered the pattimar. We will also observe that it was another when our sable Portuguese "butler," as he terms himself, ecstasied by his propinquity to home—sweet home, and forgetting respect and self-possession in an *elan* of patriotism, abruptly directed our vision towards the white-washed farol, or lighthouse, which marks the north side of the entrance to the Goa creek. And now, as we glide rapidly in, we will take a short military *coup d'œil* at the outward defences of the once celebrated Portuguese capital.

The hill, or steep, upon which the farol stands, is crowned with batteries, called the Castello de Agoada, as ships touch there to water. There are other works, *à fleur d'eau,* all round the point. These defences, however, are built of stone, without any embankments of earth, and suggest uncomfortable ideas of splinters. In fact, a few gun-boats would drive any number of men out of them in half an hour. The entrance of the creek is at least two miles broad, and the southern prong, the "Cabo de Convento," is occupied, as its name shows, by a monastery instead of a fort. Moreover, none but a native general would ever think of thrusting an invading force through the jaws of the bay, when it might land with perfect safety and convenience to itself a few miles to the north or south.

"What are we pulling up for?"

The Tindal informs us that we may expect a visit from the "Portingal Captain," who commands the Castello, for the purpose of ascertaining our rank, our wealth, and our object in visiting Goa. He warns us to conceal our sketch-book, and not to write too much; otherwise, that our ardour for science may lead us into trouble. But, mind, we laugh him to scorn; natives must have something mysterious to suspect, or expect, or affect.

But here comes the officer, after keeping us waiting a good hour. He is a rhubarb-coloured man, dressed in the shabby remains of a flashy uniform; his square inch of blackish brown mustachio, and expression of countenance, produce an appearance which we should pronounce decidedly valiant, did we not know that valour here seldom extends below or beyond the countenance. How respectfully our butler bows to him, and with what fellow-feeling the same valuable domestic grasps the hand of that orderly in shell jacket, but not in pantaloons, who composes the guard of his superior officer! Behold! he has a bundle of *cigarettos*, made of the blackest tobacco, rolled up in bits of plantain leaf; and he carries his "weeds" in a very primitive cigar-case, namely, the pouch formed by the junction of his huge flap of an ear, with the flat and stubby poll behind it. As the favourite narcotic goes round, no Portuguese refuses it. The Hindoos shake their heads politely and decliningly, the Moslems grimly and with a suspicion of a curse.

But we must summon our domestic to mediate between us and our visitor, who speaks nothing but most Maharatta-like Portuguese and Portuguese-like Maharatta.

We begin by offering him a glass of wine, and he inquires of Salvador, our acting interpreter, —"Why?" Being assured that such is the practice among the barbarous Anglo-Indians, he accepts it with a helpless look, and never attempts to conceal the contortions of countenance produced by the operation of a glass of Parsee sherry, fiery as their own divinity, upon a palate accustomed to tree-toddy and thin red wine. However, he appears perfectly satisfied with the inspection, and after volunteering an introductory epistle to one Ioaõ Thomas—*i.e.* John Thomas, a cicerone of Goanese celebrity—which we accept without the slightest intention of delivering, he kindly gives us permission to proceed, shakes our hand with a cold and clammy palm, which feels uncommonly like a snake, and with many polite bows to our servants, disappears over the side, followed by his suite. Whilst the anchor is being re-weighed, before we forget the appearance of the pair, we will commit them to the custody of the sketch-book.

The old lateen creeps creaking crankily up the

mast once more, and the Durrya Prashad recommences to perambulate the waters as unlike a thing of life as can be imagined. Half an hour more will take us in. Perched upon the topmast angle of our penthouse, we strain our eyes in search of the tall buildings and crowded ways that denote a capital: we can see nought but a forest of lanky cocoa-nut trees, whose stems are apparently growing out of a multitude of small hovels.

Can this be Goa?

Rendered rabid by the query our patriotic domestic, sneering as much as he safely can, informs us that *this* is the village of Verim, *that* St. Agnes, and proceeds to display his store of topographical lore by naming or christening every dirty little mass of hut and white-washed spire that meets the eye.

Bus, Bus,—enough in the name of topography! We will admire the view to-morrow morning when our minds are a little easier about John Thomas, a house, &c.

We turn the last corner which concealed from view the town of Panjim, or as others call it, the city of New Goa, and are at last satisfied that we are coming to something like a place. Suddenly the Tindal, and all his men, begin to chatter like a wilderness of provoked baboons; they are debating as to what part of the narrow creek which runs parallel with the town should be selected for anchor ground. Not with an eye to our comfort in landing, observe, but solely bearing in mind that they are to take in cargo to-morrow.

At length our apology for an anchor once more slides down the old side of the Durrya Prashad, and she swings lazily round with the ebb tide, like an elephant indulging in a solitary roll. It is dark, we can see nothing but a broken line of dim oil-lamps upon the quay, and hear nought save the unharmonious confusion of native music with native confabulation. Besides the wind that pours down the creek feels damp and chilly, teeming with unpleasant reminiscences of fever and ague. So after warning our domestics, that instant dismissal from the service will follow any attempt to land to-night, a necessary precaution if we wish to land to-morrow, we retire to pass the last of three long nights in slapping our face in the desperate hope of crushing mosquitos, dreaming of De Gama and Albuquerque, starting up every two hours with jaws glowing like those of a dark age dragon, scratching our legs and feet, preferring positive excoriation to the exquisite titillation produced by the perpetual perambulation, and occasional morsication (with many other -ations left to the reader's discrimination) of our nocturnal visitations, and in uttering emphatic ejaculations concerning the man with the rhinoceros hide and front of brass who invented and recommended to his kind the pattimar abomination.

CHAPTER II.

NEW GOA.

Early in the morning, rudely roused by curiosity, we went on deck to inspect the celebrated view of the Rio de Goa.

The air was soft and fragrant, at the same time sufficiently cool to be comfortable. A thin mist rested upon the lower grounds and hovered half way up the hills, leaving their palm-clad summits clear to catch the silvery light of dawn. Most beautiful was the hazy tone of colour all around contrasted with the painfully vivid tints, and the sharp outlines of an Indian view seen a few hours after sunrise. The uniformity of the cocoa-nut groves, which at first glance appeared monotonous, gradually became tolerable. We could now remark that they were full of human habitations, and intersected by numbers of diminutive creeks. Close by lay Panji Panjim, Panjem or New Goa, with its large palace and little houses, still dark in the shadow of the hill behind it. As for Goa Velha (the Old Goa) we scarcely ventured to look towards it, such were our recollections of Tavernier, Dillon, and Amine Vanderdecken, and so strong our conviction that a day at least must elapse before we could tread its classic ground. An occasional peep, however, discovered huge masses of masonry—some standing out from the cloudless sky, others lining the edge of the creek,—ruins of very picturesque form, and churches of most unpicturesque hue.

Precisely at six A.M. appeared Mr. John Thomas, whose aristocratic proper name, by the by, is the Señor Ioaõ Thomas de Sonza. After perpetrating a variety of congees in a style that admirably combined the Moorish salaam with the European bow, he informed us in execrable English that "he show de Goa to de Bombay gentlemens." We rapidly pass over the preliminary measures of securing a house with six rooms, kitchen, stable and back court, for fourteen shillings *per mensem*—a low rate of rent for which the owner was soundly rated by his compatriots, who have resolved that treble that sum is the minimum chargeable to Englishmen—of landing our bag and baggage, which were afterwards carried to our abode by coolies*—the primitive style of transportation universally used here, —and finally of disembarking our steeds by means of a pigmy crane, the manipulation of which called together a herd of admiring gazers.

Then the Señor began to take command. He obligingly allowed us to breakfast, but insisted upon our addressing a note to the aide-de-camp in waiting to ascertain the proper time for waiting upon his Excellency the Governor of Goa. This the Señor warned us was *de rigueur*, and he bade us be prepared to face the burning sun between eleven and twelve, such being the hour usually appointed. Then with our missive between his sable fingers he performed another ceremonious bow and departed for a while.

Just as the Señor disappeared, and we were preparing to indulge in our morning meal *en deshabille*, as best suits the climate, an uncomely face, grinning prodigiously, and surmounted by a scampish looking cap, introduced itself through the open window, and commenced a series of felicitations and compliments in high-flown Portuguese.

Who might our visitor be? A medical student, a poet, or a thief? Confused in mind, we could

* Porters and labourers.

only look at him vacantly, with an occasional involuntary movement of the head, respondent to some gigantic word, as it gurgled convulsively out of his throat. He must have mistaken the sign for one of invitation, for, at the close of his last compliment to the British nation, he withdrew his head from the window, and deliberately walked in by the door, with the usual series of polite bows.

Once in the house, he seemed determined to make himself at home.

We looked up from our breakfast with much astonishment. Close to our elbow stood our new friend in the form of a tall ugly boy about seventeen, habited in a green cloth surtout, with plaited plaid unmentionables, broad-toed boots, and a peculiar appearance about the wrists, and intervals between the fingers, which made us shudder at the thought of extending to him the hand of fellowship. Rapidly deciding upon a plan of action, we assumed ignorance of the *lingoa Baxa*,* and pronounced with much ceremony in our vernacular,

"Whom have I the honour to address?"

Horror of horrors! Our visitor broke out in disjointed English, informed us that his name was

* The Portuguese tongue.

the Señor Gaetano de Gama, son of the collector of Ribandar, and a lineal descendant from the Gran Capitaõ; that he had naturally a great admiration for the British, together with much compassion for friendless strangers; and finally, that he might be of the utmost use to us during our stay at Goa. Thereupon he sat down, and proceeded to make himself comfortable. He pulled a cigar out of our box, called for a glass of water, but preferred sherry, ate at least a dozen plantains, and washed down the sherry with a coffee-cup full of milk. We began to be amused.

"Have you breakfasted?"

Yes, he had. At Goa they generally do so betimes. However, for the sake of companionship he would lay down his cigar and join us. He was certainly a good trencher-companion, that young gentleman. Witness his prowess upon a plate of fish, a dish of curry, a curd cheese, a water melon, and half-a-dozen cups of *café au lait*. Then after settling the heterogeneous mass with a glass of our *anisette*, he re-applied himself to his cheroot.

We were in hopes that he had fallen into a state of torpor. By no means! The activity of his mind soon mastered the inertness of the flesh. Before the first few puffs had disappeared in the thin air, our friend arose, distinctly for the purpose of surveying the room. He walked slowly and calmly around it, varying that recreation by occasionally looking into our bed, inspecting a box or two, opening our books, addressing a few chance words to us, generally in the style interrogative, trying on our hat before the looking-glass, defiling our brushes and combs with his limp locks, redolent of rancid cocoa-nut oil, and glancing with fearful meaning at our tooth-brushes.

Our amusement now began to assume the form of indignation. Would it be better to disappear into an inner room, send for Salvador to show our *bête noire* the door, or lead him out by the ear? Whilst still deliberating, we observed with pleasure the tawny face of John Thomas.

The Señor Ioaõ Thomas de Sonza no sooner caught sight of the Señor Gaetano de Gama than his countenance donned an expression of high indignation, dashed with profound contempt; and the latter Señor almost simultaneously betrayed outward and visible signs of disappointment and considerable confusion. The ridiculous scene ended with the disappearance of the unsuccessful aspirant to ciceronic honours, a homily from John Thomas upon the danger of having anything to do with such rabble, and an injunction to Salvador never to admit the collector's son again.

"His Excellency the Governor General of all the Indies cannot have the exalted honour of receiving your Excellency this morning, on account of the sudden illness of Her Excellency the Lady of the Governor General of all the Indies; but the Governor General of all the Indies will be proud to receive your Excellency to-morrow—if Heaven be pleased!" said John Thomas, tempering dignity with piety.

Thank Goodness for the reprieve!

"So, if the measure be honoured with your Excellency's approval, we will now embark in a covered canoe, and your servant will have the felicity of pointing out from the sea the remarkable sites and buildings of New Goa; after which, a walk through our celebrated city will introduce your Excellency to the exteriors and interiors of its majestic edifices, its churches, its theatre, its hospital, its library, and its barracks."

Very well!

A few minutes' rowing sufficed to bring our canoe to the centre of the creek, along side and in full view of the town. Around us lay the shipping, consisting of two or three vessels from Portugal and

China, some score of native craft, such as pattimars, cottias, canoes, and bunderboats, with one sloop of war, composing the Goanese navy.

Panjim is situated upon a narrow ledge, between a hill to the south, and, on the north, the Rio de Goa, or arm of the sea, which stretches several miles from west to east. A quay of hewn stone, well built, but rather too narrow for ornament or use, lines the south bank of the stream, if we may so call it, which hereabouts is a little more than a quarter of a mile in breadth. The appearance of the town is strange to the Indian tourist. There are many respectable-looking houses, usually one story high, solidly constructed of stone and mortar, with roofs of red tile, and surrounded by large court-yards overgrown with cocoa-nut trees. Bungalows are at a discount; only the habitations of the poor consist solely of a ground floor. In general the walls are whitewashed,—an operation performed regularly once a year, after the Monsoon rains; and the result is a most offensive glare. Upon the eminence behind the town is a small telegraph, and half-way down the hill, the Igreja (church) de Conceicaô, a plain and ill-built pile, as usual, beautifully situated. The edifices along the creek which catch the eye, are the Palacio, where the Governor resides, the Archbishop's Palace, the Contadorin or Accomptant's Office, and the Alfandega or Custom House. All of them are more remarkable for vastness than neatness of design.

"We will now row down the creek, and see the Aldeas or villages of St. Agnes and Verim," quoth our guide, pointing towards a scattered line of churches, villas, and cottages, half concealed from view by the towering trees, or thrown forward in clear relief by the green background.

To hear was to obey: though we anticipated little novelty. On landing we were surprised to find the shore so thickly inhabited. Handsome residences, orientally speaking, appeared here and there; a perfect network of footpaths ramified over the hills; in a word, every yard of ground bore traces of life and activity. Not that there was much to be seen at St. Agnes, with its huge, rambling old pile, formerly the archiepiscopal palace, or at Verim, a large village full of Hindoos, who retreat there to avoid the places selected for residence by the retired officers, *employés* of government, students, and Christian landed proprietors.

"And now for a trip to the eastward!"

"What!" we exclaimed, "is n't the lionizing to stop here?"

"By no means," replied John Thomas, solemnly; "all English gentlemen visit Ribandar, Britona, and the Seminary of Chorão."

Ribandar is about two miles to the east of Panjim, and is connected with it by a long stone bridge, built by the viceroy Miguel de Noronha. It seems to be thriving upon the ruins of its neighbour, San Pedro or Panelly, an old village, laid waste by the devastator of Velha Goa—intermittent fever. From some distance we saw the noble palace, anciently inhabited by the archbishops, and the seat of the viceroys and governors, called the Casa de Polvora, from a neighbouring manufactory of gunpowder. Here, however, we became restive, and no persuasion could induce us to walk a mile in order to inspect the bare walls.

Being somewhat in dread of Britona, which appeared to be a second edition of St. Agnes and Verim, we compounded with John Thomas, and secured an exemption by consenting to visit and inspect the Seminary.

Chorão was formerly the noviciate place of the Jesuits.* It is an island opposite Ribandar, small

* Their other great clerical establishment being the Seminary

and thinly populated, the climate being confessedly most unwholesome. We were informed that the director was sick and the rector suffering from fever. The pallid complexion of the resident pupils told a sad tale of malaria.

The building is an immense mass of chapels, cloisters, and apartments for the professors and students. There is little of the remarkable in it. The walls are ornamented with abominable frescoes and a few prints, illustrating the campaigns of Napoleon and Louis Quatorze. The crucifixes appear almost shocking. They are, generally speaking, wooden figures as large as life, painted with most livid and unnatural complexions, streaked with indigo-coloured veins, and striped with streams of blood. More offensive still are the representations of the Almighty, so common in Roman Catholic countries.

In the sacristy, we were shown some tolerable heads of apostles and saints. They were not exactly original Raphaels and Guidos, as our black friends declared, but still it was a pleasure to see

at Rachol, a town which, when the Portuguese first came to India, was the capital of the province of Salsette. In Tavernier's time the Jesuits had no less than five religious houses at Goa.

good copies of excellent exemplars in India, the land of coloured prints and lithographs of Cerito and Taglioni.

Ah! now we have finished our peregrinations.

"Yes," responded John Thomas; "your Excellency has now only to walk about and inspect the town of Panjim."

Accordingly we landed and proceeded to make our observations there.

That Panjim is a Christian town appears instantly from the multitude and variety of the filthy feeding hogs, that infest the streets. The pig here occupies the social position that he does in Ireland, only he is never eaten when his sucking days are past. Panjim loses much by close inspection. The streets are dusty and dirty, of a most disagreeable brick colour, and where they are paved, the pavement is old and bad. The doors and window-frames of almost all the houses are painted green, and none but the very richest admit light through anything more civilized than oyster-shells. The balcony is a prominent feature, but it presents none of the gay scenes for which it is famous in Italy and Spain.

We could not help remarking the want of horses and carriages in the streets, and were informed that the whole place did not contain more than half a dozen vehicles. The popular conveyance is a kind of palanquin, composed of a light sofa, curtained with green wax cloth, and strung to a bamboo pole, which rests upon the two bearers' heads or shoulders. This is called a *mancheel,* and a most lugubrious-looking thing it is, forcibly reminding one of a coffin covered with a green pall.

At length we arrived at the Barracks, a large building in the form of an irregular square, fronting the Rio, and our British curiosity being roused by hearing that the celebrated old thief, Phonde Sawunt,* was living there under surveillance, we determined to visit that rebel on a small scale. His presence disgraces his fame ; it is that of a wee, ugly, grey, thin, old and purblind Maharatta. He received us, however, with not a little dignity and independence of manner, motioned us to sit down with a military air, and entered upon a series of queries concerning the Court of Lahore, at that time the only power on whose exertions the agitators of India could base any hopes. Around the feeble, decrepit old man stood about a dozen stalworth sons, with naked shoulders, white cloths round their waists and topknots of hair, which

* He raised the standard of revolt against the Indian government spiritedly but unsuccessfully.

the god Shiva himself might own with pride. They have private apartments in the barracks, full of wives and children, and consider themselves personages of no small importance ; in which opinion they are, we believe, by no means singular. Their fellow-countrymen look upon them as heroes, and have embalmed, or attempted to embalm their breakjaw names in immortal song. They are, in fact, negro Robin Hoods and Dick Turpins—knights of the road and the waste it is true, but not accounted the less honourable for belonging to that celebrated order of chivalry. The real Maharatta is by nature a thorough-bred plunderer, and well entitled to sing the Suliot ditty—

"Κλεφτες ποτε Παργαν,"*

with the slight variation of locality only. Besides, strange to say, amongst Orientals, they have a well-defined idea of what patriotism means, and can groan under the real or fancied wrongs of the "stranger" or the "Sassenach's" dominion as loudly and lustily as any Hibernian or Gael in the land.

We now leave Phonde Sawunt and the Barracks to thread our way through a numerous and disagreeable collection of yelping curs and officious boatmen.

* "All thieves at Parga."

"Would your Excellency prefer to visit the hospital, the churches of St. Sebastian and Conceiçaõ, the jail, the library, the printing-house, and the bazaars now or to-morrow morning?"

"Neither now nor ever—thank you—we are going to the promenade."

After a few minutes' walk we came to the west end of Panjim, where lies a narrow scrap of sea-beach appropriated to "constitutionals." On our way there we observed that the Goanese, with peculiar good taste, had erected seats wherever a pretty *point de vue* would be likely to make one stand and wish to sit awhile.

Had we expected a crowded *corso*, we should have been disappointed; half-a-dozen mancheels, two native officers on horseback, one carriage, and about a dozen promenaders, were moving lazily and listlessly down the lugubrious-looking strand.

Reader, has it ever been your unhappy fate to be cooped up in a wretched place called Pisa? If so, perhaps you recollect a certain drive to the Cascine—a long road, down whose dreary length run two parallel rows of dismal poplars, desolating to the eye, like mutes at a funeral. We mentally compared the Cascine drive and the Panjim corso, and the result of the comparison was, that we wished a very good evening to the Señor, and went home.

"Salvador, what is that terrible noise—are they slaughtering a pig—or murdering a boy?"

"Nothing," replied Salvador, "nothing whatever—some Christian beating his wife."

"Is that a common recreation?"

"Very."

So we found out to our cost. First one gentleman chastised his spouse, then another, and then another. To judge by the ear, the fair ones did not receive the discipline with that patience, submission, and long-suffering which Eastern dames are most apocryphally believed to practise. In fact, if the truth must be told, a prodigious scuffling informed us that the game was being played with similar good will, and nearly equal vigour by both parties. The police at Goa never interfere with these little domesticalities; the residents, we suppose, lose the habit of hearing them, but the stranger finds them disagreeable. Therefore, we should strongly advise all future visitors to select some place of residence where they may escape the martial sounds that accompany such *tours de force* when displayed by the lords and ladies of the creation. On one occasion we were obliged to change our lodgings for others less exposed to the nuisance. Conceive inhabiting a snug corner of a locality devoted to the conversion of pig into pork!

"Sahib," exclaimed Salvador, "you had better go to bed, or retire into another room, for I see the Señor Gaetano coming here as fast as his legs can carry him."

"Very well," we whispered, slipping rapidly through the open door, "tell him we are out." And behind the wall we heard the message duly delivered.

But the Señor saw no reason in our being out why he should not make himself at home. He drew two chairs into the verandah, called for cigars and sherry, fanned himself with his dirty brown cotton pocket-handkerchief, and sat there patiently awaiting our return.

We did not forcibly eject that Señor. The fact is, memory began to be busily at work, and dim scenes of past times, happy days spent in our dear old distant native land were floating and flashing before our mental eye. Again we saw our neat little rooms at —— College, Oxford, our omnipresent dun, Mr. Joye—what a name for a tailor!—comfortably ensconsed in the best arm-chair, with the best of our regalias in his mouth, and the best of our Port wine at his elbow, now warming his lean hands before the blazing coal fire—it was very near Christmas—now dreamily gazing at the ceiling, as if £ *s. d.* were likely to drop through its plaster.

And where were we?

Echo cannot answer, so we must.

Standing in the coal-hole—an aperture in the wall of our bedchamber—whence seated upon a mass of coke, we could distinctly discern through the interstices of the door, Mr. Joye enjoying himself as above described.

Years of toil and travel and trouble had invested that coal-hole with the roseate hue which loves to linger over old faces and old past times; so we went quietly to bed, sacrificing at the shrine of Mnemosyne the sherry and the cheroots served to us, and the kick-out deserved by the Señor Gaetano de Gama, son of the Collector of Ribandar, and a lineal descendent of the Gran Capitaõ.

CHAPTER III.

OLD GOA AS IT WAS.

"SEÑOR," said our cicerone, entering unannounced, at about ten A. M., "it is time for your Excellency to prepare for an interview with his Excellency the Governor-General of all the Indies; and if it meet with your approbation, we can see the library, and the celebrated statue of Alfonso de Albuquerque on our way to the palacio."

The horses were soon saddled, and the Señor was with some difficulty persuaded to mount. *En route* his appearance afforded no small amusement to his fellow townsmen, who grinned from ear to ear seeing him clinging to the saddle, and holding on by the bridle, with his back hunched, and his shoulders towering above his ears like those of an excited cat. The little Maharatta "man-eater"* was dancing

* The name given to that breed of ponies on account of their extraordinary viciousness.

with disgust at this peculiar style of equitation, and the vivacity of his movements so terrified the Señor, that, to our extreme regret, he chose the first moment to dismount under pretext of introducing us to Albuquerque.

The statue of that hero stands under a white-washed dome, in a small square opposite the east front of the Barracks. It is now wrapped up in matting, having lately received such injuries that it was deemed advisable to send to Portugal for a new nose and other requisites.

The library disappointed us. We had heard that it contained many volumes collected from the different religious houses by order of the government, and thus saved from mildew and the white ants. Of course, we expected a variety of MSS. and publications upon the subject of Oriental languages and history, as connected with the Portuguese settlements. The catalogue, however, soon informed us that it was a mere ecclesiastical library, dotted here and there with the common classical authors; a few old books of travels; some volumes of history, and a number of musty disquisitions on ethics, politics, and metaphysics. We could find only three Oriental works—a Syriac book printed at Oxford, a manuscript Dictionary, and a Grammar of the Concanee dialect of Maharatta.

Arrived at the palace, we sent in our card, and were desired to walk up. We were politely received by an aide-de-camp, who, after ascertaining that we could speak a few words of Portuguese, left the room to inform the Governor of that prodigious fact, which, doubtless, procured us the honour of an interview with that exalted personage. It did not last long enough to be tedious, still we were not sorry when his Excellency retired with the excuse of public business, and directed the aide-de-camp to show us about the building. There was not much to be seen in it, except a tolerably extensive library, a private chapel, and a suite of lofty and spacious saloons, with enormous windows, and without furniture; containing the portraits of all the Governors and Viceroys of Portuguese India. The collection is, or rather has been, a valuable one; unfortunately some Goth, by the order of some worse than Goth, has renewed and revived many of the best and oldest pictures, till they have assumed a most ludricrous appearance. The handsome and chivalrous-looking knights have been taught to resemble the Saracen's Head, the Marquis of Granby, and other sign-post celebrities in England. An artist is, however, it is said, coming from Portugal, and much scraping and varnishing may do something for the De Gamas and de Castros at present so miserably disfigured.

And now, thank Goodness, all our troubles are over. We can start as soon as we like for the "ruin and the waste," merely delaying to secure a covered boat, victual it for a few days, and lay in a store of jars of fresh water—a necessary precaution against ague and malaria. Salvador is to accompany us, and John Thomas has volunteered to procure us a comfortable lodging in the Aljube, or ecclesiastical prison.

A couple of hours' steady rowing will land us at old Goa. As there is nothing to be said about the banks which are lined with the eternal succession of villages, palaces, villas, houses, cottages, gardens, and cocoa-nut trees; instead of lingering upon the uninteresting details, we will pass the time in drawing out a short historical sketch of the hapless city's fortunes.

It is not, we believe, generally known that there are two old Goas. Ancient old Goa stood on the south coast of the island, about two miles from its more modern namesake. Ferishteh, and the other Moslem annalists of India allude to it as a great and celebrated seaport in the olden time. It was governed by its own Rajah, who held it in fief from the Princes of Beejanugger and the Carnatic. In the fifteenth century it was taken by the Moslem monarchs of the Bahmani line. Even before the arrival of the Portuguese in India the inhabitants began to desert their old seaport and migrate to the second Goa. Of the ancient Hindoo town no traces now remain, except some wretched hovels clustering round a parish church. Desolation and oblivion seem to have claimed all but the name of the place, and none but the readers of musty annals and worm-eaten histories are aware that such a city ever existed.

The modern old Goa was built about nineteen years before the arrival of Vasco de Gama at Calicut, an event fixed by the historian, Faria, on 20th of May, 1498. It was taken from the Moors or Moslems by Albuquerque, about thirty years after its foundation—a length of time amply sufficient to make it a place of importance, considering the mushroom-like rapidity with which empires and their capitals shoot up in the East. Governed by a succession of viceroys, many of them the bravest and wisest of the Portuguese nation, Goa soon rose to a height of power, wealth, and magnificence almost incredible. But the introduction of the Jesuits, the Holy Tribunal, and its fatal offspring, religious persecution; pestilence, and wars with European and native powers, disturbances arising from an unsettled home government, and, above all things, the slow but sure workings of the short-sighted policy of the Portuguese in intermarrying and identifying themselves with Hindoos of the lowest castes, made her fall as rapid as her rise was sudden and prodigious. In less than a century and a half after De Gama landed on the shore of India, the splendour of Goa had departed for ever. Presently the climate changed in that unaccountable manner often witnessed in hot and tropical countries. Every one fled from the deadly fever that raged within the devoted precincts, and the villages around began to thrive upon the decay of the capital. At last, in 1758, the viceroy, a namesake of Albuquerque, transferred his habitual residence to Panjim. Soon afterwards the Jesuits were expelled, and their magnificent convents and churches were left all but utterly deserted. The Inquisition * was suppressed when the Portuguese court

* At that time, however, this horrible instrument of religious tyranny seems to have lost much of its original activity.

was at Rio Janeiro, at the recommendation of the British Government—one of those good deeds with which our native land atones for a multitude of minor sins.

The descriptions of Goa in her palmy days are, thanks to the many travellers that visited the land, peculiarly graphic and ample.

First in the list, by seniority, stands Linschoten, a native of Haarlem, who travelled to the capital of Portuguese India about 1583, in company with the Archbishop Fre Vincent de Fonçega. After many years spent in the East, he returned to his native country, and published his travels, written in old French. The book is replete with curious information. Linschoten's account of the riches and splendour of Goa would be judged exaggerated, were they not testified to by a host of other travellers. It is described as the finest, largest, and most magnificent city in India: its villas almost merited the title of palaces, and seemed to be built for the purpose of displaying the wealth and magnificence of the erectors. It is said that during the prosperous times of the

When the dungeons were thrown open there was not a single prisoner within the walls, and Mons. de Kleguen asserts that no one then living remembered having seen an Auto da Fé.

Portuguese in India, you could not have seen a bit of "iron in any merchant's house, but all gold and silver." They coined an immense quantity of the precious metals, and used to make pieces of workmanship in them for exportation. They were a nation of traders, and the very soldiers enriched themselves by commerce. After nine years' service, all those that came from Portugal were entitled to some command, either by land or sea; they frequently, however, rejected government employ on account of being engaged in the more lucrative pursuit of trade. The viceroyalty of Goa was one of the most splendid appointments in the world. There were five other governments, namely — Mozambique, Malacca, Ormus, Muscat, and Ceylon, the worst of which was worth ten thousand crowns (about two thousand pounds) per annum — an enormous sum in those days.

The celebrated Monsieur Tavernier, Baron of Aubonne, visited Goa twice; first in 1641, the second time seven years afterwards. In his day the city was declining rapidly,* and even during

* About the end of the sixteenth century the Dutch sent ships round the Cape, and soon managed to secure the best part of the Eastern trade, formerly monopolized by the Portuguese.

the short period that elapsed between his two voyages, he remarked that many whom he had known as people of fashion, with above two thousand crowns revenue, were reduced to visiting him privately in the evening, and begging for alms. Still, he observed, "they abated nothing, for all that, of their inherent pride and haughtiness." He pays no compliment to the Portuguese character: "They are the most revengeful persons, and the most jealous of their wives in the world, and where the least suspicion creeps into their saddles, they rid themselves of them either by poison or dagger." The baron had no cause for complaint in his reception at Goa by the viceroy, Don Philip de Mascaregnas, who "made him very welcome, and esteeming much a pistol, curiously inlaid," which the traveller presented to him, sent for him five or six times to the Powder-house, or old palace. That viceroy seems, however, to have been a dangerous host. He was a most expert poisoner, and had used his skill most diligently, ridding himself of many enemies, when governor of Ceylon. At Goa he used to admit no one to his table—even his own family was excluded. He was the richest Portuguese noble that ever left the East, especially in diamonds, of which he had a large parcel containing none but stones between ten and forty carats weight. The Goanese hated him, hung him in effigy before his departure, and when he died on the voyage, reported that he had been poisoned in the ship—a judgment from Heaven.

Monsieur Tavernier visited the Inquisition, where he was received with sundry "searching questions" concerning his faith, the Protestant. During the interview, the Inquisitor "told him that he was welcome, calling out at the same time, for some other persons to enter. Thereupon, the hangings being held up, came in ten or twelve persons out of a room hard by." They were assured that the traveller possessed no prohibited books; the prudent Tavernier had left even his Bible behind him. The Inquisidor Mor * discoursed with him for a couple of hours, principally upon the subject of his wanderings, and, three days afterwards, sent him a polite invitation to dinner.

But a well-known practice of the Holy Tribunal—namely, that of confiscating the gold, silver, and jewels of every prisoner, to defray the expenses of the process—had probably directed the Inquisitor's attention to so rich a traveller as the baron was. Tavernier had, after all, rather a narrow escape from

* The Grand Inquisitor.

the Holy Office, in spite of its civilities. When about to leave Goa, he imprudently requested and obtained from the Viceroy, permission to take with him one Mons. de Belloy, a countryman in distress. This individual had deserted from the Dutch to the Portuguese, and was kindly received by them. At Macao, however, he lost his temper at play, and "cursed the portraiture of some Papistical saint, as the cause of his ill-luck." For this impiety he was forthwith sent by the Provincial Inquisitor to Goa, but he escaped the stake by private interest with the Viceroy,* and was punished only by "wearing old clothes, which were all to tatters and full of vermin." When Tavernier and his friend set sail, the latter "became very violent, and swore against the Inquisition like a madman." That such procedure was a dangerous one was proved by Mons. de Belloy's fate. He was rash enough to return some months afterwards to Goa, where he remained two years in the dungeons of the Holy Office, "from which he was not discharged but with a sulphured

* The Holy Office had power over all but the Viceroy and Archbishop, and they did not dare openly to interpose in behalf of any prisoner, under pain of being reported to the Inquisitor and his Council in Portugal, and being recalled. Even the Papal threats were disregarded by that dread tribunal.

shirt, and a St. Andrew's cross upon his stomach." The unfortunate man was eventually taken prisoner by the enraged "Hollanders," put into a sack, and thrown into the sea, as a punishment for desertion.

About twenty-five years after Tavernier's departure, Dellon, the French physician, who made himself conspicuous by his "Relation de l'Inquisition de Goa," visited the city. By his own account, he appears to have excited the two passions which burn fiercest in the Portuguese bosom—jealousy and bigotry. When at Daman, his "innocent visits" to a lady, who was loved by Manuel de Mendonça, the Governor, and a black priest, who was secretary to the Inquisition, secured for him a pair of powerful enemies. Being, moreover, an amateur of Scholastic Theology, a willing disputer with heretics and schismatics, a student of the Old as well as the New Testament, and perhaps a little dogmatical, as dilettanti divines generally are, he presently found himself *brouillé* at the same place with a Dominican friar. The Frenchman had refused to kiss the figure of the Virgin, painted upon the lids of the alms boxes: he had denied certain effects of the baptism, called "flaminis," protested against the adoration of images, and finally capped the whole by declaring that the decrees of the

Holy Tribunal are not so infallible as those of the Divine Author of Christianity. The horror-struck auditor instantly denounced him with a variety of additions and emendations sufficient to make his case very likely to conclude with strangling and burning.

Perceiving a storm impending over him, our physician waited upon the Commissary of the Inquisition, if possible to avert the now imminent danger. That gentlemanly old person seems to have received him with uncommon urbanity, benevolently offered much good advice, and lodged him in jail with all possible expedition.

The prison at Daman is described as a most horrible place; hot, damp, fetid, dark, and crowded. The inmates were half starved, and so miserable that forty out of fifty Malabar pirates, who had been imprisoned there, preferred strangling themselves with their turbans to enduring the tortures of such an earthly Hades.

The first specimen of *savoir faire* displayed by the Doctor's enemies was to detain him in the Daman jail till the triennial Auto da Fé at Goa had taken place; thereby causing for him at least two years' delay and imprisonment in the capital before he could be brought to trial. Having succeeded in this they sent him heavily ironed on board a boat which finally deposited him in the Casa Santa.* There he was taken before the Mesa, or Board, stripped of all his property, and put into the *chambrette* destined for his reception.

Three weary years spent in that dungeon gave Dellon ample time to experience and reflect upon the consequences of amativeness and disputativeness. After being thrice examined by the grand Inquisitor, and persuaded to confess his sins by the false promise of liberty held out to him, driven to despair by the system of solitary imprisonment, by the cries of those who were being tortured, and by anticipations of the noose and the faggot, he made three attempts to commit suicide. During the early part of his convalescence he was allowed the luxury of a negro fellow-prisoner in his cell; but when he had recovered strength this indulgence was withdrawn. Five or six other examinations rapidly succeeded each other, and finally, on the 11th of January, 1676, he was

* No description of the building and its accommodations is given. Captain Marryat's graphic account of it in the "Phantom Ship," must be fresh in the memory of all readers. The novelist seems to have borrowed his account from the pages of Dellon.

fortunate enough to be present at the Auto da Fé in that garb of good omen, the black dress with white stripes. The sentence was confiscation of goods and chattels, banishment from India, five years of the galleys in Portugal, and a long list of various penances to be performed during the journey.

On arriving at Lisbon he was sent to the hulks, but by the interest of his fellow-countrymen he recovered his liberty in June, 1677. About eleven years afterwards he published anonymously a little volume containing an account of his sufferings. By so doing he broke the oaths of secrecy administered to him by the Holy Tribunal, but probably he found it easy enough to salve his conscience in that matter.

The next in our list stands the good Capt. Hamilton, a sturdy old merchant militant, who infested the Eastern seas about the beginning of the eighteenth century.

The captain's views of the manners and customs of the people are more interesting than his description of the city. After alluding to their habits of intoxication he proceeds to the subject of religion, and terms both clergy and laity "a pack of the most atrocious hypocrites in the world;" and, at the same time, "most zealous bigots." There were not less than eighty churches, convents, and monasteries within view of the town, and these were peopled by "thirty thousand church vermin who live idly and luxuriously on the labour and sweat of the miserable laity." Our voyager then falls foul of the *speciosa miracula* of St. Francis de Xavier. He compares the holy corpse to that of "new scalded pig," opines that it is a "pretty piece of wax-work that serves to gull the people," and utterly disbelieves that the amputated right-arm, when sent to Rome to stand its trial for sainthood, took hold of the pen, dipped it in ink and fairly wrote "Xavier" in full view of the sacred college.

The poverty of Goa must have been great in Capt. Hamilton's time, when "the houses were poorly furnished within like their owners' heads, and the tables and living very mean." The army was so ill-paid and defrauded that the soldiers were little better than common thieves and assassins. Trade was limited to salt and arrack, distilled from the cocoa-nut. The downfall of Goa had been hastened by the loss of Muscat to the Arabs, a disaster brought on by the Governor's insolent folly,* by an

* An Arab chieftain sent a civil request to the governor, desiring liberty to buy provisions. The answer was a bit of

attack made in 1660 upon the capital by a Dutch squadron, which, though it failed in consequence of the strength of the fortifications, still caused great loss and misery to the Portuguese, and finally by the Maharatta war. In 1685, Seevagee, the Robert Bruce of Southern India, got a footing in the island, and would have taken the city had he not been—

"Foiled by a woman's hand before a broken wall."

The "Maid of Goa" was one Donna Maria, a Portuguese lady, who travelled to Goa dressed like a man in search of a perfidious swain who had been guilty of breach of promise of marriage. She found him at last and challenged him to the duello with sword and pistol, but the gentleman declined the invitation, preferring to marry than to fight Donna Maria.

A few years afterwards the Maharatta war began, and the heroine excited by her country's losses, and, of course, directed by inspiration, headed a sally against Seevagee, took a redoubt, and cut

pork wrapped up in paper, and a message, that such was the only food likely to be furnished. The chieftain's wife, who was a Sayyideh, a woman of the Prophet's tribe, and a lady of proper spirit, felt the insult so keenly, that she persuaded her husband and his tribe to attack Muscat and massacre all its defenders. This event took place in 1650.

all the heathen in it to pieces. The enemy, probably struck by some superstitious terror, precipitately quitted the island, and the Donna's noble exploit was rewarded with a captain's pay for life.

We conclude with the Rev. Mons. Cottineau de Kleguen, a French missionary, who died at Madras in 1830. His "Historical Sketch of Goa" was published the year after his death. It is useful as a guide-book to the buildings, and gives much information about ecclesiastical matters. In other points it is defective in the extreme. As might be expected from a zealous Romanist, the reverend gentleman stands up stoutly for the inquisition in spite of his "entire impartiality," and displays much curious art in defending the Jesuits' peculiar process of detaching the pagans from idol worship, by destroying their temples and pagodas.

CHAPTER IV.

OLD GOA AS IT IS.

THE setting sun was pouring a torrent of crimson light along the Rio as the prow of our canoe bumped against the steps of the wharf, warning us that we had at length reached our destination. The landing-place is a little beyond the arsenal, and commands a full view of the cathedral and other conspicuous objects. The first glance around convinced us that we were about to visit a city of the dead, and at once swept away the delusion caused by the distant view of white-washed churches and towers, glittering steeples and domes.

As such places should always, in our humble opinion, be visited for the first time by moonlight, we spent an hour or two in ascertaining what accommodations the Aljube, or ecclesiastical prison, would afford. Dellon's terrible description of the place had prepared us for "roughing it," but we were agreeably disappointed.* The whole building, with the exception of a few upper rooms, had been cleaned, plastered, and painted, till it presented a most respectable appearance. Salvador, it is true, had ventured into the garrets, and returned with his pantaloons swarming with animal life. This, however, only suggested the precaution of placing water-pots under the legs of our "Waterloo," and strewing the floor with the leaves of the "sacred grass," a vegetable luxury abounding in this part of the world.

When the moon began to sail slowly over the eastern hills, we started on our tour of inspection, and, as a preliminary measure, walked down the wharf, a long and broad road, lined with double rows of trees, and faced with stone, opposite the sea. A more suggestive scene could not be conceived than the utter desolation which lay before us. Everything that met the eye or ear seemed teeming with melancholy associations; the very rustling of the trees and the murmur of the waves sounded like a dirge for the departed grandeur of the city.

A few minutes' walk led us to a conspicuous

* He calls it the "Aljouvar." It is probably a corrupted Arabic word الجبر Al-jabr, "the prison."

object on the right hand side of the wharf. It was a solitary gateway, towering above the huge mass of ruins which flanks the entrance to the Strada Diretta.* On approaching it we observed the statue of Saint Catherine,† shrined in an upper niche, and a grotesque figure of Vasco de Gama in one beneath. Under this arch the newly-appointed viceroys of Goa used to pass in triumphal procession towards the palace.

Beyond the gateway a level road, once a populous thoroughfare, leads to the Terra di Sabaio, a large square, fronting the Se Primaçial or Cathedral of Saint Catherine, and flanked by the Casa Santa. Before visiting the latter spot we turned to the left, and ascending a heap of ruins, looked down upon the excavation, which now marks the place where the Viceregal Palace rose. The building, which occupied more than two acres of ground, has long been razed from the very foundations, and the ground on which it stood is now covered with the luxuriant growth of poisonous plants and thorny trees. As we wandered amidst them, a solitary

* The Straight Street, so called because almost all the streets of Goa were laid out in curvilinear form.

† St. Catherine was appointed patron saint of Goa, because the city was taken by the Portuguese on her day.

R. Burton del.

Printed by Hullmandel & Walton

THE CATHEDRAL OF GOA.

London: Richard Bentley, New Burlington Street, 1851

jackal, slinking away from the intruder, was the only living being that met our view, and the deep bell of the cathedral, marking the lapse of time for dozens, where hundreds of thousands had once hearkened to it, the only sound telling of man's presence that reached our ear.

In the streets beyond, nothing but the foundations of the houses could be traced, the tall cocoa and the lank grass waving rankly over many a forgotten building. In the only edifices which superstition has hitherto saved, the churches, convents, and monasteries, a window or two, dimly lighted up, showed that here and there dwells some solitary priest. The whole scene reminded us of the Arab's eloquent description of the "city with impenetrable gates, still, without a voice or a cheery inhabitant: the owl hooting in its quarters, and birds skimming in circles in its areas, and the raven croaking in its great thoroughfare streets, as if bewailing those that had been in it." What a contrast between the moonlit scenery of the distant bay, smiling in all eternal Nature's loveliness, and the dull grey piles of ruined or desolate habitations, the short-lived labours of man!

We turned towards the Casa Santa, and with little difficulty climbed to the top of the heaps which mark the front where its three gates stood. In these remains the eye, perhaps influenced by imagination, detects something more than usually dreary. A curse seems to have fallen upon it; not a shrub springs between the fragments of stone, which, broken and blackened with decay, are left to encumber the soil, as unworthy of being removed.

Whilst we were sitting there, an old priest, who was preparing to perform mass in the cathedral, came up and asked what we were doing.

"Looking at the Casa Santa," we answered. He inquired if we were Christian, meaning, of course, Roman Catholic. We replied in the affirmative, intending, however, to use the designation in its ampler sense.

"Ah, very well," replied our interrogator. "I put the question, because the heretics from Bombay and other places always go to see the Casa Santa first in order to insult its present state."

And the Señor asked us whether we would attend mass at the cathedral; we declined, however, with a promise to admire its beauties the next day, and departed once more on our wanderings.

For an hour or two we walked about without

meeting a single human being. Occasionally we could detect a distant form disappearing from the road, and rapidly threading its way through the thick trees as we drew near. Such precaution is still deemed necessary at Goa, though the inducements to robbery or violence, judging from the appearance of the miserable inhabitants, must be very small.

At last, fatigued with the monotony of the ruins and the length of the walk, we retraced our steps, and passing down the Strada Diretta, sat under the shade of a tree facing the Rio. Nothing could be more delicately beautiful than the scene before us—the dark hills, clothed with semi-transparent mist, the little streams glistening like lines of silver over the opposite plain, and the purple surface of the creek stretched at our feet. Most musically too, the mimic waves splashed against the barrier of stone, and the soft whisperings of the night breeze alternately rose and fell in unison with the voice of the waters.

Suddenly we heard, or thought we heard, a groan proceeding from behind the tree. It was followed by the usual Hindoo ejaculation of "Ram! Ram!" *

* Calling upon the name of the Almighty.

Our curiosity was excited. We rose from our seat and walked towards the place whence the sound came.

By the clear light of the moon we could distinguish the emaciated form and features of an old Jogee.* He was sparingly dressed, in the usual ochre-coloured cotton clothes, and sat upon the ground, with his back against the trunk of the tree. As he caught sight of us, he raised himself upon his elbow, and began to beg in the usual whining tone.

"Thy gift will serve for my funeral," he said with a faint smile, pointing to a few plantain leaf platters, containing turmeric, red powder, rice, and a few other similar articles.

We inquired into what he considered the signs and symptoms of approaching dissolution. It was a complaint that must have caused him intense pain, which any surgeon could have instantly alleviated. We told him what medical skill could do, offered to take him at once where assistance could be procured, and warned him that the mode of suicide which he proposed to carry out, would be one of most agonising description.

"I consider this disease a token from the Bhag-

* A particular class of Hindoo devotee and beggar.

wán (the Almighty) that this form of existence is finished!" and he stedfastly refused all aid.

We asked whether pain might not make him repent his decision, perhaps too late. His reply was characteristic of his caste. Pointing to a long sabre cut, which seamed the length of his right side, he remarked,

"I have been a soldier—under your rule. If I feared not death in fighting at the word of the Feringee, am I likely, do you think, to shrink from it when the Deity summons me?"

It is useless to argue with these people; so we confined ourselves to inquiring what had made him leave the Company's service.

He told us the old story, the cause of half the asceticism in the East—a disappointment in an *affaire de cœur*. After rising to the rank of *naick*, or corporal, very rapidly, in consequence of saving the life of an officer at the siege of Poonah, he and a comrade obtained leave of absence, and returned to their native hamlet, in the Maharatta hills. There he fell in love, desperately, as Orientals only can, with the wife of the village Brahman. A few months afterwards the husband died, and it was determined by the caste brethren that the relict should follow him, by the Suttee rite. The soldier, however, resolved to save her, and his comrade, apprised of his plans, promised to aid him with heart and hand.

The pyre was heaped up, and surrounded by a throng of gazers collected to witness the ceremony, so interesting and exciting to a superstitious people.

At length the Suttee appeared, supported by her female relations, down the path opened to her by the awe-struck crowd. Slowly she ascended the pile of firewood; and, after distributing little gifts to those around, sat down, with the head of the deceased in her lap. At each of the four corners of the pyre was a Brahman, chaunting some holy song. Presently the priest who stood fronting the south-east, retired to fetch the sacred fire.

Suddenly a horseman, clad in yellow clothes,* dashed out of a neighbouring thicket. Before any had time to oppose him, his fierce little Maharatta pony clove the throng, and almost falling upon his haunches with the effort, stood motionless by the side of the still unlit pyre. At that instant the widow, assisted by a friendly hand, rose from her seat, and was clasped in the horseman's arms.

* Yellow is the colour usually chosen by the Hindoo when about to "do some desperate deed."

One touch of the long Maharatta spur, and the pony again bounds, plunging through the crowd, towards the place whence he came. Another moment and they will be saved!

Just as the fugitives are disappearing behind the thicket, an arrow shot from the bow of a Rankari,* missing its mark, pierces deep into the widow's side.

The soldier buried his paramour under the tree where we were sitting. Life had no longer any charms for him. He never returned to his corps, and resolved to devote himself to futurity.

It was wonderful, considering the pain he must have been enduring, to hear him relate his tale so calmly and circumstantially.

The next morning, when we passed by the spot, three or four half-naked figures, in the holy garb, were sitting like mourners round the body of the old Jogee.

Strange the contempt for life shown by all these metempsychosists. Had we saved that man by main force—an impossibility, by the by, under the circumstances of the case—he would have cursed us, during the remnant of his days, for committing an

* A "forester," and generally a regular sylvan or savage man.

act of bitter and unprovoked enmity. With the Hindoo generally, death is a mere darkening of the stage in the mighty theatre of mundane life. To him the Destroyer appears unaccompanied by the dread ideas of the Moslem tomb-torments, or the horror with which the Christian* looks towards the Great Day; and if Judgment, and its consecutive state of reward or punishment, be not utterly unknown to him, his mind is untrained to dwell upon such events. Consequently, with him Death has lost half his sting, and the Pyre can claim no victory over him.

Old Goa has few charms when seen by the light of day. The places usually visited are the Se Primaçial (Cathedral), the nunnery of Santa Monaca, and the churches of St. Francis, St. Gaetano, and Bom Jesus. The latter contains the magnificent tomb of St. Francis Xavier. His saintship, however, is no longer displayed to reverential gazers in mummy or "scalded pig" form. Altogether we reckoned about thirty buildings. Many of them were falling to ruins, and others were being, or had been, partially demolished. The extraordinary

* This is said particularly of the Eastern Christian, whose terror of the tomb is most remarkable.

amount of havoc committed during the last thirty* years, is owing partly to the poverty of the Portuguese. Like the modern Romans, they found it cheaper to carry away cut stone, than to quarry it; but, unlike the inhabitants of the Eternal City, they have now no grand object in preserving the ruins. At Panjim, we were informed that even the woodwork that decorates some of the churches, had been put up for sale.

The edifices, which are still in good repair, may be described in very few words. They are, generally speaking, large rambling piles, exposing an extensive surface of white-washed wall, surmounted by sloping roofs of red tile, with lofty belfries and small windows. The visitor will admire the vastness of the design, the excellence of the position, and the adaptation of the architecture to the country and climate. But there his praise will cease. With the exception of some remarkable wood-work, the minor decorations of paintings and statues are inferior to those of any Italian village church. As there is no such thing as coloured marble in the country, parts of the walls are painted

* For a detailed list and description of the buildings, we must refer readers to the work of Monsieur de Kleguen, alluded to in the third chapter.

exactly in the style of a small *cabaret* in the south of France. The frescoes are of the most grotesque description. Pontius Pilate is accommodated with a huge Turkish turban; and the other saints and sinners appear in costumes equally curious in an historical and pictorial point of view. Some groups, as for instance the Jesuit martyrs upon the walls of Saint Francis, are absolutely ludicrous. Boiled, roasted, grilled and hashed missionaries, looking more like seals than men, gaze upon you with an eternal smile. A semi-decapitated individual stands bolt upright during the painful process which is being performed by a score of grim-looking heathen. And black savages are uselessly endeavouring to stick another dart in the epidermis of some unfortunate, whose body has already become more

"Like an Egyptian porcupig"

than aught human. One may fancy what an exhibition it is, from the following fact. Whenever a picture or fresco fades, the less brilliant parts are immediately supplied with a coating of superior vividness by the hand of a common house-decorator. They reminded us forcibly of the studio of an Anglo-Indian officer, who, being devotedly fond of pictorial pursuits, and rather pinched for time withal, used to teach his black servants to lay the blue, green, and brown on the canvas, and when he could spare a leisure moment, return to scrape, brush, and glaze the colour into sky, trees, and ground.

Very like the paintings is the sculpture: it presents a series of cherubims, angels, and saints, whose very aspect makes one shudder, and think of Frankenstein. Stone is sometimes, wood the material generally used. The latter is almost always painted to make the statue look as unlike life as possible.

Yet in spite of these disenchanting details, a feeling not unallied to awe creeps over one when wandering down the desert aisles, or through the crowdless cloisters. In a cathedral large enough for a first-rate city in Europe, some twenty or thirty native Christians may be seen at their devotions, and in monasteries built for hundreds of monks, a single priest is often the only occupant. The few human beings that meet the eye, increase rather than diminish the dismal effect of the scene; as sepulchral looking as the spectacle around them, their pallid countenances, and emaciated forms seem so many incarnations of the curse of desolation which still hovers over the ruins of Old Goa.

We felt curious to visit the nunnery of Santa Monaca, an order said to be strict in the extreme. The nuns are called madres (mothers) by the natives, in token of respect, and are supposed to lead a very correct life. Most of these ladies are born in the country; they take the veil at any age when favoured with a vocation.

Our curiosity was disappointed. All we saw was a variety of black handmaids, and the portress, an antiquated lay sister, who insisted upon our purchasing many rosaries and sweetmeats. Her garrulity was excessive; nothing would satisfy her desire for mastering the intricacies of modern Portuguese annals but a long historical sketch by us fancifully impromptued. Her heart manifestly warmed towards us when we gave her the information required. Upon the strength of it she led us into a most uninteresting chapel, and pointed out the gallery occupied by the nuns during divine service. As, however, a close grating and a curtain behind it effectually conceal the spot from eyes profane, we derived little advantage from her civility. We hinted and hinted that an introduction to the prioress would be very acceptable—in vain; and when taking heart of grace we openly asked permission to view the cloisters, which are said to be worth seeing, the amiable old *soror* replied indignantly, that it was utterly impossible. It struck us forcibly that there was some mystery in the case, and accordingly determined to hunt it out.

"Did the Sahib tell them that he is an Englishman?" asked Salvador, after at least an hour's hesitation, falsification, and prevarication produced by a palpable desire to evade the subject.

We answered affirmatively, and inquired what our country had to do with our being refused admittance?

"Everything," remarked Salvador. He then proceeded to establish the truth of his assertion by a variety of distorted and disjointed fragments of an adventure, which the labour of our ingenious cross-questioning managed to put together in the following form.

"About ten years ago," said Salvador, "I returned to Goa with my master, Lieut. ——, of the — Regt., a very clever gentleman, who knew everything. He could talk to each man of a multitude in his own language, and all of them would appear equally surprised by, and delighted with him. Besides, his faith was every man's faith. In a certain Mussulmanee country he married a girl, and divorced her a week afterwards. Moreover, he chaunted the Koran, and the circumcised dogs considered him a kind of saint. The Hindoos also respected him, because he always eat his beef in secret, spoke religiously of the cow, and had a devil, (*i. e.*, some heathen image) in an inner room. At Cochin he went to the Jewish place of worship, and read a large book, just like a priest. Ah! he was a clever Sahib that! he could send away a rampant and raging creditor playful as a little goat, and borrow more money from Parsees at less interest than was ever paid or promised by any other gentleman in the world.

"At last my master came to Goa, where of course he became so pious a Christian that he kept a priest in the house—to perfect him in Portuguese—and attended mass once a day. And when we went to see the old city, such were the fervency of his lamentations over the ruins of the Inquisition, and the frequency of his dinners to the Padre of Saint Francis, that the simple old gentleman half canonized him in his heart. But I guessed that some trick was at hand, when a pattimar, hired for a month, came and lay off the wharf stairs, close to where the Sahib is now sitting; and presently it appeared that my officer had indeed been cooking a pretty kettle of fish!

"My master had been spending his leisure hours with the Prioress of Santa Monaca, who—good lady—when informed by him that his sister, a young English girl, was only waiting till a good comfortable quiet nunnery could be found for her, not only showed her new friend about the cloisters and dormitories, but even introduced him to some of the nuns. Edifying it must have been to see his meek countenance as he detailed to the Madres his well-digested plans for the future welfare of that apocryphal little child, accompanied with a thousand queries concerning the style of living, the moral and religious education, the order and the discipline of the convent. The Prioress desired nothing more than to have an English girl in her house—except, perhaps, the monthly allowance of a hundred rupees which the affectionate brother insisted upon making to her.

"You must know, Sahib, that the madres are, generally speaking, by no means good-looking. They wear ugly white clothes, and cut their hair short, like a man's. But, the Latin professor—"

"The who?"

"The Latin professor, who taught the novices and the younger nuns learning, was a very pretty white girl, with large black eyes, a modest smile, and a darling of a figure. As soon as I saw that Latin professor's face, I understood the whole nature and disposition of the affair.

"My master at first met with some difficulty, because the professor did not dare to look at him, and, besides, was always accompanied by an elder sister."

"Then, how did he manage?"

"Hush, sir, for Santa Maria's sake; here comes the priest of Bom Jesus, to return the Sahib's call."

CHAPTER V.

RETURN TO PANJIM.

ONCE more the canoe received us under its canopy, and the boatmen's oars, plunging into the blue wave, sounded an adieu to old Goa. After the last long look, with which the departing vagrant contemplates a spot where he has spent a happy day or two, we mentally reverted to the adventure of the Latin professor, and made all preparations for hearing it to the end.

"Well, Sahib," resumed Salvador, "I told you that my master's known skill in such matters was at first baffled by the professor's bashfulness, and the presence of a grim-looking sister. But he was not a man to be daunted by difficulties: in fact, he became only the more ardent in the pursuit. By dint of labour and perseverance, he succeeded in bringing the lady to look at him, and being rather a comely gentleman, that was a considerable point gained. Presently her eternal blushings gave way, though occasionally one would pass over her fair face when my master's eyes lingered a little too long there: the next step in advance was the selection of an aged sister, who, being half blind with conning over her breviary, and deaf as a dead donkey, made a very suitable escort."

"Pray, how did you learn all these particulars?"

"Ah, Sahib," replied Salvador, "my master became communicative enough when he wanted my services, and during the trip which we afterwards made down the coast.

"I was now put forward in the plot. After two days spent in lecturing me as carefully as a young girl is primed for her first confession, I was sent up to the nunnery with a bundle of lies upon my tongue, and a fatal necessity for telling them under pain of many kicks. I did it, but my repentance has been sincere, so may the Virgin forgive me!" ejaculated Salvador, with fervent piety, crossing himself at the same time.

"And, Sahib, I also carried a present of some Cognac—called European medicine—to the prioress, and sundry similar little gifts to the other officials, not excepting the Latin professor. To her, I presented a nosegay, containing a little pink note, whose corner just peeped out of the chambeli * blossoms. With fear and trembling I delivered it, and was overjoyed to see her presently slip out of the room. She returned in time to hear me tell the prioress that my master was too ill to wait upon them that day, and by the young nun's earnest look as she awaited my answer to the superior's question concerning the nature of the complaint, I concluded that the poor thing was in a fair way for perdition. My reply relieved their anxiety. Immediately afterwards their curiosity came into play. A thousand questions poured down upon me, like the pitiless pelting of a monsoon rain. My master's birth, parentage, education, profession, travels, rank, age, fortune, religion, and prospects, were demanded and re-demanded, answered and re-answered, till my brain felt tired. According to instructions, I enlarged upon his gallantry in action, his chastity and temperance, his love for his sister, and his sincere devotion to the Roman Catholic faith."

"A pretty specimen of a rascal you proved yourself, then!"

"What could I do, Sahib?" said Salvador, with a hopeless shrug of the shoulders, and an expression

* The large flowered jessamine.

of profound melancholy. "My master never failed to find out a secret, and had I deceived him—"

"Well!"

"My allusion to the sister provoked another outburst of inquisitiveness. On this subject, also, I satisfied them by a delightful description of the dear little creature, whose beauty attracted, juvenile piety edified, and large fortune enchanted every one. The eyes of the old prioress glistened from behind her huge cheeks, as I dwelt upon the latter part of the theme especially: but I remarked the Latin professor was so little interested by it, that she had left the room. When she returned, a book, bound in dirty white parchment, with some huge letters painted on the back of the binding, was handed over to me for transmission to my master; who, it appears, had been very anxious to edify his mind by perusing the life of the holy Saint Augustine.

"After at least three hours spent in perpetual conversation, and the occasional discussion of mango cheese, I was allowed to depart, laden with messages, amidst a shower of benedictions upon my master's head, prayers for his instant recovery, and anticipations of much pleasure in meeting him.

"I should talk till we got to Calicut, Sahib, if I were to detail to you the adventures of the ensuing fortnight. My master passed two nights in the cloisters—not praying, I suppose; the days he spent in conversation with the prioress and sub-prioress, two holy personages who looked rather like Guzerat apes than mortal women. At the end of the third week a swift-sailing pattimar made its appearance.

"I was present when my master took leave of the Superior, and an affecting sight it was; the fervour with which he kissed the hand of his 'second mother,' his 'own dear sister's future protectress.' How often he promised to return from Bombay, immediately that the necessary preparations were made! how carefully he noted down the many little commissions entrusted to him! And, how naturally his eyes moistened as, receiving the benediction, he withdrew from the presence of the reverend ladies!

"But that same pattimar was never intended for Bombay; I knew THAT!

"My master and I immediately packed up everything. Before sunset all the baggage and servants were sent on board, with the exception of myself, who was ordered to sit under the trees on the side of the wharf, and an Affghan scoundrel, who went out walking with the Sahib about eleven o'clock that night. The two started, in native dresses, with their turbans concealing all but the parts about their eyes; both carried naked knives, long and bright enough to make one shake with fear, tucked under their arms, with dark lanterns in their hands. My master's face—as usual when he went upon such expeditions—was blackened, and with all respect, speaking in your presence, I never saw an English gentleman look more like a Mussulman thief!"

"But why make such preparations against a house full of unprotected women?"

"Because, Sahib," replied Salvador, "at night there are always some men about the nunnery. The knives, however, were only in case of an accident; for, as I afterwards learned, the Latin professor had mixed up a little datura* seed with the tobacco served out to the guards that evening.

"A little after midnight I felt a kick, and awoke. Two men hurried me on board the pattimar, which had weighed anchor as the clock struck twelve. Putting out her sweeps she glided down the Rio swiftly and noiselessly.

"When the drowsiness of sleep left my eyelids I observed that the two men were my master and

* The *Datura stramonium*, a powerful narcotic.

that ruffian Khudadad. I dared not, however, ask any questions, as they both looked fierce as wounded tigers, though the Sahib could not help occasionally showing a kind of smile. They went to the head of the boat, and engaged in deep conversation, through the medium of some tongue to me unknown; and it was not before we had passed under the guns of the Castello, and were dancing merrily over the blue water, that my officer retired to his bed.

"And what became of the Latin professor?"

"The Sahib shall hear presently. In the morning I was called up for examination, but my innocence bore me through that trial safely. My master naturally enough suspected me of having played him some trick. The impression, however, soon wore off, and I was favoured with the following detail of his night's adventure.

"Exactly as the bell struck twelve, my Sahib and his cut-throat had taken their stand outside the little door leading into the back-garden. According to agreement previously made, one of them began to bark like a jackal, while the other responded regularly with the barking of a watch-dog. After some minutes spent in this exercise they carefully opened the door with a false key, stole through the cloisters, having previously forced the lock of the grating with their daggers, and made their way towards the room where the Latin professor slept. But my master, in the hurry of the moment, took the wrong turning, and found himself in the chamber of the sub-prioress, whose sleeping form was instantly raised, embraced, and borne off in triumph by the exulting Khudadad.

"My officer lingered for a few minutes to ascertain that all was right. He then crept out of the room, closed the door outside, passed through the garden, carefully locked the gate, whose key he threw away, and ran towards the place where he had appointed to meet Khudadad, and his lovely burthen. But imagine his horror and disgust when, instead of the expected large black eyes and the pretty little rosebud of a mouth, a pair of rolling yellow balls glared fearfully in his face, and two big black lips, at first shut with terror, began to shout and scream and abuse him with all their might.

"'Khudadad, we have eaten filth,' said my master, 'how are we to lay this she-devil?'

"'Cut her throat?' replied the ruffian.

"'No, that won't do. Pinion her arms, gag her with your handkerchief, and leave her—we must be off instantly.'

"So they came on board, and we set sail as I recounted to your honour."

"But why didn't your master, when he found out his mistake, return for the Latin professor?"

"Have I not told the Sahib that the key of the garden-gate had been thrown away, the walls cannot be scaled, and all the doors are bolted and barred every night as carefully as if a thousand prisoners were behind them?"

The population of Goa is composed of three heterogeneous elements, namely, pure Portuguese, black Christians, and the heathenry. A short description of each order will, perhaps, be acceptable to the reader.

The European portion of Goanese society may be subdivided into two distinct parts—the officials, who visit India on their tour of service, and the white families settled in the country. The former must leave Portugal for three years; and if in the army get a step by so doing. At the same time as, unlike ourselves, they derive no increase of pay from the expatriation, their return home is looked forward to with great impatience. Their existence in the East must be one of endurance. They complain bitterly of their want of friends, the disagreeable state of society, and the dull stagnant life they are compelled to lead. They despise their dark brethren, and consider them uncouth in manner, destitute of *usage* in society, and deficient in honour, courage,* and manliness. The despised retort by asserting that the white Portuguese are licentious, ill-informed, haughty, and reserved. No better proof of how utterly the attempt to promote cordiality between the European and the Asiatic by a system of intermarriage and equality of rights has failed in practice can be adduced, than the utter contempt in which the former holds the latter at Goa. No Anglo-Indian Nabob sixty years ago ever thought less of a "nigger" than a Portuguese officer now does. But as there is perfect equality, political † as well as social, between the two colours, the "whites," though reduced to the level

* The European Portuguese can fight bravely enough, as many a bloody field in the Peninsular war has testified. Their Indian descendants, however, have never distinguished themselves for that quality.

† Formerly, only the Reinols, as the Portuguese who came directly from Europe were called, could be viceroys, governors of Ceylon, archbishops, or grand inquisitors of Goa. Tavernier tells us that all the adventurers who passed the Cape of Good Hope forthwith became fidalgos, or gentlemen, and consequently assumed the title of Don.

of the herd, hold aloof from it; and the "blacks" feel able to associate with those who despise them but do so rarely and unwillingly. Few open signs of dislike appear to the unpractised observer in the hollow politeness always paraded whenever the two parties meet; but when a Portuguese gentleman becomes sufficiently intimate with a stranger to be communicative, his first political diatribe is directed against his dark fellow-subjects. We were assured by a high authority that the native members of a court-martial, if preponderating, would certainly find a European guilty, whether rightly or wrongly, *n'importe.* The same gentleman, when asked which method of dealing with the natives he preferred, Albuquerque's or that of Leadenhall Street, unhesitatingly replied, "the latter, as it is better to keep one's enemies out of doors." How like the remark made to Sir A. Burnes by Runjeet Singh, the crafty old politician of Northern India.

The reader may remember that it was Albuquerque* who advocated marriages between the European settlers and the natives of India. How-

* As that "greatest hero of Portuguese Asia" governed for the short space of six years a country of which he and all around him were utterly ignorant, his fatal measure must have been suggested entirely by theory.

ever reasonable it might have been to expect the amalgamation of the races in the persons of their descendants, experience and stern facts condemn the measure as a most delusive and treacherous political day dream. It has lost the Portuguese almost everything in Africa as well as Asia. May Heaven preserve our rulers from following their example! In our humble opinion, to tolerate it is far too liberal a measure to be a safe one.

The white families settled in the country were formerly called Castissos to distinguish them from Reinols. In appearance there is little difference between them; the former are somewhat less robust than the latter, but both are equally pallid and sickly-looking — they dress alike, and allow the beard and mustachios* to grow. This colonist class is neither a numerous nor an influential one. As soon as intermarriage with the older settlers takes place the descendants become Mestici—in plain English, mongrels. The flattering term is occasionally applied to a white family which has been settled

* If our rulers only knew what the natives of Central Asia generally think of a "clean shaved" face, the growth of the mustachio would soon be the subject of a general order. We doubt much if any shaven race could possibly hold Affghanistan. In Western Arabia the Turks were more hated for shaving the beard than for all their flogging and impaling.

in the country for more than one generation, "for although," say the Goanese, "there is no mixture of blood, still there has been one of air or climate, which comes to the same thing." Owing to want of means, the expense of passage, and the unsettled state of the home country, children are very seldom sent to Portugal for education. They presently degenerate, from the slow but sure effects of a debilitating climate, and its concomitant evils, inertness, and want of excitement. Habituated from infancy to utter idleness, and reared up to consider the *far niente* their *summum bonum*, they have neither the will nor the power of active exertion in after years.

There is little wealth among the classes above described. Rich families are rare, landed property is by no means valuable; salaries small;* and in so cheap a country as Goa anything beyond 200*l.* or 300*l.* a-year would be useless. Entertainments are not common; a ball every six months at Government House, a few dinner parties, and an occasional

* Compared with those of British India. Probably there are not three fortunes of 500*l.* per annum amongst the half million of souls that own the rule of the successor of the viceroys. A large family can live most comfortably upon one-fifth of that sum.

soirée or *nautch*, make up the list of gaieties. In the different little villages where the government *employés* reside, once a week there is quadrilling and waltzing, *à l'antique*, some flirting, and a great deal of smoking in the verandah with the ladies, who are, generally speaking, European. Gambling is uncommon ; high play unknown. The theatre is closed as if never to open again. No serenades float upon the evening gale, the *guitarra* hangs dusty and worm-eaten against the wall, and the *cicisbeo* is known only by name. Intrigue does not show itself so flauntingly as in Italy, and other parts of Southern Europe. Scandal, however, is as plentiful as it always is in a limited circle of idle society. The stranger who visits Goa, persuaded that he is to meet with the freedom of manners and love of pleasure which distinguish the people of the Continent, will find himself grievously mistaken. The priesthood is numerous, and still influential, if not powerful. The fair sex has not much liberty here, and their natural protectors are jealous as jailers.

The ancient Portuguese *costume de dame*, a plain linen cap, long white waistcoat, with ponderous rosary slung over it, thick striped and coloured petticoat, and, out of doors, a huge white, yellow, blue, or black calico sheet, muffling the whole figure—is now confined to the poor—the ladies dress according to the Parisian fashions. As, however, steamers and the overland route have hitherto done little for Goa, there is considerable grotesqueness to be observed in the garments of the higher as well as the lower orders. The usual mode of life among the higher orders is as follows:—They rise early, take a cold bath, and make a light breakfast at some time between seven and nine. This is followed by a dinner, usually at two; it is a heavy meal of bread, meat, soup, fish, sweetmeats, and fruits, all served up at the same time, in admirable confusion. There are two descriptions of wine, in general use; the *tinto* and *branco*,* both imported from Portugal. About five in the evening some take tea and biscuits, after awaking from the siesta and bathing; a stroll at sunset is then indulged in, and the day concludes with a supper of fish, rice, and curry. Considering the little exercise in vogue, the quantity of food consumed is wonderful. The Goanese smoke all day, ladies as well as gentlemen; but cheroots, cigars, and the hookah are too expensive to be common. A pinch of Virginia or Maryland, uncomfortably wrapped up in a dried

* Red and white wine: the latter is the favourite.

plantain leaf, and called a *cannudo*, is here the poor succedaneum for the charming little *cigarita* of Spain. The talented author of a "Peep at Polynesian Life" assures us, that, "strange as it may seem, there is nothing in which a young and beautiful female appears to more advantage than in the act of smoking." We are positive that nothing is more shocking than to see a Goanese lady handling her *biree*,* except to hear the peculiarly elaborate way in which she ejects saliva when enjoying her weed.

The reader who knows anything of India will at once perceive the difference between English and Portuguese life in the East. The former is stormy from perpetual motion, the latter stagnant with long-continued repose. Our eternal "knocking about" tells upon us sooner or later. A Portuguese lieutenant is often greyheaded before he gets his company; whereas some of our captains have scarcely a hair upon their chins. But the former eats much and drinks little, smokes a pinch of tobacco instead of Manillas, marries early, has a good roof over his head, and, above all things, knows not what marching and counter-marching mean. He never rides, seldom shoots, cannot

* The Hindostanee name for the cannudo.

hunt, and ignores mess tiffins and guest nights. No wonder that he neither receives nor gives promotion.

An entertainment at the house of a Goanese noble presents a curious contrast to the semi-barbarous magnificence of our Anglo-Indian "doings." In the one as much money as possible is lavished in the worst way imaginable; the other makes all the display which taste, economy, and regard for effect combined produce. The balls given at the palace are, probably, the prettiest sights of the kind in Western India. There is a variety of costumes, which if not individually admirable, make up an effective *tout ensemble;* even the dark faces, in uniforms and ball dresses, tend to variegate and diversify the scene. The bands are better than the generality of our military musicians, European as well as Native, and the dancing, such as it is, much more spirited. For the profusion of refreshments,—the ices, champagne, and second suppers, which render a Bombay ball so pernicious a thing in more ways than one, here we look in vain.

The dinner parties resemble the other entertainments in economy and taste; the table is decorated, as in Italy, with handsome China vases, containing bouquets, fruits, and sweetmeats, which remain there all the time. Amongst the higher classes the cookery is all in the modified French style common to the South of Europe. The wines are the white and red *vins ordinaires* of Portugal; sometimes a bottle of port, or a little bitter beer from Bombay, are placed upon the table. The great annoyance of every grand dinner is the long succession of speeches which concludes it. A most wearisome recreation it is, certainly, when people have nothing to do but to propose each other's healths in long orations, garnished with as many facetious or flattering platitudes as possible. After each speech all rise up, and with loud "vivas" wave their glasses, and drain a few drops in honour of the accomplished *caballero* last lauded. The language used is Portuguese; on the rare occasions when the person addressed or alluded to is a stranger, then, probably, Lusitanian French will make its appearance. We modestly suggest to any reader who may find himself in such predicament the advisability of imitating our example.

On one occasion after enduring half an hour's encomium delivered in a semi-intelligible dialect of Parisian, we rose to return thanks, and for that purpose selecting the English language, we launched into that inexhaustible theme for declamation, the glories of the Portuguese eastern empire, beginning at De Gama, and ending with his Excellency the Governor-General of all the Indies, who was sitting hard by. It is needless to say that our oratory excited much admiration, the more, perhaps, as no one understood it. The happiest results ensued—during our stay at Goa we never were urged to address the company again.

CHAPTER VI.

THE POPULATION OF PANJIM.

THE black Christians, like the whites, may be subdivided into two orders; first, the converted Hindoos; secondly, the mixed breed of European and Indian blood. Moreover, these latter have another distinction, being either Brahman Christians, as they ridiculously term themselves, on account of their descent from the Hindoo pontifical caste, or common ones. The only perceptible difference between them is, we believe, a moral one; the former are justly renowned for extraordinary deceitfulness and treachery. They consider themselves superior to the latter in point of dignity, and anciently enjoyed some peculiar privileges, such as the right of belonging to the orders of the *Theatins*, or regular clerks, and Saint Philip Nerius.* But in manners, appear-

* Goez, who travelled in India about 1650, says that he was surprised to see the image of a black saint on the altars,

ance, customs, and education, they exactly resemble the mass of the community.

The Mestici, or mixed breed, composes the great mass of society at Goa; it includes all classes, from the cook to the government official. In 1835 one of them rose to the highest post of dignity, but his political career was curt and remarkably unsuccessful. Some half-castes travel in Europe, a great many migrate to Bombay for service and commerce, but the major part stays at Goa to stock professions, and support the honour of the family. It would be, we believe, difficult to find in Asia an uglier or more degraded looking race than that which we are now describing. The forehead is low and flat, the eyes small, quick, and restless; there is a mixture of sensuality and cunning about the region of the mouth, and a development of the lower part of the face which are truly unprepossessing, not to say revolting. Their figures are short and small, with concave chests, the usual calfless Indian leg, and a remarkable want of muscularity. In personal attractions the fair sex is little superior to the other. During the whole period of our stay at Goa we

and to hear that a black native was not thought worthy to be a "religious" in this life, though liable to be canonized when he departs it.

scarcely ever saw a pretty half-caste girl. At the same time we must confess that it is difficult to pronounce judgment upon this point, as women of good mixed family do not appear before casual visitors. And this is of course deemed a sign of superior modesty and chastity, for the black Christians, Asiatically enough, believe it impossible for a female to converse with a strange man and yet be virtuous. The dark ladies affect the old Portuguese costume, described in the preceding chapter; a few of the wealthiest dress like Europeans. Their education is purposely neglected—a little reading of their vernacular tongue, with the Ave and other prayers in general use, dancing, embroidery, and making sweetmeats,* are considered *satis superque* in the way of accomplishments. Of late years, a girls' school has been established by order of government at Panjim, but a single place of the kind is scarcely likely to affect the mass of the community. The life led by the fair sex at Goa must be, one would think, a dull one. Domestic occupations,

* Bernier, the traveller, in 1655 remarks, that "Bengala is the place for good comfits, especially in those places where the Portuguese are, who are dexterous in making them, and drive a great trade with them." In this one point their descendants have not degenerated.

smoking, a little visiting, and going to church, especially on the *ferie*, or festivals, lying in bed, sitting *en deshabille*, riding about in a mancheel, and an occasional dance—such are the blunt weapons with which they attack Time. They marry early, begin to have a family probably at thirteen, are old women at twenty-two, and decrepit at thirty-five. Like Indians generally, they appear to be defective in amativeness, abundant in philoprogenitiveness, and therefore not much addicted to intrigues. At the same time we must record the fact, that the present archbishop has been obliged to issue an order forbidding nocturnal processions, which, as they were always crowded with lady devotees, gave rise to certain obstinate scandals.

The mongrel men dress as Europeans, but the quantity of clothing diminishes with the wearer's rank. Some of the lower orders, especially in the country, affect a full-dress costume, consisting *in toto*, of a cloth jacket and black silk knee breeches. Even the highest almost always wear coloured clothes, as, by so doing, the washerman is less required. They are intolerably dirty and disagreeable :—verily cleanliness ought to be made an article of faith in the East. They are fond of spirituous liquors, and seldom drink, except honestly for the purpose of intoxication. As regards living, they follow the example of their white fellow-subjects in all points, except that they eat more rice and less meat. Their characters may be briefly described as passionate and cowardly, jealous and revengeful, with more of the vices than the virtues belonging to the two races from which they are descended. In early youth, especially before arriving at years of puberty, they evince a remarkable acuteness of mind, and facility in acquiring knowledge. They are equally quick at learning languages, and the lower branches of mathematical study, but they seem unable to obtain any results from their acquirements. Goa cannot boast of ever having produced a single eminent literato, or even a second-rate poet. To sum up in a few words, the mental and bodily development of this class are remarkable only as being a strange *mêlange* of European and Asiatic peculiarities, of antiquated civilization and modern barbarism.

We before alluded to the deep-rooted antipathy between the black and the white population: the feeling of the former towards an Englishman is one of dislike not unmingled with fear. Should Portugal ever doom her now worse than useless colony to form part payment of her debts, their fate would be rather a hard one. Considering the wide spread of perhaps too liberal opinions concerning the race quaintly designated as "God's images carved in ebony," they might fare respectably as regards public estimation, but scarcely well enough to satisfy their inordinate ambition. It is sufficiently amusing to hear a young gentleman, whose appearance, manners, and colour fit him admirably to become a band-boy to some Sepoy corps, talk of visiting Bombay, with letters of introduction to the Governor and Commander-in-chief. Still more diverting it is when you know that the same character would invariably deduct a perquisite from the rent of any house he may have procured, or boat hired for a stranger. Yet at the same time it is hard for a man who speaks a little English, French, Latin, and Portuguese to become the lower clerk of some office on the paltry pay of 70*l.* per annum; nor is it agreeable for an individual who has just finished his course of mathematics, medicine, and philosophy to sink into the lowly position of an assistant apothecary in the hospital of a native regiment. No wonder that the black Indo-Portuguese is an utter radical; he has gained much by Constitution, the "dwarfish demon" which sets everybody by the ears at Goa. Hence it is that he will take the first opportunity in conversation with a foreigner to extol Lusitanian liberty to the skies, abuse English tyranny over, and insolence to, their unhappy Indian subjects, and descant delightedly upon the probability of an immediate crash in our Eastern empire. And, as might be expected, although poverty sends forth thousands of black Portuguese to earn money in foreign lands, they prefer the smallest competence at home, where equality allows them to indulge in a favourite independence of manner utterly at variance with our Anglo-Indian notions concerning the proper demeanour of a native towards a European.

The native Christian is originally a converted Hindoo, usually of the lowest castes;* and though he has changed for centuries his manners, dress, and religion, he retains to a wonderful extent the ideas, prejudices, and superstitions of his ancient state. The learned *griff*, Bishop Heber, in theorizing upon the probable complexion of our First Father, makes a remark about these people, so curiously erroneous, that it deserves to be mentioned. "The Portuguese have, during a three hundred years' residence in India, become as black as Caffres; surely this goes

* Many tribes, however, are found among them. Some have African features.

far to disprove the assertion which is sometimes made, that climate alone is insufficient to account for the difference between the Negro and the European." Climate in this case had nothing whatever to do with the change of colour. And if it had, we might instance as an argument against the universality of such atmospheric action, the Parsee, who, though he has been settled in the tropical lands of India for more than double three hundred years, is still, in appearance, complexion, voice, and manners, as complete an Iranian as when he first fled from his native mountains. But this is *par parenthèse.*

The native Christians of Goa always shave the head; they cultivate an apology for a whisker, but never allow the beard or mustachios to grow. Their dress is scanty in the extreme, often consisting only of a dirty rag, worn about the waist, and their ornaments, a string of beads round the neck. The women are equally badly clothed: the single long piece of cotton, called in India a saree, is their whole attire,* consequently the bosom is unsupported and uncovered. This race is decidedly the lowest in the scale of civilized humanity we have

* Without the cholee or bodice worn by Hindoo and Moslem women in India.

yet seen. In appearance they are short, heavy, meagre, and very dark; their features are uncomely in the extreme; they are dirtier than Pariahs, and abound in cutaneous diseases. They live principally on fish and rice, with pork and fruit when they can afford such luxuries. Meat as well as bread* is holiday diet; clarified butter, rice, water, curry, and cocoa-nut milk are every-day food.

These people are said to be short lived, the result of hard labour, early marriages, and innutritious food. We scarcely ever saw a man that looked fifty. In disposition they resemble the half-castes, but they are even more deficient in spirit, and quarrelsome withal, than their "whitey-brown" brethren. All their knowledge is religious, and consists only of a few prayers in corrupt Maharatta, taught them by their parents or the priest; these they carefully repeat three times *per diem*—at dawn, in the afternoon, and before retiring to rest. Loudness of voice and a very Puritanical snuffle being *sine qua nons* in their devotional exercises, the neighbourhood of a pious family is anything

* Leavened bread is much better made here than in any other part of Western India; moreover, it is eaten by all those who can afford it.

but pleasant. Their superiority to the heathen around them consists in eating pork, drinking toddy to excess, shaving the face, never washing, and a conviction that they are going to paradise, whereas all other religionists are emphatically not. They are employed as sepoys, porters, fishermen, seamen, labourers, mancheel bearers, workmen and servants, and their improvident indolence renders the necessity of hard labour at times imperative. The carpenters, farriers, and other trades, not only ask an exorbitant sum for working, but also, instead of waiting on the employer, scarcely ever fail to keep him waiting for them. For instance, on Monday you wanted a farrier, and sent for him. He politely replied that he was occupied at that moment, but would call at his earliest convenience. This, if you keep up a running fire of messages, will probably be about the next Saturday.

The visitor will not find at Goa that number and variety of heathen castes which bewilder his mind at Bombay. The capital of Portuguese India now stands so low amongst the cities of Asia that few or no inducements are offered to the merchant and the trader, who formerly crowded her ports. The Turk, the Arab, and the Persian have left them for a wealthier mart, and the only strangers are a few

Englishmen, who pass through the place to visit its monuments of antiquity.

The Moslem population at Panjim scarcely amounts to a thousand. They have no place of worship, although their religion is now, like all others, tolerated.* The distinctive mark of the Faithful is the long beard. They appear superior beings by the side of the degenerate native Christians.

Next to the Christians, the Hindoos are the most numerous portion of the community. They are held in the highest possible esteem and consideration, and no office unconnected with religion is closed to them. This fact may account for the admirable ease and freedom of manner prevalent amongst them. The Gentoo will enter your room with his slippers on, sit down after shaking hands as if the action were a matter of course, chew his betel, and squirt the scarlet juice all over the floor, in a word, make himself as offensive as you can conceive. But at Goa all men are equal. Moreover, the heathens may be seen in Christian churches,† with covered feet, pointing at, putting

* Anciently, neither Moslem nor Jew could, under pain of death, publicly perform the rites of his religion in any Indo-Portuguese settlement.

† At the same time we were not allowed to pass the threshold of the little pagoda to the southward of the town.

questions concerning, and criticising the images with the same quite-at-home *nonchalance* with which they would wander through the porticoes of Dwarka or the pagodas of Aboo. And these men's fathers, in the good old times of Goa, were not allowed even to burn their dead * in the land!

In appearance the Hindoos are of a fair, or rather a light yellow complexion. Some of the women are by no means deficient in personal charms, and the men generally surpass in size and strength the present descendants of the Portuguese heroes. They wear the mustachio, but not the beard, and dress in the long cotton coat, with the cloth wound round the waist, very much the same as in Bombay. The head, however, is usually covered with a small red velvet skullcap, instead of a turban. The female attire is the saree, with the long-armed bodice beneath it; their ornaments are numerous; and their caste is denoted by a round spot of kunkun, or vermilion, upon the forehead between the eyebrows.

As usual among Hindoos, the pagans at Goa are divided into a number of sub-castes. In the Brah-

* Tavernier says of them, "the natives of the country called Canarins are not permitted to bear any office but only in reference to the law, *i. e.*, as solicitors, advocates, and scriveners. If a Canarin happened to strike a European, his hand was amputated."

man we find two great subdivisions, the Sashteekar, or inhabitants of Salsette, and the Bardeskar, or people of Bardes. The former is confessedly superior to the latter. Both families will eat together, but they do not intermarry. Besides these two, there are a few of the Chitpawan, Sinart, Kararee and Waishnau castes of the pontifical order.

The Brahmans always wear the tika, or sectarian mark, perpendicularly, to distinguish them from the Sonars, or Goldsmiths, who place it horizontally on the forehead. They are but superficially educated, as few of them know Sanscrit, and these few not well. All read and write Maharatta fluently, but they speak the inharmonious Concanee dialect.

Next to the Brahmans, and resembling them in personal appearance, are the Banyans, or traders. They seem to be a very thriving portion of the population, and live in great comfort, if not luxury.

The Shudra, or servile class of Hindoos, is, of course, by far the most numerous; it contains many varieties, such as Bhandan (toddy-makers), Koonbee (potters), Hajjam (barbers), &c.

Of mixed castes we find the goldsmith, who is descended from a Brahman father and servile mother, and the Kunchanee, or Εταιρη, whose maternal parent is always a Maharatta woman, whatever the other progenitor may chance to be. The outcasts are principally Chamars, or tanners, and Parwars (Pariahs).

These Hindoos very rarely become Christians, now that fire and steel, the dungeon and the rack, the rice-pot and the rupee, are not allowed to play the persuasive part in the good work formerly assigned to them. Indeed, we think that conversion of the heathen is almost more common in British than in Portuguese India, the natural result of our being able to pay the proselytes more liberally. When such an event does occur at Goa, it is celebrated at a church in the north side of the creek, opposite Panjim, with all the pomp and ceremony due to the importance of spoiling a good Gentoo by making a bad Christian of him.

We were amused to witness on one occasion a proof of the high importance attached to Hindoo opinion in this part of the world. Outside the church of St. Agnes, in a little chapel, stood one of the lowest orders of black priests, lecturing a host of naked, squatting, smoking, and chattering auditors. Curiosity induced us to venture nearer, and we then discovered that the theme was a rather imaginative account of the birth and life of the Redeemer. Presently a group of loitering Gentoos, who had been strolling about the church, came up and stood by our side.

The effect of their appearance upon his Reverence's discourse was remarkable, as may be judged from the peroration, which was very much in these words :—

"You must remember, sons, that the *avatár*, or incarnation of your blessed Lord, was in the form of a rajah, who ruled millions of men. He was truly great and powerful; he rode the largest elephant ever trapped; he smoked a hookah of gold, and when he went to war he led an army the like of which for courage, numbers, and weapons was never seen before. He would have conquered the whole world, from Portugal to China, had he not been restrained by humility. But, on the last day, when he shall appear even in greater state than before, he will lead us his people to most glorious and universal victory."

When the sermon concluded, and the listeners had wandered away in different directions, we walked up to his Reverence and asked him if he had ever read the Gospel.

"Of course."

"Then where did you find the historical picture you so graphically drew just now about the rajah-ship?"

"Where?" said the fellow, grinning and pointing to his forehead: "here, to be sure. Didn't you see those Gentoos standing by and listening to every word I was saying? A pretty thing it would have been to see the pagans laughing and sneering at us Christians because the Founder of our Blessed Faith was the son of a Burhaee." *

Such reasoning was conclusive.

If our memory serve us aright, there is a story somewhat like the preceding in the pages of the Abbé Dubois. Such things we presume must constantly be taking place in different parts of India. On one occasion we saw an unmistakable Lakhshmi † borne in procession amongst Christian images, and, if history be trusted, formerly it was common to carry as many Hindoo deities as European saints in the palanquins. On the other hand, many a Gentoo has worn a crucifix for years, with firm faith in the religious efficacy of the act, yet utterly ignorant of the nature of the symbol he was bearing, and we have ourselves written many and many a charm for

* A carpenter, one of the lowest castes amongst Hindoos.

† The Hindoo goddess of plenty and prosperity.

ladies desirous of becoming prolific, or matrons fearful of the evil eye being cast upon their offspring.

On our return from old Goa to Panjim we visited an establishment, which may be considered rather a peculiar one. It is called the Caza de Misericordia, and contains some forty or fifty young ladies, for the most part orphans, of all colours, classes, and ages. They are educated by nuns, under the direction of a superior and a committee, and when grown up, remain in the house till they receive and accept suitable offers of marriage.

Hearing that it was not unusual to propose oneself as a suitor; with a view of inspecting the curiosities of the establishment, we repaired to the Caza, and were politely received by the old lady at the gate. After showing us over the chapel and other public portions of the edifice, she perceived that we had some other object, and presently discovered that we were desirous of playing the part of Cœlebs in search of a wife. Thereupon she referred us to another and more dignified relic of antiquity, who, after a long and narrow look at our outward man, proceeded to catechise us in the following manner.

"You say, señor, that you want a wife; what may be your name?"

"Peter Smith."

"Your religion?"

"The Christian, señora."

"Your profession?"

"An ensign in H. E. I. Company's Navy.

Not satisfied with such authentic details, the inquisitive old lady began a regular system of cross-questioning, and so diligently did she pursue it, that we had some difficulty to prevent contradicting ourselves. At length, when she had, as she supposed, thoroughly mastered the subject, she requested us to step into a corridor, and to dispose of ourselves upon a three-legged stool. This we did, leaning gracefully against the whitewashed wall, and looking stedfastly at the open grating. Presently, a wrinkled old countenance, with a skin more like a walnut's than a woman's, peered through the bars, grinned at us, and disappeared. Then came half-a-dozen juveniles, at the very least, tittering and whispering most diligently, all of which we endured with stoical firmness, feeling that the end of such things was approaching.

At last, a sixteen-year old face gradually drew within sight from behind the bars. That was clearly one of the young ladies. Now for it.—

"Good day, and my respects to you, senorita!"

"The same to you, sir."

Hem! It is rather a terrible thing to make love under such circumstances. The draw upon one's imagination in order to open the dialogue, is alone sufficient to frighten Cupid out of the field. It was impossible to talk of the weather, in that country where it burns, deluges, and chills with the regularity of clock-work. So we plunged at once *in medias res.*

"Should you like to be married, senorita?"

"Yes, very much, señor."

"And why, if you would satisfy my curiosity?"

"I don't know."

Equally unsatisfactory was the rest of the conversation. So we bowed politely, rose from our three-legged stool, and determined to seek an interview with the Superior. Our request was at last granted, and we found a personage admirably adapted, in point of appearance, to play dragon over the treasures committed to her charge. She had a face which reminded us exactly of a white horse, a body answerable, and manners decidedly repulsive. However, she did not spare her tongue.

She informed us that there were twelve marriageable young ladies then in the establishment, named them, and minutely described their birth, parentage, education, mental and physiological development. She also informed us that they would receive a dowry from the funds of the house, which, on further inquiry, proved to be the sum of ten pounds.

At length we thought there was an opportunity to put in a few words about our grievance—how we had been placed on a three-legged stool before a grating — exposed to the inquisitiveness of the seniors, and subjected to the ridicule of the junior part of the community. We concluded with a modest hint that we should like to be admitted within, and be allowed a little conversation with the twelve marriageable young ladies to whom she had alluded.

The old lady suddenly became majestic.

"Before you are admitted to such a privilege, señor, you must be kind enough to address an official letter to the mesa, or board, explaining your intentions, and requesting the desired permission. We are people under government, and do not keep a naughty house. Do you understand me, señor?"

" Perfectly, madam."

Upon which we arose, scraped the ground thrice, with all the laboriousness of Indo-Portuguese politeness, promised compliance in our best phraseology, and rapidly disappeared, resolving never to near the Caza de Misericordia again.

CHAPTER VII.

SERODA.

After an unusually protracted term of isolation and friendlessness, we were agreeably surprised by meeting Lieutenants L—— and T——, walking in their shooting-jackets, somewhat slowly and disconsolately, down the dusty wharf of New Goa.

It is, we may here observe, by no means easy for a stranger— especially if he be an Englishman — to get into Goanese society: more difficult still to amuse himself when admitted. His mother tongue and Hindostanee will not be sufficient for him. French, at least, or, what is more useful, Portuguese should be well understood, if not fluently spoken. As the generality of visitors pass merely a few days at Panjim, call at the palace, have a card on the secretary, rush to the ruins, and then depart, they expect and receive little attention. There are no messes to invite them to — no public amusements or places of resort, and private families do not easily open their doors. Besides, as might be expected, the Goanese have occasionally suffered severely from individuals terming themselves "British Officers." It were well too, had the offenders been always of the male sex: unfortunately for our national reputation, such is by no means the case. However, a stranger may be sure that with his commission, some knowledge of languages, and any letter of introduction, he will be most hospitably received in society, such as it is.

The unlearned in such matters may be disposed to inquire whether there are no resident Englishmen at Goa.

Certainly, there are a few; but they are, generally speaking, of that class who have made Bombay too hot for them. Once in the Portuguese territory, they may laugh at the bailiff, and fearlessly meet the indignant creditor. The cheapness of the locality is, to certain characters, another inducement; so that, on the whole, it is by no means safe to become acquainted with any compatriot one may chance to meet at Goa.

Now it so happened that all three of us had been reading and digesting a rich account of Seroda, which had just appeared in one of the English periodicals. We remembered glowing descriptions of a village, inhabited by beautiful Bayaderes, governed by a lady of the same class — Eastern Amazons, who permitted none of the rougher sex to dwell beneath the shadow of their roof-trees— high caste maidens, who, having been compelled to eat beef by the "tyrannical Portuguese in the olden time," had forfeited the blessings of Hindooism, without acquiring those of Christianity, — lovely patriots, whom no filthy lucre could induce to quit their peaceful homes: with many and many etceteras, equally enchanting to novelty-hunters and excitement-mongers.

We unanimously resolved to visit, without loss of time, a spot so deservedly renowned. Having been informed by our old friend John Thomas, that we should find everything in the best style at Seroda, we hired a canoe, cursorily put up a few cigars, a change of raiment, and a bottle of Cognac to keep out the cold; and, a little after sunset, we started for our Fool's Paradise.

Our course lay towards the south-east. After about an hour's rowing along the coast, we entered a narrow channel, formed by the sea and innumerable little streams that descend towards the main, winding through a dense mass of bright green underwood. It was a lovely night, but the thick dew soon compelled us to retreat under the mats destined to defend our recumbent forms. The four boatmen that composed the crew must have been sadly addicted to sleeping on duty, for, although the distance was only fifteen miles, the sun appeared high in the heavens next morning before we arrived at the landing-place. A guide was soon procured, and under his direction we toiled up two miles of a steep and rocky path, through a succession of cocoa groves, and a few parched-up fields scattered here and there, till at last we saw, deep in a long narrow hollow, surrounded by high hills, the bourne of our pilgrimage.

The appearance of Seroda is intensely that of a Hindoo town. Houses, pagodas, tombs, tanks, with lofty parapets, and huge flights of steps, peepul trees, and bazaars, are massed together in chaotic confusion. No such things as streets, lanes, or alleys exist. Your walk is invariably stopped at the end of every dozen steps by some impediment, as a loose wall, or a deep drop, passable only to the well practised denizens of the place. The town is dirty in the extreme, and must be fearfully hot in summer, as it is screened on all sides from the wind. The houses are raised one story above the ground, and built solidly of stone and mortar: as there is no attempt at order or regularity, their substantial appearance adds much to the strangeness of the *coup d'œil.*

To resume our personal adventures. Descending the slope which leads through the main gate we wandered about utterly at a loss what to do, or where to go, till a half-naked sample of the Hindoo male animal politely offered to provide us with a lodging. Our hearts felt sad at witnessing this practical proof of the presence of *man*kind, but sleepy, tired, and hungry withal, we deferred sentimentalizing over shattered delusions and gay hopes faded, till a more opportune moment, and followed him with all possible alacrity. A few minutes afterwards we found ourselves under the roof of one of the most respectable matrons in the town. We explained our wants to her. The first and most urgent of the same being breakfast. She stared at our ideas of that meal, but looked not more aghast than we did when informed that it was too late to find meat, poultry, eggs, bread, milk, butter, or wine in the market—in fact, that we must be contented with "kichree"—a villanous compound of boiled rice and split vetches—as a *pièce de resistance*, and whatever else Providence might please to send us in the way of "kitchen."

Rude reality the second !—

We had left all our servants behind at Panjim, and not an iota of our last night's supper had escaped the ravenous maws of the boatmen.—

Presently matters began to mend. The old lady recollected that in days of yore she had possessed a pound of tea, and, after much unlocking and rummaging of drawers, she produced a remnant of that luxury. Perseverance accomplished divers other feats, and after about an hour more of half starvation we sat down to a breakfast composed of five eggs, a roll of sour bread, plantains, which tasted exactly like edible cotton dipped in *eau sucrée*, and a "fragrant infusion of the Chinese leaf," whose perfume vividly reminded us of the haystacks in our native land. Such comforts as forks or spoons were unprocurable, the china was a suspicious looking article, and the knives were apparently intended rather for taking away animal life than for ministering to its wants. Sharp appetites, however, removed all our squeamishness, and the board was soon cleared. The sting of hunger blunted, we lighted our "weeds," each mixed a cordial potion in a tea-cup, and called aloud for the nautch, or dance, to begin.

This was the signal for universal activity. All the fair dames who had been gazing listlessly or giggling at the proceedings of their strange guests, now starting up as if animated with new life rushed off to don their gayest apparel : even the grey-haired matron could not resist the opportunity of displaying her gala dress, and enormous pearl nose-ring. The tables were soon carried away, the rebec and kettledrum sat down in rear of the *figurantes*, and the day began in real earnest. The singing was tolerable for India, and the voices good. As usual, however, the highest notes were strained from the chest, and the use of the *voix de gorge* was utterly neglected. The verses were in Hindostanee and Portuguese, so that the performers understood about as much of them as our young ladies when they perform Italian bravura songs. There was little to admire either in the persons, the dress or the ornaments of the dancers : common looking Maharatta women, habited in the usual sheet and long-armed bodice, decked with wreaths of yellow flowers, the red mark on the brow, large nose and ear-rings, necklaces, bracelets, bangles, and chain or ring anklets, studded with strings of coarsely made little brass bells. Some of them were very fair, having manifestly had the advantage of one European progenitor: others showed the usual dark yellow hue; the features were seldom agreeable, round heads, flat foreheads, immense eyes, increased by the streaks of black dye along the thickness of the eyelid, projecting noses, large lips, vanishing chins, and a huge development of "jowl," do not make up a very captivating physiognomy. A few, but very few, of quite the youngest *figurantes*, were tolerably pretty. They performed in sets for about four hours, concluding with the *pugree*, or turban dance, a peculiar performance, in which one lady takes the part of a man.

Our matron informed us that Seroda contains about twenty establishments, and a total number of fifty or sixty dancing-girls. According to her account all the stars were at the time of our visit engaged at Panjim, or the towns round about: personal experience enabled us to pronounce that the best were in her house, and, moreover, that there is scarcely a second-rate station in the Bombay Presidency that does not contain prettier women and as good singers. The girls are bought in childhood—their price varies from 3*l.* to 20*l.* according to the market value of the animal.

The offspring of a Bayadere belongs of right to her owner. When mere children they are initiated in the mysteries of *nautching,* — one young lady who performed before us could scarcely have been five years old. Early habit engenders much enthusiasm for the art. The proportion of those bought in distant lands to those born at Seroda is said to be about one to five. Of late years the nefarious traffic has diminished, but unhappily many are interested in keeping it up as much as possible.

Several of these *nautch* women can read and write. Our matron was powerful at reciting Sanscrit shlokas (stanzas), and as regards Pracrit, the popular dialect, she had studied all the best known works, as the " Panja Tantra," together with the legends of Vikram, Rajah Bhoj, and other celebrated characters. Their spoken language is the corrupt form of Maharatta, called the Concanee,* in general use throughout the Goanese territory ; the educated mix up many Sanscrit vocables with it, and some few can talk a little Portuguese. Their speaking voices are loud, hoarse, and grating : each sentence,

* Opposite to the Desha, the pure dialect of Maharatta They are about as different as English spoken in the south of England and Lowland Scotch.

moreover, ends in a sing-song drawl, which is uncommonly disagreeable to a stranger's ear. These ladies all smoke, chew betel-nut, drink wine and spirits, and eat fowls and onions, an unequivocal sign of low caste. They do not refuse to quit Seroda, as is generally supposed, but, of course, prefer their homes to other places. Living being extremely cheap most of the money made by *nautching* is converted into pearl and gold ornaments; and these are handed down from generation to generation. Some of the coins strung together into necklaces are really curious. An old English five-guinea-piece may be found by the side of a Portuguese St. Thomas, a French *Louis d'or*, and a Roman medal of the Lower Empire. We should be puzzled to account for how they came there, did we not know that India has from the earliest ages been the great sink for Western gold. Many of the matrons have collected a considerable stock of linen, pictures, and furniture for their houses, besides dresses and ornaments. Our countrymen have been liberal enough to them of late, and numerous, too, as the initials upon the doors and shutters prove. Each establishment is violently jealous of its neighbour, and all appear to be more remarkable for rapacity than honesty. In spite of the general belief, we venture to assert that a chain, a ring, or a watch, would find Seroda very dangerous quarters. As a stranger soon learns, everything is done to fleece him ; whether he have five or five hundred rupees in his pocket, he may be sure to leave the place without a farthing. This seems to be a time-honoured custom among the Bayaderes cherished by them from immemorial antiquity.

When the rising shades of evening allowed us to escape from the house of dancing, we sallied forth to view the abode in which Major G—— passed his last years. The matron soon found a boy who preceded us to the place, threading his way through a multitude of confused dwellings, climbing over heaps of loose stones, walking along the walls of tanks, and groping through the obscurity of the cocoa groves. At the end of this unusual kind of walk, we found ourselves at the house, asked, and obtained leave to enter it. There was nothing to attract attention in the building, except a few old books ; the peculiar character of its owner will, perhaps, plead our excuse to the reader, if we dwell a little upon the circumstances which led him to make Seroda his home.

Major G—— was an officer who had served with

distinction for many years in a Native Regiment. He was a regular old Indian, one of the remnants of a race which, like its brethren in the far west, is rapidly disappearing before the eastward progress of civilisation in the shape of rails, steamers, and overland communication. By perpetual intercourse with the natives around him he had learned to speak and write their language as well as, if not better than, his own. He preferred their society to that of his fellow-countrymen; adopted the Hindoo dress; studied their sciences, bowed to their prejudices, and became such a proficient in the ritual of their faith as to be considered by them almost a fellow-religionist. Having left England at an early age, with a store of anything but grateful reminiscences, he had determined to make India his country and his home, and the idea once conceived, soon grew familiar to his mind. Knowing that there is no power like knowledge amongst a semi-civilised people, and possibly inclined thereto by credulity, he dived deep into the "dangerous art," as the few books preserved at Seroda prove. Ibn Sirin,* and Lily, the Mantras,† and Casaubon,

* A celebrated Arabic author on the interpretation of dreams.

† Magical formula and works on "Gramarye," generally in the Sanscrit, sometimes in the Pracrit, tongue.

works on Geomancy, Astrology, Ihzar or the Summoning of Devils, Osteomancy, Palmistry, Oneiromancy, and Divination. The relics of his library still stand side by side there, to be eaten by the worms.

Late in life Major G—— fell in love with a Seroda Nautch girl living under his protection; not an usual thing in those days: he also set his mind upon marrying her, decidedly a peculiar step. His determination gave rise to a series of difficulties. No respectable Hindoo will, it is true, wed a female of this class, yet, as usual amongst Indians, the caste has at least as much pride and prejudice as many far superior to it. So Sita would not accept a *mlenchha* (infidel) husband, though she was perfectly aware that she had no right to expect a *dwija*, or twice born one.

But Major G——'s perseverance surmounted every obstacle. Several times the lady ran away, he followed and brought her back by main force at the imminent risk of his commission. At last, finding all opposition in vain, possibly thinking to prescribe too hard a trial, or, perhaps, in the relenting mood, she swore the most solemn oath that she would never marry him unless he would retire from the service to live and die with her in her native town.

Major G—— at once sold out of his regiment, disappeared from the eyes of his countrymen, bought a house at Seroda, married his enchantress, and settled there for the remainder of his years. Many of the elder inhabitants recollect him; they are fond of describing to you how regularly every morning he would repair to the tank, perform his ablutions, and offer up water to the manes of his *pitris,* or ancestors, how religiously he attended all the festivals, and how liberal he was in fees and presents to the Brahmans of the different pagodas.

We were shown his tomb, or rather the small pile of masonry which marks the spot where his body was reduced to ashes—a favour granted to him by the Hindoos on account of his pious munificence. It is always a melancholy spectacle, the last resting-place of a fellow-countryman in some remote nook of a foreign land, far from the dust of his forefathers—in a grave prepared by strangers, around which no mourners ever stood, and over which no friendly hand raised a tribute to the memory of the lamented dead. The wanderer's heart yearns at the sight. How soon may not such fate be his own?

The moonlight was falling clear and snowy upon

the tranquil landscape, and except the distant roar of a tiger, no noise disturbed the stillness that reigned over the scene around, as we slowly retraced our steps towards Seroda. Passing a little building, whose low doomed roof, many rows of diminutive columns, and grotesque architectural ornaments of monkeys and elephants' heads, informed us was a pagoda, whilst a number of Hindoos lounging in and out, showed that some ceremony was going on, we determined to attempt an entrance, and passed the threshold unopposed. Retiring into a remote corner we sat down upon one of the mats, and learned from a neighbour that the people were assembled to hear a Rutnageree Brahman celebrated for eloquence, and very learned in the Vedas. The preacher, if we may so call him, was lecturing his congregation upon the relative duties of parents and children; his discourse was delivered in a kind of chaunt, monotonous, but not rude or unpleasing, and his gesticulation reminded us of many an Italian Predicatore. He stood upon a strip of cloth at the beginning of each period, advancing gradually as it proceeded, till reaching the end of his sentence and his carpet, he stopped, turned round, and walked back to his standing place, pausing awhile to take breath and to allow the words of wisdom to sink deep into his hearers' hearts. The discourse was an excellent one, and we were astonished to perceive that an hour had slipped away almost unobserved. However, the heat of the place, crowded as it was with all ages and sexes—for the ladies of Seroda, like the frail sisterhood generally in Asia, are very attentive to their *dharma*, or religious duties—the cloud of incense which hung like a thick veil under the low roof, and the overpowering perfume of the huge bouquets and garlands of jessamine with which the assembly was profusely decorated, compelled us to forfeit the benefit we might have derived from the peroration of the learned Brahman's discourse.

Our night was by no means a pleasant one; the Seroda vermin, like the biped population, were too anxious to make the most of the stranger. Early the next morning we arose to make our exit; but, alas! it was not destined to be a triumphant one. The matron and her damsels, knowing us to be English, expected us to be made of money, and had calculated upon easing our breeches pockets of more gold than we intended to give silver. Fearful was the din of chattering, objurgating, and imprecating, when the sum decided upon was gracefully tendered to our entertainers, the rebec and the kettle-drum seemed inclined to be mutinous, but *they* were more easily silenced than the ladies. At length, by adding the gift of a pair of slippers adorned with foil spangles, to which it appeared the company had taken a prodigious fancy, we were allowed to depart in comparative peace.

Bidding adieu to Seroda, we toiled up the hill, and walked dejectedly towards the landing-place, where we supposed our boat was awaiting us. But when we arrived there, the canoe, of course, was not to be found. It was breakfast time already, and we expected to be starved before getting over the fifteen miles between us and Panjim. One chance remained to us; we separated, and so diligently scoured the country round that in less than half an hour we had collected a fair quantity of provender; one returning with a broiled spatchcock and a loaf of bread; another with a pot full of milk and a cocoa-nut or two, whilst a third had succeeded in "bagging" divers crusts of stale bread, a bunch of onions, and a water-melon. The hospitable portico of some Banyan's country-house afforded us a breakfast-room; presently the boat appeared, and the crew warned us that it was time to come on board. It is strange that these people must tell lies, even when truth would be in their favour.

This we found to our cost, for wind and tide proved both against us.

Six hours' steaming and broiling under a sun which penetrated the matting of our slow conveyance, as if it had been water within a few degrees of boiling heat, brought us on towards evening. Seeing some difficulty in rowing against every disadvantage, we proposed to our rascally boatmen—native Christians, as usual—to land us at the most convenient place. Coming to a bluff cape, the wretches swore by all that was holy, that we were within a mile's walk of our destination. In an evil hour, we believed the worse than pagans, and found that by so doing we had condemned ourselves to a toilsome trudge over hill and dale, at least five times longer than they had asserted it to be. Our patience being now thoroughly exhausted, we relieved our minds a little by administering periodical chastisements to the fellow whom our bad luck had sent to deceive and conduct us, till, at length, hungry, thirsty, tired, and sleepy, we found ourselves once more in the streets of Panjim.

Reader, we have been minute, perhaps unnecessarily so, in describing our visit to Seroda. If you be one of those who take no interest in a traveller's "feeds," his sufferings from vermin, or his "rows about the bill," you will have found the preceding pages uninteresting enough. Our object is, however, to give you a plain programme of what entertainment you may expect from the famed town of the Bayaderes, and, should your footsteps be ever likely to wander in that direction, to prepare you for the disappointment you will infallibly incur.

CHAPTER VIII.

EDUCATION, PROFESSIONS, AND ORIENTAL STUDIES.

PANJIM and Margao (a large town in the province of Salsette, about fifteen miles south-east of Goa), are the head-quarters of the Indo-Portuguese muses. The former place boasts of mathematical and medical schools, and others in which the elements of history, and a knowledge of the Portuguese, Latin, English, French, and Maharatta languages are taught gratis. The students are, generally speaking, proficients in the first,* tolerable in the second, and execrable in the third and fourth dialects above specified. As regards the Maharattas, the study of its literature has been rendered obligatory by government, which however, in its wisdom, appears

* As, however, the Maharatta is the mother tongue of the Goanese, it communicates its peculiar twang to every other language they speak. The difference of their Portuguese from the pure Lusitanian, is at once perceptible to a practised ear.

to have forgotten, or perhaps never knew, that certain little aids called grammars and dictionaries are necessary to those who would attain any degree of proficiency in any tongue. For the benefit of the fair sex there is a school at Panjim. Dancing and drawing masters abound. Music also is generally studied, but the Portuguese here want the "furore," as the Italians call it, the fine taste, delicate ear, and rich voice of Southern Europe.

At Panjim there is also a printing office, called the Imprensa Naçional, whence issues a weekly gazette, pompously named the *Boletim do Governo do Estado da India.* It is neatly printed, and what with advertisements, latest intelligence borrowed from the Bombay papers, and government orders, it seldom wants matter. At the Imprensa also, may be found a few Portuguese books for sale, but they are, generally speaking, merely elementary, besides being extravagantly dear.

Physic as well as jurisprudence may be studied at Margao. The same town also has schools of theology, philosophy, Latin, Portuguese, and the rude beginnings of a Societade Estudiosa, or Literary Society. The latter is intended for learned discussion: it meets twice a week, does not publish but keeps MS. copies of its transactions, and takes from each member an annual subscription of about 1*l*.

Upon the whole, education does not thrive in the Indo-Portuguese settlement. It seldom commences before the late age of nine or ten, and is very soon ended. After entering some profession, and coquetting a little with modern languages and general literature, study is considered a useless occupation. Moreover, if our observation deceive us not, the description of talent generally met with at Goa is rather of the specious and shallow order. A power of quick perception, an instinctive readiness of induction, and even a good memory, are of little value when opposed to constitutional inertness, and a mind which never proposes to itself any high or great object. Finally, the dispiriting influence of poverty weighs heavy upon the student's ambition, and where no rewards are offered to excellence, no excellence can be expected. The romantic, chivalrous, and fanatic rage for propagating Christianity which animated the first conquerors of Goa, and led their immediate descendants to master the languages and literature of the broad lands won by their sharp swords, has long since departed, in all human probability for ever.

The religion of Goa is the Roman Catholic. The primate is appointed from home, and is expected to pass the rest of his life in exile. In the ceremonies of the church we observed a few, but not very important deviations from the Italian ritual. The holy week and other great festivals are still kept up, but the number of *ferie* (religious holidays) has of late been greatly diminished, and the poverty of the people precludes any attempt at display on these occasions. All ecclesiastical matters are settled with the utmost facility. By the constitution lately granted, the clergy have lost the power of excommunication. The Papal see, who kept so jealous and watchful an eye upon Goa in the days of her wealth and grandeur, seems now almost to have forgotten the existence of her froward daughter.* As regards the effect of religion upon the community in general, we should say that the mild discipline of the priesthood has produced so far a happy result, that the free-thinking spirit roused by ecclesiastical intolerance in Europe, is all but unknown here.

* And yet as late as 1840, the Government of Goa was obliged to issue an order confiscating the property of all priests who should submit to the Vicar-apostolic appointed by the Pope.

The priests always wear out of doors the clerical cap and cassock. They are now very poorly provided for, and consequently lead regular lives. The archbishop's prison is almost always empty, and the amount of profligacy which in Rome would be smiled at in a polite young abbate, would certainly incur the severest penalty at Goa. It is said that the clergy is careful to maintain the reputation of the profession, and that any little peccadilloes, such as will and must occur in a warm climate, and an order of celibataires, are studiously concealed from public observation. As might be expected, the ecclesiastical party prefers Don Miguel to Donna Maria, the favourite of the laity, the more so as that "excellent son of Don John of Portugal," were he even to set his august foot on the floors of the Adjuda, would probably humour them in such trifles as readmitting the Jesuits, and reestablishing the Inquisition. The only objection to the holy profession at Goa is, that the comparatively idle life led by its members offers strong inducements to a poor, careless, and indolent people, who prefer its inutility to pursuits more advantageous to themselves, as well as more profitable to the commonweal.

The ecclesiastical education lasts about seven years, three of which are devoted to studying Latin, one is wasted upon moral philosophy, dialectics and metaphysics, and the remainder is deemed sufficient for theology. On certain occasions, students at the different seminaries are taught the ceremonies of the church, and lectured in the Holy Scriptures. There are two kinds of pupils, the resident, who wear the clerical garb, and are limited in number, and the non-resident, who dress like the laity, unless they intend to take orders. In this course of education much stress is laid upon, and pride taken in, a knowledge of Latin, whose similarity to Portuguese enables the student to read and speak it with peculiar facility. Many authors are perused, but the niceties of scholarship are unknown, good editions of the poets and orators being unprocurable here. Few Goanese write the classical language well; and though all can master the words, they seldom read deeply enough to acquire the idiom. And lastly, the strange pronunciation of the consonants in Portuguese is transferred to Latin, imparting to it an almost unrecognisable sound. The clergy belonging to the country, of course understand and speak the Concanee Maharattas. Sermons are sometimes preached, and services performed in this dialect: it boasts of a printed volume of oraçoens (prayers) dated 1660, for the benefit of the lowest and most ignorant classes.

The military profession is by no means a favourite one, on account of poor pay and slow promotion. The aspirante, or cadet, enters the service as a private, wears the uniform of that rank, and receives about 10s. *per mensem* for attending lectures. After learning Portuguese, the course of study is as follows:—

1st Term. Geometry, Trigonometry (plane and spherical), Geodesy and Surveying.

2nd Term. Algebra, differential and integral calculus.

3rd Term. Mechanics, Statics, Dynamics, Hydrodynamics, Hydrostatics, Hydraulics, &c.

4th Term. Gunnery, Mining, Practice of Artillery.

5th Term. Navigation and the Use of Instruments.

6th Term. Fortification and Military Architecture.

Infantry cadets study geometry and field-fortification during two or three years. Those intended for the Artillery and Engineers, go through all the course above mentioned, except navigation. Drawing, in all its branches, is taught by professors who are, generally speaking, retired officers superintended by a committee. After passing their examinations, the names of the cadets are put down in the Roster, and they are promoted, in due order, to the rank of alferez, or ensign.

The total number of the Goanese army may be estimated at about two thousand * men on actual duty, besides the Mouros, or Moors, who act as police and guards at Panjim. The regiments are—two of infantry, stationed at Bicholim and Ponda; two battalions of caçadores (chasseurs not mounted), at Margao and Mapuca; a provincial battalion, and a corps of artillery at Panjim. In each regiment there are six companies, composed of between sixty and seventy men: a full band reckons thirty musicians. The officers are about as numerous as in a British corps on foreign service.

The army is poorly paid; † the privates receive no salary when in sick quarters, and the consequence is that they are frequently obliged to beg their bread. We cannot therefore wonder that the

* Francklin, who visited Goa in 1786, says that the army was about five thousand men, two regiments of which were Europeans. Even in his day the Home Government was obliged to send large sums of money annually to defray the expenses of their Indian possessions.

† A colonel receiving about 15*l.*, an ensign, 3*l.* *per mensem.*

European soldiery is considered the least respectable part of the whole community. Most of the officers belong to some family resident in India; consequently, they do not live upon their pay. Moreover, they have no expensive establishments to keep up, and have little marching or change of stations.

The corps are seldom paraded; once every two days is considered ample work during the cold season. Except on particular occasions, there are no mounted officers on the ground, a peculiarity which gives a remarkably "National Guard" like appearance to the field. They are well dressed, but very independent in such movements as in carrying the sword, or changing flanks: after a few manœuvres, which partake more of the character of company than battalion exercise, the men order arms, and the captains, lieutenants, and ensigns all fall out for a few minutes, to smoke a leaf-full of tobacco, and chat with the commanding officer. They then return to their places, and the parade proceeds. The appearance of the privates on the drill-ground is contemptible in the extreme The smallest regiment of our little Maharattas would appear tolerable sized men by the side of them; and as for a corps of Bengalees, it ought to be able to walk over an equal number of such opponents, without scarcely a thrust of the bayonet. Europeans and natives, in dirty clothes, and by no means of a uniform colour—some fiercely "bearded like the pard," some with moustachios as thick as broomsticks, others with meek black faces, religiously shaven and shorn — compose admirably heterogeneous companies which, moreover, never being sized from flanks to centre, look as jagged as a row of shark's teeth. Drill is the last thing thought of. The sergeant, when putting his recruits through their manual and platoon, finds it necessary to refer to a book. When the pupils are not sufficiently attentive, a spiteful wring of the ear, or poke between the shoulders, reminds them of their duty. To do justice to their spirit, we seldom saw such admonition received in silence; generally, it was followed by the description of dialogue affected by two irritated fishwives. So much for the outward signs of discipline. As regards the effects of drill, the loose, careless, and *draggling* way in which the men stand and move, would be the death of a real English martinet. We could not help smiling at the thought of how certain friends of ours who, after a march of fifteen miles, will keep an unhappy regiment ordering and shouldering arms for half an hour in front of their tents, would behave themselves, if called to command such corps.

Till lately, no books of tactics have been published for the instruction of the Goanese army. At present there are several, chiefly elementary, and translated from the English and French. The manual and platoon, the sword exercise, and other small works were prepared by Major G——n, an officer and linguist of some talent. We saw few publications upon the subject of military law. Courts-martial are rare compared with the absurd number yearly noted in the annals of the Indian army, where a boy of eighteen scarcely ever commits a fault for which he would be breeched at school, without being solemnly tried upon the charge of "conduct highly unbecoming an officer and a gentleman."

To conclude the subject of the Goanese army, it is evident that there are two grand flaws in its composition. The officers are compelled to be scientific, not practical men, and the soldiers are half-drilled. This propensity for mathematics is, of course, a European importation. Beginning with France, it has spread over the Western Continent till at last, like sundry other new-fangled fashions, it has been seized upon and applied to the British army. Why a captain commanding a company, or a colonel in charge of a battalion, should be required to have Geometry, History, and Geography at his fingers' ends, we cannot exactly divine. With respect to drill, it may be remarked that, when imperfectly taught, it is worse than useless to the soldier. We moderns seem determined to discourage the personal prowess, gymnastics, and the perpetual practice of weapons in which our forefathers took such pride. We are right to a certain extent: the individual should be forced to feel that his safety lies in acting in concert with others. At the same time, in our humble opinion, they carry the principle too far who would leave him destitute of the means of defending himself when obliged to act singly. How many good men and true have we lost during the late wars, simply in consequence of our neglecting to instruct them in the bayonet exercise! And may not this fact in some wise account for the difficulty experienced of late by disciplined troops in contending with semi-civilised tribes, whose military studies consist of athletic exercises which prepare the body for hardship and fatigue, and the skilful use of weapons that ensures success in single combat? The English, French, and Russians have, within the last fifteen years, all suffered more or less severely from the undrilled valour, and the irregular attacks of the Affghans, Arabs, and Circassians.

Young aspirants to the honours which Justinian gives, have no public schools to frequent, nor can they study gratis. In a community which so decidedly prefers coppers to knowledge, this is perhaps one of the most judicious measures imaginable for limiting the number of this troublesome order. The law students frequent private establishments at Margão, and a course of two years is generally considered sufficient to qualify them for practice. After a very superficial examination in the presence of a committee composed of two judges and a president, they receive, if found competent, a diploma, and proceed to seek employment in one of the courts.

Justice at Goa, as in British India, seems to have adapted herself to the peculiarities of the country much better than one might have expected from a character so uncompromising as hers is generally represented to be. The great difference between us and the Portuguese is, that whereas we shoot and hang upon the authority of our civil and military courts, no Goanese can be brought to the gallows till the death-warrant, bearing her majesty's signature, arrives from Europe,—a pleasant state of suspense for the patient! Murder and sacrilege are the only crimes which lead to capital punishment; for lesser offences, criminals are transported to the Mozambique, or imprisoned in the jail — a dirty building, originally intended for a Mint—or simply banished from Goa.

Those covetous of the riches which Galen is said to grant, are prepared for manslaughter—to use a Persian phrase—by a course of five years' study. They are expected to attend lectures every day, except on Thursdays and Sundays, the principal religious festivals, and a long vacation that lasts from the fifteenth of March to the middle of June. On the first of April every year, the students are examined, and two prizes are given. The professors are four in number, three surgeons and one physician, together with two assistants. The course commences with Anatomy and Physiology; during the second year Materia Medica and Pharmacy are studied; the surgical and chemical branches of the profession occupy the third; and the last is devoted to Pathology and Medical Jurisprudence. The hospital must be visited every day during the latter half of the course. It is a large edifice, situated at the west end of the town, close to the sea, but by no means, we should imagine, in a favourable position for health, as a channel of fetid mud passes close under the walls. The building can accommodate about three hundred patients and is tolerably but not scrupulously clean. It contains two wards, one for surgical, the other for medical cases, a chapel, an apartment for sick prisoners and a variety of different lecture-rooms. After his four years of study, the pupil is examined, and either rejected or presented with a diploma and permission to practise.

The elementary works upon the subjects of Anatomy and Materia Medica are, generally speaking, Portuguese; the proficient, however, is compelled to have recourse to French books, which have not been translated into his vernacular tongue. The English system of medicine is universally execrated, and very justly. Dieting, broths, and ptisanes, cure many a native whose feeble constitution would soon sink beneath our blisters, calomel, bleeding, and drastic purges. As might be expected, all the modern scientific refinements, or quackeries, are known here only by name. We were surprised, however, by the general ignorance of the properties of herbs and simples—a primitive science in which the native of India is, usually speaking, deeply read.

The principal Oriental tongues studied by the early Portuguese in their mania for converting the heathens were the Malabar, Maharatta, Ethiopic, and Japanese, the dialects of Congo, and the Canary Isles, the Hebrew, and the Arabic. The Portuguese Jews, in the fifteenth century, were celebrated for their proficiency in Biblical, Talmudic, and Rabbinical lore; and the work of João de Souza, entitled, "Documentos Arabios de Historia Portugueza copiades dos originaes da Torre do' Tombo," is a fair specimen of Orientalism, considering the early times in which it was composed. Of late years, Portuguese zeal for propagating the faith, depressed by poverty, and worn out by the slow and sure spiritual *vis inertiæ*, which the natives of the East have opposed to the pious efforts of Modern Europe, appears to have sunk into the last stage of decline, and with it their ancient ardour for the study of so many, and, in some cases, such unattractive languages.

Our case is very different from theirs. In addition to religious incentives, hundreds of our nation have more solid and powerful inducements to labour held out to them. We fondly hope and believe that the days are passed when Oriental study and ruin were almost synonymous. Within the last few years we have more or less facilitated the acquisition, and rifled the literature of between thirty and forty eastern dialects—a labour of which any nation might be proud. Our industry, too, is apparently still unabated. Societies for the translation and publication of new works, Oriental libraries; and, perhaps, the most useful step of all, the lithographic process, which has lately supplanted the old and unseemly moveable types, are fast preparing a royal road for the Oriental learner. It may be observed that the true means of promoting the study is to diminish its laboriousness, and still more its expense. So far we have been uncommonly successful. For instance, an excellent and correct lithograph of Mirkhond's celebrated history, the "Rauzat el Safa," may now be bought for 3*l.* or 4*l.*; a few years ago the student would have paid probably 70*l.* or 80*l.* for a portion of the same work in the correct MS.

At the same time we quite concur in the opinion of the eminent Orientalist,* who declared, *ex cathedrâ*, that our literary achievements in this branch

* The translator of Ibn Batuta's Travels.

bear no flattering proportion to the vastness of our means as a nation. It is true, to quote one of many hard cases, that we must send to Germany or Russia for grammars and publications in the Affghan language, although the country lies at our very doors. But the cause of this is the want of patronage and assistance, not any deficiency in power or ability. There are many unknown D'Herbelots in India, unfortunately England has not one Ferdinand.*

* Ferdinand, the second Duke of Tuscany, was the munificent patron of the father of Western Orientalism.

CHAPTER IX.

ADIEU TO PANJIM.

At a time when public attention is so deeply interested in the twin subjects of colonization and conversion, some useful lessons may be derived from the miserable state of the celebrated Portuguese settlement; even though our present and their past positions be by no means parallel in all points, and though a variety of fortuitous cases, such as the pestilence and warfare which led to their decadence, cannot or may not affect our more extended Indian empire.

The Portuguese, it must be recollected, generally speaking, contented themselves with seizing the different lines of sea-coast, holding them by means of forts, stations, and armed vessels, and using them for the purpose of monopolising the export and import trade of the interior. In the rare cases when they ventured up the country they made a point of colonising it. We, on the contrary, have hitherto acted upon the principle of subjugating whole provinces to our sway, and such has been our success, that not only the Christian, but even the heathen, sees the finger of Providence directing our onward course of conquest.

Of late years, climates supposed to be favourable to the European constitution, such as the Neilgherry hills and the lower slopes of the Himalayas, have been discovered, tested, and approved of. Determined to make use of them, our legislators have taken the wise step of establishing barracks for the British soldiery in places where they may live in comparative health and comfort during peaceful times, and yet be available for immediate active service, whenever and wherever their presence may be required.

But we are not willing to stop here, we argue that such salubrious and fertile tracts of country would form excellent permanent settlements for half-pay officers, pensioners, worn-out soldiers, and others, who prefer spending the remainder of their days in the land of their adoption. Here, then, we have the proposed beginning of a colony.

To the probability of extensive success, or public

utility in such a scheme, there are two important objections.

In the first place, supposing the offspring of the colonists to be of pure European blood, we must expect them to degenerate after the second generation. All who have sojourned long in the southern parts of Europe, such as Italy or Spain, must have remarked the deleterious effects of a hot and dry climate upon a race that thrives only in a cold and damp one. An English child brought up in Italy is, generally speaking, more sickly, more liable to nervous and hepatic complaints, and, consequently, more weakened in mind as well as body, than even the natives of the country. If this remark hold true in the South of Europe, it is not likely to prove false in tropical latitudes.

But, secondly, if acting upon Albuquerque's fatal theory, we encourage intermarriage with the natives of the country, such colony would be worse than useless to us. We cannot but think that the Hindoos are the lowest branch of the Caucasian or Iranian family; and, moreover, that, contrary to what might be expected, any intermixture of blood with the higher classes of that same race produces a still inferior development. Some have accounted for the mental inferiority of the mixed breed by a supposed softness or malformation of the brain, others argue that the premature depravity and excess to which they are prone, enervate their bodies, and, consequently, affect their minds. Whatever may be the cause of the phenomenon its existence is, we humbly opine, undeniable. Neither British nor Portuguese India ever produced a half-caste at all deserving of being ranked in the typical order of man.

Our empire in the East has justly been described as one of opinion, that is to say, it is founded upon the good opinion entertained of us by the natives, and their bad opinion of themselves. In the old times of the Honourable East India Company, when no Englishman or Englishwoman was permitted to reside in India, without formal permission, the people respected us more than they do now. Admitting this assertion, it is not difficult to account for the reason why, of late years, a well-appointed British force has more than once found it difficult to defeat a rudely-drilled Indian army. We are the same men we were in the days of Clive and Cornwallis ; the people of India are not ; formerly they fought expecting to be defeated, now they enter the field flushed with hopes of success. We cannot but suspect that the lower estimate they have formed of their antagonists has more to do with their increased formidableness, than any other of the minor causes to which it is usually attributed. But if not contented with exposing individuals to their contempt, we offer them whole colonies, we may expect to incur even greater disasters. Every one knows that if the people of India could be unanimous for a day they might sweep us from their country as dust before a whirlwind. There is little danger of their combining so long as they dread us. Such fear leads to distrust; every man knows himself, and, consequently, suspects his neighbour, to be false. Like the Italians in their late war of independence the cry of *tradimento* (treachery) is sufficient to paralyse every arm, however critical be the hour in which it is raised. So it is in India. But their distrust of each other, as well as their respect for us, is founded entirely upon their fear of our bayonets.

In whatever way, then, we propose to populate our settlement, we place ourselves in a position of equal difficulty and danger. Such colonies would, like Goa, be born with the germs of sure and speedy decline, and well for our Indian empire in general, if the contagious effects of their decay did not extend far and wide through the land.

The conversion of the natives of India to Christianity has of late years become a species of excitement in our native country, and, consequently, many incorrect, prejudiced and garbled statements of the progress and success of the good work have gone forth to the world. Not a few old Indians returned home, have been very much surprised by hearing authentic accounts and long details of effectual missionary labour which they certainly never witnessed. Our candour may not be appreciated—it is so difficult for the enthusiastic to avoid running down an opinion contrary to their own—we cannot, however, but confess that some years spent in Western India have convinced us that the results hitherto obtained are utterly disproportionate to the means employed for converting the people. Moreover, study of the native character forces us to doubt whether anything like success upon a grand scale can ever reasonably be anticipated. We have often heard it remarked by those most conversant with the deep-rooted prejudices and the fanatic credulity of the Hindoos that with half the money and trouble we have lavished upon them they could have made double the number of converts to their heathenism in Europe.

The splendid success of the Portuguese in converting the Hindoos, was owing to two main causes, the first, their persecution,* which compelled many natives to assume European names, adopt the dress, manners, and customs of the West, and gradually to lapse, if we may use the expression, into Christianity. After once entering a church, the proselytes were under the strict surveillance of the Inquisition, who never allowed a "new Christian" to apostatize without making a signal example of him. In the second place, the Portuguese sent out in all directions crowds of missionaries, who, as Tavernier informs us, assumed the native dress, and taught under the disguise of Jogees and other Hindoo religious characters, a strange, and yet artful mixture of the two faiths. That these individuals sacrificed the most vital points of their religion to forward the end they proposed to themselves, we have ample proof; at the same time that they were eminently successful, is equally well known. The virulent animosity that existed between the Jesuits and Jansenists disclosed to astonished Europe the system of adaptation adopted by

* When Vasco de Gama returned to India, part of his freight was "eight Franciscan friars, eight chaplains, and one chaplain major, who were instructed to begin by preaching, and, if that failed, to proceed to the decision of the sword."

the former, and Benedict XIV., by a violent bull, put an end at once to their unjustifiable means, and their consequent successfulness of conversion.*

We by no means mean to insinuate that our holy faith is unfavourable to the development or progression of the human species. Still it cannot be concealed that, generally speaking, throughout the East the Christian is inferior, as regards strength, courage, and principle to the average of the tribes which populate that part of the world. His deficiency of personal vigour may be accounted for by the use of impure meats, and the spirituous liquors in which he indulges. The want of ceremonial ablutions, also, undoubtedly tends to deteriorate the race. It may be observed, that from Zoroaster and Moses downwards, no founder of an Eastern faith has ever omitted to represent his dietetic or ablusive directions as inspired decrees, descending from Heaven. Care applied to public health, ensures the prosperity of a people, especially amongst semi-barbarous races, where health engenders bodily vigour, strength begets courage, and bravery a rude principle of honour.

* The curious reader will find the subject of Jesuitical conversion in India most ably treated in Sir J. E. Tennent's late work on "Christianity in Ceylon."

What Goa has done may serve as a lesson to us. She compelled or induced good Hindoos and Moslems to become bad Christians. The consequence has been the utter degeneracy of the breed, who have been justly characterized by our House of Commons as "a race the least respected and respectable, and the least fitted for soldiers of all the tribes that diversify the populous country of India."

In conclusion, we have only to inform our reader that the opinions thus boldly proposed to him are, we believe, those entertained by many of the acutest judges of native character and native history. It is easy to understand why they are not more often offered to public attention.

After addressing a note to the Secretary for permission to leave Goa, we set out in quest of a conveyance; and deeply we had to regret that we did not retain our old pattimar. The owners of vessels, knowing that we must pay the price they asked, and seeing that we were determined to migrate southwards, became extortionate beyond all bounds. At last we thought ourselves happy to secure a wretched little boat for at least double the usual hire. After duly taking leave of our small circle of acquaintances, we transferred ourselves and luggage on board the San Ignacio awaiting the pleasure of the Tindal — a hard-featured black Portuguese — to quit the land of ruins and cocoa trees. Before preparing for rest we went through the usual ceremony of mustering our crew, and ascertaining the probable hour of our departure: we presently found, as we might have guessed, that they were all on shore except a man and a diminutive boy, and that consequently we were not likely to weigh anchor before 2 A.M., at least five hours later than was absolutely necessary. As we felt no desire to encounter the various Egyptian plagues of the cabin, we ordered a table to be placed under the awning, and seated ourselves upon the same with the firm determination of being as patient and long-suffering as possible.

The night was a lovely one — fair and cool as ever made amends for a broiling and glaring April day in these detestable latitudes. A more beautiful sight, perhaps, was never seen than the moon rising like a ball of burnished silver through the deep azure of the clear sky, and shedding her soft radiance down the whole length of the Rio. The little villages almost hidden from view by the groves of impending trees, whose heads glistened as if hoar-frost had encrusted them; the solemn forms of the towering churches, the ruins of Old Goa dimly perceptible in the far distance, and nearer, Panjim, lying in darkness under the shadow of the hills, all looked delightfully tranquil and peaceful. Besides, we were about to bid adieu to scenes in which we had spent a pleasant hour or two, and they are epochs in the traveller's life, these farewells to places or faces we admire. Will then the reader wonder if we confess that, under the circumstances of the case, we really had no resource but to feel poetically disposed? And, as happens in such cases, the Demon of Doggrel emboldened by the presence of those two kindred spirits, the naughty Herba Nicotiana and the immodest "Naiad of the Phlegethontic Rill Cogniac," tempted us so long and sorely, that he at last succeeded in causing us to perpetrate the following

LINES.

Adieu, fair land, deep silence reigns
O'er hills and dales and fertile plains;
Save when the soft and fragrant breeze
Sighs through the groves of tufted trees;
Or the rough breakers' distant roar,
Is echoed by the watery shore.
Whilst gazing on the lovely view,
How grating sounds the word "adieu!"
What tongue ——

Aye, what tongue indeed? In an instant the demon fled, as our crew, in the last stage of roaring intoxication, scaled the side of what we were about poetically to designate our "bark." A few minutes' consideration convinced us that energetic measures must be adopted if we wished to restore order or quiet. In vain were the efforts of our eloquence; equally useless some slight preliminary exertions of toe and talon. At last, exasperated by the failure, and perhaps irritated by thinking of the beautiful lines we might have indited but for the inopportune interruption, we ventured to administer a rapid succession of small double raps to the Tindal's shaven and cocoanut-like pericranium. The wretch ceased his roaring, rose from off his hams, and after regarding us for a minute with a look of intense drunken ferocity, precipitated himself into the water. Finding the tide too strong for him he began to shriek like a dying pig; his crew shouted because he shouted, sympathetically yelled the sailors in the neighbouring boats, and the sentinels on shore began to give the alarm. Never, perhaps, has there been such confusion at Goa since the Maharatta rode round her walls. Up rushed the harbour master, the collector of customs, the military, and the police—even his Excellency the

Governor General of all the Indies, did not deem it beneath his dignity to quit the palace for the purpose of ascertaining what had caused the turmoil. The half-drowned wretch, when hurried into the high presence, declared, in extenuation of his conduct, that he had imprudently shipped on board the San Ignacio, an Inglez or Englishman, who had deliberately commenced murdering the crew the moment they came on board. The Governor, however, seeing the truth of things, ordered him immediately to be placed in the nearest quarter guard till midnight, at which time it was calculated that, by virtue of the ducking, he might be sober enough to set sail.

As we rapidly glided by the Castle of Agoada, all our crew stood up, and with hands reverentially upraised, said their prayers. They did not, however, pay much respect to the patron saint of the boat, whose image, a little painted doll, in a wooden box, occupied a conspicuous position in the "cuddy." A pot of oil with a lighted wick was, it is true, regularly placed before him every night to warn the vermin against molesting so holy a personage : the measure, however, failed in success, as the very first evening we came on board, a huge rat took his station upon the saint's back and glared at us, stretching his long sharp snout over the unconscious San Ignacio's head. One evening, as the weather appeared likely to be squally, we observed that the usual compliment was not offered to the patron, and had the curiosity to inquire why.

"Why?" vociferated the Tindal indignantly, "if that chap can't keep the sky clear, he shall have neither oil nor wick from me, d—n him!"

"But I should have supposed that in the hour of danger you would have paid him more than usual attention?"

"The fact is, Sahib, I have found out that the fellow is not worth his salt: the last time we had an infernal squall with him on board, and if he doesn't keep this one off, I'll just throw him overboard, and take to Santa Caterina: hang me, if I don't—the brother-in-law!"*

And so saying the Tindal looked ferocious things at the placid features of San Ignacio.

The peculiar conformation of our captain's mind, recalled to memory a somewhat similar phenomenon which we noticed in our younger days. We were toiling up a steep and muddy mountain-road over the Apennines, on foot, to relieve our panting steeds, whom the vetturino was fustigating, *con amore*, at

* A common term of insult.

the same time venting fearful imprecations upon the soul of Sant' Antonino Piccino, or the younger.

At length, tired of hearing the cadet so defamed, we suggested that our friend should address a few similar words to the other Sant' Antonino — the elder.

"The elder!" cried the vetturino, aghast with horror. "Oh, *per Bacco che bestemmia*—what a blasphemy! No, I daren't abuse His Sanctity; but as for this little *rufiano* of a younger, I 've worn his portrait these ten years, and know by this time that nothing is to be got out of him without hard words."

On the fourth day after our departure from Panjim, a swarm of canoes full of fishermen, probably the descendants of the ancient Malabar pirates, gave us happy tidings of speedy arrival. They were a peculiar-looking race dressed in head-gear made of twisted palm leaves, and looking exactly as if an umbrella, composed of matting, had been sewn on to the top of a crownless hat of the same material.

And now we are in the Malabar seas.

CHAPTER X.

CALICUT.

Can those three or four bungalows, with that stick-like light-house between them and the half-dozen tiled and thatched roofs peeping from amongst the trees, compose Calicut—the city of world-wide celebrity, which immortalised herself by giving a name to calico?

Yes; but when we land we shall find a huge mass of huts and hovels, each built in its own yard of cocoas with bazaars, vast and peculiar-looking mosques, a chapel or two, courts and cutcherries, a hospital, jail, barracks, and a variety of bungalows. Seen from the sea, all the towns on this coast look like straggling villages, with a background of distant blue hill,* and a middle

* The mountains distinctly visible from the sea off Calicut, in clear weather, are the Koondah range of the Neilgherries, or Blue Hills.

space of trees, divided by a strip of sand from the watery plain.

Calicut is no longer the

Cidade—nobre e rica *

described by Camoens' tuneful muse. Some, indeed, declare that the present city is not the one alluded to in the Lusiad. There is a tradition amongst the natives of the country, that the ancient Calicut was merged beneath the waves; but in the East, tradition is always a terrible romancer. So we will still continue to believe that here old De Gama first cast anchor and stepped forth from his weather-beaten ship, at the head of his mail-clad warriors, upon the land of promise.

D'Anville assigns two dates to the foundation of Calicut, the earlier one †—A.D. 805—will suit historical purposes sufficiently well. There is nothing to recommend the position selected. During the monsoon, no vessel can approach the anchorage-ground with safety, and even in the fine season many have been wrecked upon the reefs of rocks which line the coast. Very little wind suffices to raise the surf: Nature has made no attempt at a harbour, and the ships lying in an open roadstead, are constantly liable

* "Noble and wealthy city."

† The later is A.D. 907.

to be driven on the sand and mud-banks around them. Tippoo Sultan— a very long-headed individual, by the bye—saw the defects of the situation, and determining to remove the town about six miles southward to the mouth of the Beypoor, or Arricode river, where a natural port exists, adopted the energetic measure of almost destroying the old city, that the inhabitants might experience less regret in leaving their homes. The Moslem emperor regarded Calicut with no peculiar good-will. He and his subjects were perpetually engaged in little squabbles, which by no means tended to promote kindly feeling between them.* On one occasion, offended by the fanaticism of the Nair and Tiyar Hindoos, their ruler pulled down almost every pagoda in the place, and with the stones erected a splendid tank in the middle of the large open space where the travellers' bungalow now stands.

* In 1788, Tippoo was induced by ill-timed zeal or mistaken policy to order the circumcision and conversion of the Malabar Hindoos, and compelled the Brahmans to eat beef, as an example to the other inferior castes. A general insurrection of the oppressed was the natural consequence of the oppressive measure.

Tradition asserts that there was a forcible but partial circumcision of the natives of Malabar by the people of Arabia long before Hyder's time. So the grievance was by no means a new one.

Tippoo unfortunately failed in this project of removal, and when the British became supreme in Malabar, the natives all returned to their ancient haunts. Calicut, for many reasons, is not likely to be deserted under the present rule: it is the point to which all the lines of road which intersect the country converge; besides it would now scarcely be worth our while to bring about so violent a change for the purpose of eventual improvement.

When old Nelkunda began to decline, Calicut rose to importance, probably in consequence of its being in very early times the metropolis of the Samiry Rajah (the Zamorin of Camoens), lord paramount of Malabar. Shortly after the origin of Islam, it was visited and colonised by thousands of Arabs,* who diffused energy and activity throughout

* Who, it may be observed, are the navigators and traders *par excellence* of the Eastern world. The Jews and Phœnicians generally confined themselves to the Mediterranean and the parts about the Red Sea. The Turks were an inland nation; the Hindoos have ever been averse to any but coasting voyages, and the religion of Zoroaster forbade its followers to cross the seas. But the Arab is still what he was—the *facile princeps* of Oriental sailors.

As a proof of how strong the followers of Mohammed mustered on the Malabar coast, we may quote Barthema, who asserts, that when the Portuguese landed at Calicut, they found not less than fifteen thousand of them settled there.

the land. As trade increased, Calicut throve because of its centrical position between the countries east and west of Cape Comorin. Even in the present day, although Goa, and subsequently Bombay, have left the ancient emporium of Western India but little of its former consequence, commerce* still continues to flourish there. The export is brisker than the import trade: the latter consists principally of European piece goods and metals, the former comprises a vast variety of spices, drugs, valuable timber and cotton cloths.

We will now take a walk through the town and remark its several novelties. Monuments of antiquity abound not here: the fort erected by the Portuguese has long since been level with the ground, and private bungalows occupy the sites of the old Dutch, French, and Danish factories. We shall meet few Europeans in the streets: there are scarcely twenty in this place, including all the varieties of civilians, merchants, missionaries, and

Camoens also tells us how the friendly and disinterested plans of his hero were obstructed and thwarted by the power and influence of these infidel Moors.

* Between September 1846 and May 1847, no less than eighty ships, besides an immense number of pattimars and native craft touched at Calicut.

the officers belonging to the two seapoy companies detached from the neighbouring station — Cananore. Most of the residents inhabit houses built upon an eminence about three miles to the north of the town; others live as close as possible to the sea. A dreary life they must lead, one would suppose, especially during the monsoon, when the unhappy expatriated's ears are regaled by no other sounds but the pelting of the rain, the roaring of the blast, and the creaking of the cocoa trees, whilst a curtain of raging sea, black sky, and watery air, is all that meets his weary ken.

The first thing we observe during our perambulation, is the want of the quadruped creation: there are no horses,* sheep, or goats, and the cows are scarcely as large as English donkeys. Secondly, the abundance of sore eyes, produced, it is supposed by the offensive glare and the peculiar effect of the sun's rays, which in these regions are insufferable even to the natives of other Indian provinces. The population apparently regards us with no friendly feeling, Moslem and Hindoo, all have scowls upon their faces, and every man, moreover, carries

* Arab and other valuable horses cannot stand the climate, —a Pegu pony is the general *monture*. The sheep intended for consumption are brought down from Mysore.

a knife conveniently slung to his waistband. Those dark-faced gentlemen, in imitation European dresses, are familiar to our eyes: they are Portuguese, not, however, from Goa, but born, bred, and likely to be buried at Calicut. A little colony, of fifty or sixty families of the race is settled here; they employ themselves either in commerce, or as writers in the different government offices.

The bazaars appear to be well stocked with everything but vegetables and butcher's meat, these two articles being as scarce and bad as the poultry; fish and fruit are plentiful and good. The shops are poor; there is not a single Parsee or European store in the town, so that all supplies must be procured from the neighbouring stations. Everywhere the houses are much more comfortably and substantially built than in the Bombay presidency; the nature of the climate requires a good roof, and as much shade on and around it as possible: the streets and roads, also, look civilised compared with the narrow and filthy alleys of our native towns in general. But we shall find little amusement in inspecting the mass of huts and hovels, mosques and schools, gardens and tanks, so we might as well prolong our stroll beyond the town, and visit the venerable pagoda of Varkool.

It is, you see, a building by no means admirable in point of outward appearance; the roof is tiled, and there is little to excite your curiosity in the woodwork. Its position is remarkable — perched upon the summit of a pile of laterite rock rising abruptly from a level expanse of sand. But it is great, very great, in its historical importance. That edifice was one of the hundred and eight Maha Chaitrum, or temples of the first order, built by the demigod Parasu Rama, upon this coast, and dedicated to the Hindoo Triad. Equally notable it is for sanctity. Early in the month of October, water appears bubbling from a fissure of the rock, and this, learned Brahmans, by what test we know not, have determined to be the veritable fluid of the Ganges, which, passing under ground,* *via* Central India, displays itself regularly once a year to the devotees of Rama. Kindly observe that there is a crowd of Nairs gathered round the temple, and that some petty prince, as we may know by his retinue of armed followers, is visiting the shrine. We will not venture in, as the Hindoos generally in this part of the world, and the Nairs particularly, are accustomed to use their knives with scant ceremony.

* Subterraneous streams are still as common in India as they were in heathen Greece and Italy.

Besides, just at present, they are somewhat in a state of excitement: they expect a partial eclipse of the moon, and are prepared to make all the noise they can, with a view of frightening away the wicked monster, Rahu, who is bent upon satisfying his cannibal appetites with the lucid form of poor Luna.

The present Samiry Rajah is a proud man, who shuns Europeans, and discourages their visiting him on principle. Wishing, however, to see some sample of the regal family, we called upon a cadet of the house of Yelliah, an individual of little wealth or influence, but more sociable than the high and mighty Mana Vikram.* After a ride of about three miles, through lanes lined with banks of laterite, and over dykes stretching like rude causeways along paddy fields invested with a six-foot deep coating of mud, we arrived at the village of Mangaon. The Rajah was apparently resolved to receive us with all the honours: a caparisoned elephant stood at the gate of the "palace," and a troop of half-naked Nairs, armed as usual, crowded around to receive us. We were ushered through a succession of courts and gateways—the former full of diminutive, but seemingly most pugnacious

* The dynastical name of the Samiry.

cows—and at last, ascending a long flight of dark and narrow steps, suddenly found ourselves in the "presence." Our Rajah was a little dark man, injudiciously attired in a magnificent coat of gold cloth, a strangely-shaped cap of the same material, and red silk tights. The room was small, and choked with furniture; chairs, tables, clocks, drawers, washing-stands, boxes, book-shelves, and stools, were arranged, or rather piled up around it, with all the effect of an old curiosity-shop. The walls exhibited a collection of the cheapest and worst of coloured prints — our late gracious queen dangling in dangerous proximity to the ferocious-looking Beau Sabreur, and La Belle Americaine occupied in attentively scrutinising certain diminutive sketches of Richmond Hill, and other localities, probably torn out of some antiquated Annual. Our host met us *à l'Anglaise* —that is to say, with a warm, moist, and friendly squeeze of the hand: he was profuse in compliments, and insisted upon our sitting on the sofa opposite his chair. With the assistance of an interpreter—for the Rajah understands little Hindostani, and we less Malayalim—some twenty minutes were spent in conversation, or rather in the usual exchange of questions and answers which composes the small-talk of an Oriental visit. Presently we arose and took polite leave of our host, who accompanied us as far as the door of his little den : the regal rank and dignity forbidding him to pass the threshold. Not a little shuffling and shrieking was caused by our turning a corner suddenly and meeting in the gateway a crowd of dames belonging to the palace. They and their attendants appeared as much annoyed as we were gratified to catch a sight of Nair female beauty. The ladies were very young and pretty—their long jetty tresses, small soft features, clear dark olive-coloured skins, and delicate limbs, reminded us exactly of the old prints and descriptions of the South Sea Islanders. Their *toilette,* in all save the ornamental part of rings and necklaces, was decidedly scanty. It was the same described by old Capt. Hamilton, who, when introduced at the Court of the Samorin, observed that the queen and her daughters were " all naked above the waist, and barefooted."

People are fond of asserting that native prejudices are being rapidly subjugated by the strong arm of English civilization. We could instance numerous proofs of the contrary being the case. Two hundred years ago the white man was allowed to look upon a black princess in the presence of her husband. How long will it be before such privilege will ever be extended to him again in India?

On the way homewards our guide pointed out what he considered the great lion of Calicut. It is a square field, overgrown with grass and weeds and surrounded by a dense grove of trees. Fronting the road stands a simple gateway, composed of one stone laid horizontally across two of the same shape, planted perpendicularly in the ground. Not detecting instantly any great marvel about the place we looked our curiosity for further information.

"In days of old a strong fort, and a splendid palace adorned that spot—their only remains now those two mounds"—said the guide, pointing at what appeared to be the ruins of bastions—"and that raised platform of earth at the other end. Upon the latter a temporary festive building is erected whenever a Rajah is invested with the turban of regal dignity, in memory of the ancient dwelling-place of his ancestors, and the city which is now no more."

We had half an hour to waste, and were not unwilling to hear a detailed account of old Calicut's apocryphal destruction. So we asked the man to point out its former site. He led us towards the shore, and called our attention to a reef of rocks lying close off the mouth of the little Kullai River; they were clearly discernible as it was then low water.*

"There," said the guide,—a good Hindoo, of course—"there lies the accursed city of Cherooman Rajah!"

Our escort did not require much pressing to ease himself of a little legendary lore. After preparing his mouth for conversation by disposing of as much betel juice as was convenient, he sat down upon the ground near the log of wood occupied by ourselves, and commenced.

"When Cherooman Rajah, the last and most powerful of our foreign governors, apostatizing from the holy faith of his forefathers, received the religion of the stranger, he went forth as a pilgrim to the land of the Arab, and dwelt there for several years.†

* Captain Hamilton mentions his ship striking in six fathoms at the mainmast on some of the ruins of "*the sunken town built by the Portuguese in former times.*" But he hesitates to determine whether the place was "swallowed up by an earthquake, as some affirm, or undermined by the sea."

† A further account of Cherooman will be found in the twelfth chapter. Ferishteh, the celebrated Moslem annalist, in-

"Our ruler's return was signalized by a determination to propagate the new belief throughout Malabar, and unusual success attended upon the well-planned system of persuasion and force adopted by him. Thousands of the slaves, the cultivators and the fishermen, became Moslems, many of the Nairs, some of them men of high rank, and even a few of the Brahmans did not disdain to follow their prince's example. But the *Numboory* * stood firm in his refusal to turn from the law of Brahma; he not only toiled to counteract the monarch's influence, but on more than one occasion in solemn procession visited the palace, and denounced a curse upon the Rajah and people of Calicut if the proselytising continued.

"At length the chieftain, irritated by the deter-

forms us that the Rajah became a Mussulman in consequence of the pious exhortations of some Arab sailors who were driven into the port of Craganore. Captain Hamilton remarks that, "when the Portuguese first came to India, the Samorin of Calicut, who was lord paramount of Malabar, turned Moslem in his dotage, and to show his zeal, went to Mecca on a pilgrimage, and died on the voyage." The tradition handed down amongst the Moslems is, that the Malabar Rajah became a convert to Islam in consequence of seeing the Shakk el-Kamar, or miraculous splitting of the moon by Mohammed, and that, warned by a dream, he passed over to Arabia.

* See Chapter XII.

mined opposition of the priesthood, and urged on by his Arab advisers, swore a mighty oath that he would forcibly convert his arch enemies. The person selected to eat impure meat as a warning to his brethren was the holy Sankaracharya, the high Brahman of the Varkool pagoda.

"Slowly the old man's tottering frame bowed, and trembling with age, moved down the double line of bearded warriors that crowded the audience-hall. At the further end of the room, upon the cushion of royalty, and surrounded by a throng of foreign counsellors, sat Cherooman, looking like a Rakshasa or Spirit of Evil.

"Few words passed between the Brahman and the ruler. The threats of the latter, and the scoffs of his myrmidons, fell unheeded upon the old priest's ears.

"'It is said that a Rajah is a sword in the hand of the Almighty—but thou, Cherooman, art like the assassin's knife. Since thou art thus determined upon thine own destruction accompany me to the beach, and there, unless before sunset the dread Deity I adore vouchsafe to show thee a sign of his power, I will obey thine unhallowed orders.'

"The Rajah mounted his elephant, and followed by his mufties, his wuzeers, and guardsmen, moved slowly towards the brink of the briny wave. On foot and unattended, propping his faltering footsteps with a sandal wand, the Brahman accompanied the retinue. And all the people of Calicut, whose leaning towards the new faith made them exult in the prospect of conversion being forced upon so revered a personage as the old priest, informed of the event, hurried down in thousands to the shore, and stood there in groups conversing earnestly, and sparing neither jest nor jibe at the contrast between the champions of the two rival faiths.

"Sankaracharya sat down upon the sand where the small waves swelled and burst at his feet. Muffling his head in a cotton sheet removed from his shoulders, he drew the rosary bag over his right hand, and after enumerating the Deity's names upon his beads, proceeded to recite the charm of destruction.

"Presently, a cloud no bigger than a man's hand rose like a sea-bird above the margin of the western main. It increased with preternatural growth, and before half an hour had elapsed it veiled the midday light of heaven, and spread over the sky like the glooms of night. A low moaning sound as of a rising hurricane then began to break the drear stillness of the scene, and fierce blasts to career wildly over the heaving bosom of the waters.

"Still the Brahman continued his prayer.

"Now huge billowy waves burst like thunder upon the yellow sands, the zig-zag lightning streaking the murky sky blinded the eyes, whilst the roar of the elements deafened the ears of the trembling crowd. Yet they stood rooted to the spot by a mightier power than they could control. The Rajah, on his elephant, and the beggar crawling upon his knees, all had prepared for themselves one common doom.

"Before the bright car of Surya,* the Lord of Day, borne by its flaming steeds with agate hoofs, had entered upon their starry way, the wavelet was rippling, and the sea-gull flapping his snowy wing over the city of Cherooman the Apostate."

* *Surya*, the Hindoo Phœbus.

CHAPTER XI.

MALABAR.

THE province, now called Malabar, is part of the Kerula Rajya, the kingdom of Kerula, one of the fifty-six *deshas*, or regions, enumerated in ancient Hindoo history as forming the Bharata Khanda or Land of India. It is supposed to have been recovered from the sea by the sixth incarnation of Vishnu, who in expiation of a matricidal crime gave over to the Brahmans, particularly to those of the Moonsut tribe, the broad lands lying between Gokarna* and Kanya Kumari, or Cape Comorin. The country is also known by the names of Malayalim, the "mountain land;" Malangara and Cherun,†

* *Go-karna*, the "Cow's-ear," a celebrated place of pilgrimage in the Canara district.

† *Cherun* or *Chairun* was one of the three kingdoms contained in South India; the other two were Sholum (Tanjore) and Pundium (Madura).

from the Rajahs, who governed it at an early period. It is probably the kingdom of Pandion, described in the pages of the classical geographers.

By Malabar we now understand the little tract bounded on the north by Canara, to the south by the province of Cochin, having Coorg and Mysore to the east, and washed by the waves of the Indian Ocean on the west. Marco Polo (thirteenth century)* speaks of it as a "great kingdom," and Linschoten (sixteenth century) describes it as extending from Comorin to Goa. The natives assert that the old Kerula Rajya was divided into sixty-four *grama* or districts, of which only eight are included in the present province of Malabar.†

* We know not which to admire or to pity the more: this wonderful old traveller's accuracy and truthfulness, or the hard fate which gave him the nickname of Messer Marco Milioni. Tardy justice, however, has been done to his memory, and a learned Italian Orientalist, M. Romagnosi, now asserts, that from his adventurous wanderings "scaturirono tutte le speculazioni e teorie che condussero finalmente alla scoperta del Nuovo Mondo."

† Paolino observes, that the term Malabar ought *not* to be deduced from the Arabic *mala*, a mountain, and *bahr*, a coast. And Paolino is right; neither of those vocables are Arabic at all. The word is of Sanscrit origin, derived from *malya* (मल्य a mountain generally, but particularly the ranges called by us the Western Ghauts), and *var* (वार, a multitude). The Per-

The whole of this part of the coast acquired an early celebrity from the valuable exports* which it dispersed over the Western World. Nelkunda, the chief port, is mentioned by Ptolemy and Pliny: and the author of the "Periplus" places it near Barake or Ela Barake, the roadstead where vessels lay at anchor till their cargoes were brought down to the sea. Major Rennell has identified the ancient Nelkunda with the modern Nelisuram, as the latter place is situated twelve miles up the Cangerecora River—a distance corresponding with

sian word بار (*bar*), used in compounds, as Zang-bar, the region of blacks, or Zanguebar, is palpably a corruption of the said *var*. Thus the original Sanscrit term *malaya-desha*, the mountain land, became in Persian and Arabic *Malbar*, or *Malibar*, and hence our Malabar. A late editor of Marco Polo's travels might have been more cautious than to assert that "the very term is Arabic."

* Anciently described to be pepper, ivory, timber, and pearls. The three former articles are still produced in great abundance.

We may here notice that Vincent translates ξυλα σαγαλινα, "sandalwood," and supposes the word to have been originally written σανδαλινα. He is wrong: the *tectona grandis*, or teak, called throughout Western India *sag* (σαγ), or *sagwan*, is alluded to. So also φαλαγγες σησαμηναι is rendered "ebony in large sticks," and in a note we are informed that it is a corrupt reading, that wood of some sort is meant, but that *sesamum* is a herb. The σησαμ of the Greeks is manifestly the Indian *sisam*, or black tree.

that specified in the "Periplus." Vincent acutely guesses Ela Barake to be the spot near Cananore, called by Marco Polo "Eli," and by us Delhi*—the "Ruddy Mountain" of the ancients.

Malabar, from remote times, has been divided into two provinces, the northern and the southern: the Toorshairoo or Cottah River forming the line of demarcation. The general breadth of the country, exclusive of the district of Wynad, is about twenty-five miles, and there is little level ground. The soil is admirably fertile; in the inland parts it is covered with clumps of bamboos, bananas, mangoes, jacktrees, and several species of palms. Substantial pagodas, and the prettiest possible little villages crown the gentle eminences that rise above the swampy rice lands, and the valleys are thickly strewed with isolated cottages and homesteads, whose thatched roofs, overgrown with creepers, peep out from the masses of luxuriant

* It is variously and incorrectly written Dely, Delly, D'illi, and Dilla. The mountain derives its present name from a celebrated Moslem fakir, Mahommed of Delhi, who died there, and is invoked by the sea-faring people of the coast. Its Hindoo appellation is *Yeymullay*. No stress therefore should be laid upon the resemblance between Mount Delhi and the *Ela* Barake of the Periplus. The identity of the two places rests, however, on good local evidence.

vegetation, the embankments and the neat fences of split bamboo interlaced with thorns, that conceal them. Each tenement has its own croft planted with pepper, plantains, and the betel vine, with small tufts of cocoas, bamboos, and that most graceful species of the palm, the tall and feathery areca. These hamlets are infinitely superior in appearance to aught of the kind we have ever seen in India; the houses are generally built of brick or hewn stone and mortar, and those belonging to the wealthy have been copied from the Anglo-Indian bungalow. As the traveller passes he will frequently see the natives sitting at their doors upon chairs exactly as the rustics of Tuscany would do. The quantity of rain that annually falls* covers the ground with the bloom of spontaneous vegetation; cocoa-trees rise upon the very verge where land ends, and in some places the heaps of sand that emerge a few feet from the surface of the sea, look bright with a cap of emerald hue. In consequence of the great slope of the country the heaviest monsoon leaves little or no trace behind it, so that lines of communication once formed are easily preserved. Generally speaking

* Varying from eighty to one hundred and thirty-five inches per annum.

the roads are little more than dykes running over the otherwise impassable paddy fields, and, during wet weather, those in the lower grounds are remarkably bad. Some of the highways are macadamised with pounded laterite spread in thin layers upon the sand; the material is found in great quantities about Calicut, and it makes an admirable monsoon road, as the rain affects it but little on account of its extreme hardness. The magnificent avenues of trees,* which shade the principal lines, are most grateful to man and beast in a tropical climate. On all of them, however, there is one great annoyance, particularly during the monsoon, namely, the perpetual shifting to and from ferries† — an

* Unhappily the banyan has been selected, a tree which, though sufficiently shady when its root-like branches are allowed to reach the ground, is comparatively valueless as a protection against the sun, when planted by a roadside. Also, it is easily overthrown by high winds, for, after a time, the long and tenacious roots that uphold it rot off, and the thin branches of young shoots that cling round the parent stem have not the power to support its weight. A third disadvantage in the banyan is, that in many places the boughs grow low, and a horseman's head is in perpetual danger.

† The usual ferry-boat is a platform of planks lashed to two canoes, and generally railed round. We know not a more disagreeable predicament than half an hour's trip upon one of these vessels, with a couple of biting and kicking nags on board.

operation rendered necessary by the network of lakes, rivers, and breakwaters, that intersects the country. A great public use could be made of these inconvenient streams: with very little cutting a channel of communication might be run down the coast, and thus the conveyance of goods would remain uninterrupted even during the prevalence of the most violent monsoons. Water transit, we may observe, would be a grand boon here, as carts are rare, cattle transport is almost unknown, and the transmission of merchandise by means of coolies or porters is the barbarous, slow, and expensive method at present necessarily in general use.

The practical husbandry of Malabar is essentially rude, and yet in few countries have we seen more successful cultivation. The plough is small, of simple form, and so light, that it merely scratches the ground; a pair of bullocks, or a bullock and a woman or two, are attached to the log, and whilst the labourer dawdles over his task, he chaunts monotonous ditties to Mother Earth with more pious zeal than industry. The higher lands produce the betel vine, cocoa, areca, and jack-trees,*

* The botanical name of this tree is derived from the Malayalim *adeka*, a betel nut. The English "jackfruit" is

together with hill rice: the latter article is sown some time after the setting in of the heavy rains, and reaped about September or October. The lower rice-fields, lying in the valleys between the acclivities, are laid out in little plots, with raised footpaths between to facilitate passage and regulate the irrigation. They generally bear one, often two, and in some favoured spots, three crops a year; the average is scarcely more than six or seven fold, though a few will yield as much as thirty. The south-west monsoon, which lasts from June to September, brings forward the first harvest: the second is indebted to the south-east rains which set in about a month later. The Sama (Panicum Miliaceum) requires the benefit of wet weather; it is therefore sown in May, and reaped in August. The oil plant Yelloo (Sesamum Orientale) and the cooltie or horsegram cannot be put into the ground till the violence of the monsoon has abated.

The annual revenue of Malabar is about thirty lacs of rupees (300,000*l.*), land is valuable, the reason probably being that it is for the most part private, not government property.

the Portuguese "jacka," a corruption of the native name *chukka.*

When the Hindoo law authorizes a twelfth, an eighth, or a sixth, and at times of urgent necessity even a fourth of the crop to be taken, specifying the Shelbhaga, or one-sixth, as the rulers' usual share, it appears extraordinary that this province was exempted from all land-tax till 913,* or A.D. 1736-7. We may account for the peculiarity, however, by remembering that the country belonged, properly speaking, to the Brahmans, who were, in a religious point of view, the owners of the soil. Moreover, the avowed and legitimate sources of revenue were sufficient for the purposes of a government that had no standing army, and whose militia was supported chiefly by assignments of land. The rulers, however, were anything but wealthy: many of their perquisites were, it is true, by a stretch of authority, converted into the means of personal aggrandisement, but the influence of the Brahmans, and the jealousy of the chiefs,

* Of the Malayalim æra. It is called Kolum, from a village of that name, and dates its beginning in A.D. 824, the time when a rich Nair merchant adorned the place with a splendid palace and tank. Previous to its establishment, the natives used a cycle of twelve years, each called after some zodiacal sign. The months were also denoted by the same terms, so that the name of the year and the month were periodically identical.

generally operated as efficient checks upon individual ambition.

Malabar has been subjected to three different assessments.

1st. That of the Hindoo Rajahs.

2dly. In the days of the Moslems, and,

3dly. Under the British Government.

We propose to give a somewhat detailed account of the chief items composing the curious revenue of the Hindoo rajahs and chiefs in the olden time.

1. *Unka*, battle-wager, or trial by single combat. Quarrels and private feuds were frequent amongst the Nairs, especially when differences on the subject of the fair sex, or any of their peculiar principles of honour aroused their pugnacity. It was not indispensable that the parties who were at issue should personally fight it out. Champions were allowed by law, and in practice were frequently substituted. The combatants undertook to defend the cause they espoused till death, and a term of twelve years was granted to them that they might qualify themselves for the encounter by training and practising the use of arms. Before the onset both champions settled all their worldly matters, as the combat was *à l'outrance.*

The weapons used were sword and dagger: a small shield and a thick turban being the only articles of defensive armour. This system of duelling was a source of considerable revenue to the Rajah, as he was umpire of the battle, and levied the tax in virtue of his office. The amount of the fee varied according to the means of the parties. Sometimes it was as high as one thousand fanams.*

2. *Poorooshandrum*—a word literally meaning the "death of the man"—a relief or sum of money claimed by the ruler from Nadwallees,† Deshwallees, heads of guilds, holders of land in free gift or under conditional tenure, and generally from all persons enjoying Sthanum or official position in the state, whenever an heir succeeded to a death vacancy. The chiefs of provinces and districts, like the private proprietors, were exclusively entitled to receive Poorooshandrum from their own tenantry, as a price of entry paid upon the decease of either party, lessor or lessee. Sometimes the chiefs claimed the privilege of levying this tax from the Rajah's subjects living under their protection. It is supposed that the Hindoo rulers were entitled,

* Equal to Cos. Rs. 250, about 25*l.*

† See Chapter XII.

under the head of Poorooshandrum, to a certain share of the property left by deceased Moslems, but the prevalent opinion seems to be that in such cases there was no fixed sum payable, and, moreover, that it was not claimed from all, but only from those individuals who held situations or enjoyed privileges dependent upon the will and favour of the Rajah. This tax, so similar to one of our feudal sources of revenue in the West, often reached the extent of one thousand two hundred fanams.

3. *Polyatta Penna,* or degraded women, were another source of profit to the Rajah, who exacted various sums from Brahman families for the maintenance of such females, and for saving them from further disgrace. These persons became partial outcastes, not slaves in the full sense of the word; and yet the rulers used to sell them to the Chetties, or coast merchants. Their offspring always married into families of the same degraded class, and, after a few generations, the memory of their origin was lost in the ramifications of the race into which they had been adopted.

4. *Kaleecha*—another feudal tax, answering to the Nuzzuranah of Mussulman India. It consisted of presents made by all ranks of people to the ruler on such occasions of congratulation and con-

dolence as his ascending the throne, opening a new palace, marrying, and dying. The amount expected varied from two to one thousand fanams.

5. *Chungathum*, or protection. Whenever a person wished to place himself under the safeguard of a man of consequence, he paid from four to sixty-four fanams annually for the privilege. He might also make an assignment on particular lands for the payment. The sum was devoted to the maintenance of a kind of sentinel, similar to the belted official Peon of the Anglo-Indian settlements, furnished by the protector to his dependent. In cases of necessity, however, the former was bound to aid and assist the other with a stronger force.

6. *Recha-Bhogum*—a tax differing from Chungathum only in one point, viz., that the engagement was a general one, unlimited to any specific aid in the first instance.

7. Under the name of *Uttudukum*, the Rajah was entitled to the property of any person who, holding lands in free gift, died without heirs; moreover, no adoption was valid without his sanction. The feudal chiefs had similar privileges with respect to their tenants.

8. *Udeema punum*—the yearly payment of

one or two fanams, levied by every Tumbooran * or patron from his Udian (client).

9. *Soonka*—customs upon all imports and exports by land or sea. The amount is variously specified as two-and-a-half, three, and even ten per cent.

10. *Yela*—the systematic usurpation of territory belonging to the neighbouring rulers or chiefs, whom poverty or other causes incapacitated from holding their own. The Hindoo Scripture affirms that territorial aggrandisement is the proper object and peculiar duty of a king.

11. *Kola* or *Charadayum*—forced contributions levied by Rajahs on occasions of emergency, according to the circumstances of their subjects.

12. *Tuppa*—mulcts imposed upon those who were convicted of accidental and unintentional offences.

13. *Pala*—fines taken in the same manner for intentional crimes, according to their magnitude and the circumstances of the criminal. They sometimes extended to a total confiscation of property.

14. *Ponnarippa*—the sifting of gold. Gold dust generally was a perquisite belonging to the Rajah or Nadwallee, as the case might be.

* Tumbooran, in Malayalim, means a lord or prince. If a minor he is termed Tumban.

15. *Udeenya Oorookul*, or shipwrecked vessels, which became crown property.

16. *Chaireekul*, or private domains, which the Rajahs possessed in proprietary right, acquired either by purchase, lapses, or escheats.

17. *Aeemoola* } Cows with three and five dugs.
18. *Moomoola* }

19. *Chengkomba*, or cattle that had destroyed life, human or bestial.

20. *Kunnuda poolee*—beeves born with a peculiar white spot near the corner of the eye.

21. *Ana-pidee*—elephants caught in the jungles.

22. *Poowala*—buffalos with a white spot at the tip of the tail.

23. *Koomba*—the tusks of dead elephants.

24. *Korawa*—the leg of a hog, deer, or any other eatable animal killed in the jungles.

25. *Wala* } The tail and skin of a tiger.
26. *Tola* }

27. *Kennutil punne*—a pig that had fallen into a well.*

* Most of the matter contained in this chapter has been taken from old and valuable papers preserved in the Nuzoor Cutcherry at Calicut. By the kindness of the collector we were permitted to inspect and make any extracts from them we pleased.

This system of aid and perquisites, rather than of taxes and assessments, continued, as we have said before, till A.D. 1736. At that time the invasion of the Ikkairee, or Bednore Rajah, to whom the Canara province was then in subjection, obliged some of the rulers of Northern Malabar to levy twenty per cent. on Patum, or rent. The part of the Palghaut and Temelpooram districts, which belonged to the Calicut house, was subjected to a land tax, under the name of Kavil, or compensation for protection. With these exceptions,* Malabar was free from any land rent or regular assessment proportioned to the gross produce before Hyder's invasion in A.D. 1777.

Some are of opinion that, during Hyder's life, the land-tax assumed, in the Southern division of Malabar, the shape which it now bears in the public records. Others attribute the principles of the assessment to Arshad Beg Khan, the Foujdar, or commander of Tippoo Sultan's forces in Malabar, about A.D. 1783. His system was carefully examined by Messrs. Duncan, Page, Bodham, and

* The reader must bear in mind that in Malabar, as in all other native states, contributions carefully proportioned to the circumstances of the parties so mulcted, were called for on every occasion of emergency.

Dow, who, in 1792 and 1793, were appointed commissioners to inspect and report upon the state and condition of the country. To their laborious work* we must refer the curious reader, as the subject is far too lengthy and profound to suit such light pages as these.

* In three vols. Printed at the *Courier* press, Bombay.

CHAPTER XII.

THE HINDOOS OF MALABAR.

When Parasu Rama, the demigod, departed this transitory life, he left, as we said before, the kingdom of Malabar as a heritage to the priestly caste. For many years a hierarchy of Brahmans governed the land.* At length, finding themselves unable to defend the country, they established Nair chiefs in each Nad (province), and Desha (village),† called from their places of jurisdiction Nadwallee and Deshwallee. The main distinction between them seems to have been, that whereas the latter could not command more than a hundred

* Tradition obscurely alludes to a Rajah called Kerulam (probably from his kingdom), who reigned sixty-three years after Parasu Rama.

† In Sanscrit the word means a continent, country, or region: it is used hereabouts in a limited sense, generally signifying a village.

fighting men, the Nadwallee never went to battle with a smaller number than that under his banner; some few led as many as twenty thousand vassals to the field. Both were bound to conduct the affairs of their feofs, to preserve the peace of the country, and to assemble and head their respective forces at the summons of the Rajah. There does not appear to have been any limitation to the power of settling disputes vested in these feudal superiors, nor were they prohibited from taking fines and costs of suit;* parties appearing before them had, however, a right of appeal to the Rajah. These dignities were hereditary; still they may be considered political offices,—for, in case of demise, the heir did not succeed without a formal investiture by the ruler, and a relief, or fine of entry, taken in token of allegiance. Like the feudal landowners of England, both the Nadwallee and the Deshwallee were dependent upon the prince to whom they swore the oath of fidelity. Neither of these dignitaries was necessarily owner of all

* The Hindoo law lays down five per cent. as the amount to be levied from the plaintiff, ten from the defendant if cast in a suit, otherwise he is exempt from any tax. Some of the Rajahs were by no means content with such a moderate perquisite; the ruler of Cochin, for instance, never took less than double the sum above specified.

the landed property within his province or village boundaries: in fact he seldom was so, although there was no objection to his becoming proprietor by purchase or other means. They were not entitled to a share of the produce of the lands in their jurisdiction, nor could they claim the seignoral privileges, which the heads of villages on the eastern coast, and many other parts of India, enjoy. Under the Deshwallee of each village were several Turravattakara,* or chief burgesses. They possessed a certain hereditary dignity, but no controlling authority. In them, however, we may trace the germ of a municipal corporation, as their position entitled them to the honour of being applied to on occasions of marriages, deaths, religious ceremonies, and differences amongst the vassals. When their mediation failed the cause went before the Deshwallee.

The anarchy introduced by this complicated variety of feudalism soon compelled the hierarchy to call in the aid of the Bejanuggur, or, as it is commonly termed, the Anagundy government, and the latter, at the solicitation of the Brahmans, appointed a Peroomal, or Viceroy, whose adminis-

* Sometimes called Prumani and Mookoodee, "principal inhabitants."

tration was limited to the term of twelve years, to rule the fair lands of Malabar. These governors, who are also known by the name of Cherun,* were first appointed in the 3511th year of the Kali Yug,† about A.D. 410. Seventeen of them, curious to say, followed each other in regular succession. The last, however, Cherooman Peroomal,‡ so ingratiated himself with his temporary subjects, that he reigned thirty-six years, and, at the head of a numerous army, defeated the home government, which attempted to dispossess him of his power, in a pitched battle fought near the village of Annamalay.§ Afterwards, becoming a convert to Islam, he made a pilgrimage to Mecca. Before leaving India, he divided the province among the seventeen chiefs ‖ to whose valour he was indebted for his success in war. These were the ancestors of the present race of Rajahs.

* "Ruler of the land of Cherun." See Chapter XI.

† The current æra of the Hindoos.

‡ See Chapter X.

§ In the present talook of Temelpooram.

‖ Captain Hamilton—no great authority by the bye in such matters—relates that the Samiry divided his territories between his four nephews, and says that the partition led to long and bloody wars between the brothers. He probably confounded a Moslem with the Hindoo tradition.

Malabar was soon torn with intestine feuds, arising from the power and ambition of its host of rulers, and the Samiry, Samoory, or Calicut Rajah, soon became *de facto*—if not *de jure*—the lord paramount. He was a native of Poontoora, in the Coimbatore province, and derived his name, Mana Vikram, from Manicham and Vikram—the two brothers present on the occasion when Cheroo-man conferred dominion upon the head of the house. His superiority was acknowledged until Hyder's time, by all the chiefs from the north point of Malabar to the south extremity of Travancore.

After that Hyder had become regent of Mysore, he made use of the following pretext for invading Malabar. The Palghaut Rajah, a descendant from the Pandian sovereigns of Madura, terrified by the power of the Samiry, had, in early times, sought the alliance of the Mysore state, then governed by its Hindoo princes, and constituted himself a client of the same by paying a certain annual sum for a subsidiary force to be stationed in his territory. The ambitious Moslem, under colour of avenging his ally and protecting him against the oppressions of the Samiry and other princes, forthwith attacked them on their own ground.

The manner in which the Calicut house is and has been, from the days of hoar antiquity, broken and divided, appears curious in the extreme. It may be supposed that the Brahmans, jealous of the overgrown power of one individual, in the person of the Samiry, endeavoured to temper its force by assigning to the other members of the family certain official dignities, together with concomitant privileges. It is also possible that this partition might have taken place at the solicitation of the princes, who naturally would wish to secure for themselves a settled and independent subsistence. They were appointed to act as a council to the reigning sovereign; they could check his authority as well as aid him in his wisdom; and, finally, they were his principal officers, each having separate and particular duties to perform. By this arrangement, in case of the ruler's demise, his heir would succeed to the throne without any of the harassing disturbances and sanguinary contentions so common amongst Asiatic nations.

Where rank and property descend from father to son, there is little difficulty in settling the succession. But when families remain united for years under the Murroo-muka-tayum, or inheritance by the nephew or sister's son—the strange law which prevails among the Rajahs and Nairs of Malabar—it becomes by no means an easy matter to ascertain who is the senior in point of birth. The crafty Brahmans provided against this difficulty by establishing a system of intermediate dignities, which acted as a register, and by requiring a long interval of time, during which each individual's rights might be frequently discussed and deliberately settled, to elapse between promotion from the inferior to the superior grades.

The head of the Calicut house, who may be supposed to occupy the position of the first Samiry's mother, is called the Vullia Tumbooratee,* or principal queen. She resides in the Kovilugum, or palace of Umbadee. Priority of birth gives a claim to this dignity, and the eldest of all the princesses is entitled to it, no matter what be her relationship to the reigning sovereign. The Umbadee is the only indispensable palace; but, for the sake of convenience, an unlimited number of private dwellings have been established for the junior princesses. Thus we find the "new palace," the "eastern palace" (relatively to the Umbadee), the "western

* Tumbooratee, in Malayalim, a lady or princess; if a minor she is termed Tumbatee.

palace," and many others.* The queen and princesses are compelled to occupy the residences allotted to their several ranks; they are also prohibited from holding any commerce with men of their own family, as their paramours must either be of the Kshatriya † (military) caste, or Numboory Brahmans, and may not be changed without the consent of the Samiry and that of the whole body of near relations.

The princes are taken according to their seniority out of the above-mentioned Umbadees, and the eldest of all, when a death occurs, becomes the Samiry. There are five palaces of state allotted to the different princes—namely, the Samotree Kovilugum, or palace of the First Rajah; the Yeirumpiree Kovilugum, or palace of the Yellia Rajah—the heir apparent to the Samiry-ship; and three others, which are respectively termed the "Governments of the Third, Fourth, and Fifth Portions. After that a prince has been once established in any of these dignities, his order of rank may be considered

* The above four are the only recognised palaces.

† Some of the present chieftains of Malabar style themselves Kshatriyas, but by far the greater number derive their pedigree from the intercourse of Brahmans with the royal ladies, who principally belong to the Nair caste of Hindoos.

finally settled: he cannot be superseded, but must, if he lives, rise step by step — each time with formal investiture — till he attains the highest dignity. Whenever a superior palace becomes vacant, he is duly installed in it, and succeeds to the revenue arising from the landed property belonging to it. But he cannot remove any of the furniture, or the gold and silver utensils, from the inferior residence which he formerly occupied, as these articles are considered public goods, and, as such, are marked with distinctive stamps. Under all circumstances, however, the prince retains the right of private property.

The principles of the arrangement which we have attempted to describe, not only exist in the Calicut house but pervade all the families of the different Rajahs in Malabar.

In the intercourse between the princes there is much ceremony, and, as might be expected, little affection. No one is allowed to sit down in the presence of a superior; all must stand before the Samiry, and do obeisance to him with folded hands.

According to a census taken in 1846, the different castes were enumerated as follows in round numbers:—

1. Numboory Brahmans . .	5,500
2. Puttur, or foreign Brahmans .	15,200
3. Nairs	370,000
4. Tiyars	340,000
5. Moplahs . . .	315,000
6. Fishermen . . .	15,300
7. Chermur, or serfs . .	160,000
8. Christians and other strangers .	9,000
Total	1,230,000*

Even in India, the land of ethnologic marvels, there are few races so strange and remarkable in their customs as the people of Malabar. The soil or the climate seems to have exercised some peculiar effect upon its inhabitants: Hindoos as well as Moslems abound in peculiarities unknown to their tenets and practices in other parts of the world. The correctness of our observation will appear in the following sketches of the different castes.

The priesthood of Malabar is at present divided into two great classes; the Numboory, Numoodree or Malabar Brahmans, and the Puttur, or families of the pontifical stock that do not originally belong to the country.

* This gives upwards of two hundred souls per mile, estimating the extent of Malabar at about six thousand square miles.

The Numboory is the scion of an ancient and celebrated tree. The well known polemic Sankaracharya belonged to this race; he was born in the village of Kaludee, in the 3501st, or, according to others, the 3100th year of the Kali Yug. His fame rests principally upon his celebrated work, the sixty-four *anacharun*, or Exceptions to Established Rules, composed for the purpose of regulating and refining the customs of his fellow religionists.* No copy of the institutes which have produced permanent effects upon the people exists in Malabar. There is a history of the saint's life called Sankaracharya Chureedun, containing about seven hundred stanzas, written by a disciple.

The Numboory family is governed by several regulations peculiar to it: only the eldest of any number of brothers takes a woman of his own caste to wife. All the juniors must remain single except when the senior fails in having issue. This life of celibacy became so irksome to the Brahmans that they induced the Nair caste to permit unrestrained intercourse between their females and themselves, it being well understood that the

* It ordained, for instance, that corpses shall be burned within private premises, instead of being carried out for that purpose into the woods, &c.

priesthood was conferring an especial honour upon their disciples. Probably in order to please the compliant Shudras the more, the Numboory in many parts of the country changed their regular mode of succession for the inheritance by nephews practised amongst the Nairs. As might be supposed, the birth of female children is considered an enormous evil by these Brahmans; their daughters frequently live and die unmarried, and even when a suitable match has been found for them, their nuptials are seldom celebrated till late in life, owing to the extraordinary expense of the ceremony. Throughout India the marriage of a girl is seldom delayed after her twelfth year; in Malabar, few Numboory women are married before they reach the age of twenty-five or thirty. They are most strictly watched, and all *faux pas* are punished by a sort of excommunication pronounced by the hereditary Brahman, with the consent of the Rajah. The relations of the female delinquent are also heavily fined, and such mulcts in ancient times formed one of the items of the ruler's revenue.

There is nothing striking in the appearance of the Numboory. He is, generally speaking, a short, spare man, of a dark olive-coloured complexion, sharp features, and delicate limbs. His toilette is not elaborate; a piece of white cotton cloth fastened round the waist, and a similar article thrown loosely over the shoulders, together with the cord of the twice-born, compose the *tout ensemble*. These Brahmans are solemn in their manners and deportment, seldom appear in public, and when they do, they exact and receive great respect from their inferiors in caste. A Nair meeting a Numboory must salute him by joining the palms of the hands together, and then separating them three successive times.*

The Nairs† are a superior class of Shudra, or servile Hindoos, who formerly composed the militia,‡ or landwehr, of Malabar. Before the land-tax was introduced they held estates rent free; the only

* There is an abridged form of this salutation, which consists of joining the hands and then parting them, at the same time bending the fingers at the second joint.

† This word generally follows the name of the individual, and seems to be the titular appellation of the class. It is probably derived from the Sanscrit Nayaka (a chief), like the Teloogoo Naidoo, the Canarese and Tamul Naikum, and the Hindoo Naik.

‡ Captain Hamilton makes the number of fighting men throughout the province, of course including all castes, amount to one million two hundred and sixty-two thousand.

prestation required from them was personal service; to attend the rajah, or chief, on all official and religious occasions, and to march to battle under his banner. When absent from their homes, they were entitled to a daily subsistence, called Kole. Their arms were sword and shield, spear and matchlock, with a long knife or dagger suspended behind the back by a hook attached to a leathern waistband. Being now deprived of their favourite pastimes — fighting and plundering — they have become cultivators of the soil, and disdain not to bend over the plough, an occupation formerly confined to their slaves. And yet to the present day they retain much of their old military character, and with it the licentiousness which in Eastern countries belongs to the profession of arms. In fact, "war, wine, and women" appear to be the three ingredients of their *summum bonum,* and forced abstinence from the first, only increases the ardour of their affection for the last two. Although quite opposed to the spirit of Hindoo law, intoxication and debauchery never degrade a Nair from his caste.

Wedlock can hardly be said to exist among the Nairs. They perform, however, a ceremony called *kulleanum*, which in other castes implies marriage, probably a relic of the nuptial rite. The Nair woman has a Talee, or necklace, bound round her throat by some fellow-caste man, generally a friend of the family; a procession then ambulates the town, and by virtue thereof the lady takes the title of Ummah, or matron. But the gentleman is not entitled to the privileges of a husband, nor has he any authority over the said matron's person or property. She is at liberty to make choice of the individual with whom she intends to live—her Bhurtao, as her protector is called, she becoming his Bharya. The connection is termed Goona-doshum, words which literally signify "good and bad," and imply an agreement between the parties to take each other for better and worse; it cannot be dissolved without the simple process of one party "giving warning" to the other. In former times, the lady used always to reside in her mother's house, but this uncomfortable practice is now rapidly disappearing.

Another peculiar custom which prevails among the Nairs, is the murroo-muka-tayum,* hereditary succession by sisters' sons; or in case of their failing, by the male nearest in consanguinity from the father's grandmother. The ancient ordinances

* Opposed to muka-tayum, the succession of sons.

of Malabar forbade a Nair to leave his property by will to his offspring, and it was considered unbecoming to treat a son with the affection shown to a nephew. Of late years some heads of families have made a provision for their own children during life time, but it has been necessary to procure the assent of the rightful heirs to bequests thus irregularly made. When property is left to sons, the division follows the general Hindoo law, with two essential points of difference. In the first place, children inherit the estate of the mother only ; and, secondly, a daughter is, in certain cases, entitled to preference to a son. Thus, a female can, a male cannot, mortgage or sell land inherited from his maternal progenitor : after his death it must revert to those who were co-heirs with him ; and though a man is entitled to the same share as his sister, his right to it continues only as long as they live in the same house.

The origin of this extraordinary law is lost in the obscurity of antiquity. The Brahmans, according to some, were its inventors ; others suppose that they merely encouraged and partially adopted it. Its effects, politically speaking, were beneficial to the community at large. The domestic ties, always inconvenient to a strictly military population, were thereby conveniently weakened, and the wealth, dignity, and unbroken unity of interests were preserved for generations unimpaired in great and powerful families, which, had the property been divided among the several branches, according to the general practice of Hinduism, would soon have lost their weight and influence. As it was unnecessary that a woman should be removed from her home, or introduced into a strange family, the eldest nephew on the sister's side, when he became the senior male member of the household, succeeded, as a matter of course, to the rights, property, and dignity of Karnovun.*

We suspect that the priesthood—those crafty politicians whose meshes of mingled deceit and superstition have ever held the Hindoo mind "in durance vile"—were the originators of the murroo-muka-tayum and the goonadoshum. Both inventions, like many of the laws of Lycurgus, appear the result of well-digested plans for carrying out the one proposed object. They are audacious encroachments upon the rights of human nature; and we cannot account for their existence by any supposition except that the law-givers were determined to rear a race of warriors—no matter by

* The head of the house.

what means. As a corroboration of our theory, we may instance the fact that these strange and now objectless ordinances are gradually giving way to the tide of truer feeling. Already the succession of nephews has been partially broken through, and in the present day the control of the heads of families is nothing compared with what it was.

There is a tradition among the Nairs, that anciently, the Samiry Rajah was, by the law of the land, compelled to commit suicide by cutting his throat in public at the expiration of a twelve-years' reign. When that ceremony became obsolete, another and an equally peculiar one was substituted in its stead. A jubilee was proclaimed throughout the kingdom, and thousands flocked from all directions to the feasts and festivals prepared for them at Calicut. On an appointed day, the Rajah, after performing certain religious rites, repaired to the shore, and sat down upon a cushion, unarmed, bareheaded, and almost undressed, whilst any four men of the fighting caste, who had a mind to win a crown, were allowed to present themselves as candidates for the honour of regicide. They were bathed in the sea, and dressed in pure garments, which, as well as their persons, were profusely sprinkled over with perfumes and water coloured yellow by means of turmeric. A Brahman then putting a long sword and small round shield into each man's hand, told him to "go in and win" if he could. Almost incredible though it may appear, some cases are quoted in which a lucky desperado succeeded in cutting his way through the thirty or forty thousand armed guards who stood around the Rajah, and in striking off the sovereign's head. This strange practice has of late years been abolished.

The Nairs are rather a fair and comely race, with neat features, clean limbs, and decidedly a high caste look. They shave the head all over, excepting one long thin lock of hair, which is knotted at the end, and allowed to lie flat upon the crown. Neither cap nor turban is generally worn. Their dress consists of the usual white cotton cloth fastened round the loins: when *en grande tenue*, a similar piece hangs round their necks, or is spread over the shoulders. We have alluded to the appearance of their females in our account of Calicut, and may here observe that we were rather fortunate in having accidentally seen them. The Nair is as jealous as he is amorous and vindictive: many travellers have passed through the country without being able to catch one glimpse of their women, and the knife would be unhesitatingly used if a foreigner attempted to satisfy his curiosity by anything like forcible measures.

The Tian* of Malabar is to the Nair what the villein was to the feoffee of feudal England. These two families somewhat resemble each other in appearance, but the former is darker in complexion, and less "castey" in form and feature than the latter. It is the custom for modest women of the Tiyar family to expose the whole of the person above the waist, whereas females of loose character are compelled by custom to cover the bosom. As this class of Hindoo, generally speaking, provides the European residents with nurses and other menials, many of our countrymen have tried to make them adopt a somewhat less natural costume. The proposal, however, has generally been met pretty much in the same spirit which would be displayed were the converse suggested to an Englishwoman.

In writings the Tiyar are styled Eelavun. They are supposed to be a colony of strangers from an island of that name near Ceylon. An anomaly in the Hindoo system they certainly are: learned

* The masculine singular of this word is Tian (fem. Tiatti), in the plural Tiyar.

natives know not whether to rank them among the Shudras or not; some have designated them by the term Uddee Shudra, meaning an inferior branch of the fourth great division. Their principal employments are drawing toddy, dressing the heads of cocoa and other trees, cultivating rice lands, and acting as labourers, horse-keepers, and grass-cutters; they are free from all prejudices that would remove them from Europeans, and do not object to duties which only the lowest outcastes in India will condescend to perform. Some few have risen to respectability and even opulence by trade. They will not touch the flesh of the cow, and yet they have no objection to other forbidden food. They drink to excess, and are fond of quarrelling over their cups. Unlike the Nairs, they are deficient in spirit; they are distinguished from the natives of Malabar generally by marrying and giving in marriage. Moreover, property with them descends regularly from father to son.

Throughout the province a sort of vassalage seems to have been established universally among the Tiyar, occasionally among the Nair tribes.*

* The Moplahs, as strangers, and the merchants, tradespeople, and professional men who had no fixed places of residence, did not engage in this feudal relationship.

The latter would sometimes place himself in a state of dependency upon some Rajah, or powerful chief, and pay Chungathum,* or protection-money, for the advantage derived from the connexion. The Tiyar willingly became the Udian † of any superior whose patronage would guarantee him quiet possession of his goods and chattels. This kind of allegiance by no means amounted to slavery. The Tumbooran could not dispose of the person or property of his vassal, nor did the private tie acquit an individual of any public duty to the Rajah or his representatives upon emergent occasions. The patron was on all occasions bound to defend, protect, and procure redress for his client—favours which the latter acknowledged by yearly tribute, and by affording personal service to his superior in private quarrels. To the present day the Tian will immediately say who his Tumbooran is: the annual offerings are still kept up, and though British law entitles all parties to equality of social

* See Chapter XI.

† The word Udian, in Malayalim and Tamul, literally signifies a slave. Here it is used in its limited signification of vassal or client, as opposed to the Tumbooran or patron. The word, however, would be considered degrading to a Nair, and is therefore never applied to him.

rights, it must be an injury of some magnitude that can induce the inferior to appear against his patron in a court of justice. Some individuals became vassals of the Pagoda, which, in its turn, often subjected itself to fee a Rajah for the maintenance of its rights and the defence of its property.

The reader will remark how peculiarly characteristic of the nation this state of voluntary dependency is. In European history we find the allodialist putting himself and his estate in a condition of vassalage, but he did so because it was better to occupy the property as a fief incident to certain services than to lose it altogether, or even to be subjected to pillage and forced contributions. But the Asiatic is not comfortable without the shade of a patron over his head ; even if necessity originally compelled him to sacrifice half his freedom, habit and inclination perpetuate the practice long after all object for its continuance has ceased to exist.

The Chermur,* or serfs of Malabar, amongst the Hindoos, were entirely prædial or rustic. The sys-

* "Sons of the soil," from cher, earth, and mukkul, children. In the masculine singular the word is chermun (fem. chermee), plural, chermur.

tem of slavery is said to have been introduced by Parasu Rama, as a provision for agriculture when he gave the country to the Brahmans. We may account for it more naturally by assigning its origin and referring its subsequent prevalence to the operation of the ancient Indian laws. The rules of caste were so numerous and arbitrary that constant deviations from them would take place in a large community; and for certain offences freeborn individuals became Chandalas (outcastes), and were liable to disenfranchisement.

Servitude in Malabar offered few of the revolting, degrading, and horrible features which characterized it in the ancient, mediæval, and modern annals of the Western World. The proprietor never had the power of life or death over a slave without the sanction of the feudal chief, or more generally of the sovereign; he could inflict corporeal punishment upon him, but old established custom limited the extent as effectually as law would. Moreover, in this part of the globe serfs were born and bred in subserviency, they had no cherished memories of rights and comforts once enjoyed,—no spirit of independence conscious of a title to higher privileges and indignant at unjust seclusion from them. In their case slavery did not begin with the horrors of violent separation from country and home, the cruelties of a ship-imprisonment, forcible introduction to new habits and customs, food and dress, languages and connections. They were not degraded to the level of beasts, nor were they subjected to treatment of the worst description by strange masters, who neither understood their natures, nor sympathized with their feelings.

A proprietor in Malabar could always sell * his serfs with or without the soil, but to remove them far from their homes would have been considered a cruel and unwarrantable measure sufficient to cause and almost justify desertion. Only in some castes the wives of slaves might be sold to another master, and, generally speaking, parents were not separated from their children.† They might, however, be let out in simple rent, or mortgaged under certain deeds. The proprietors were bound to feed their slaves throughout the year. The allowance on work days was double the proportion issued at

* The price of a slave varied from *3l.* to *8l.*

† In the Calicut district, half the children belonged to the mother, or rather to her proprietor, and the other half to the father's master; the odd number was the property of the former. When both parents belonged to one owner, he of course claimed all the offspring.

other times, but it was never less than two pounds of rice to a male, and about three quarters of that quantity to a female. In Malabar there have been instances of a Chermun's holding land in lease, and being responsible to government for paying its taxes. In Canara it was by no means uncommon for slaves to have slips of rice-fields, and small pieces of land given to them by their masters for growing fruit and vegetables. When a slave possessing any property died, his owner was not entitled to it, except in the cases when no lawful heir could be found. In some places on the coast,* and near large towns, the serfs were permitted, when not labouring for their proprietor, to employ themselves in carrying grass, firewood, and other articles to market. On great occasions they expected presents of clothes, oil, grain, and small sums of money whenever the owner was wealthy enough to distribute such *largesse*. And at harvest time they were entitled to a certain portion of the produce, as a compensation for watching the crop.

There are several castes of serfs who do not intermarry or eat with each other. The Poliur is

* Generally speaking, the slaves in the maritime districts were in better condition, and far superior in bodily and mental development to their brethren in the interior.

considered the most industrious, docile, and trustworthy. Proprietors complained loudly of the pilfering propensities displayed by the others. With the exception of the Parayen and Kunnakun tribes, they abstain from slaying the cow, and using beef as an article of food. All are considered impure, though not equally so. For instance, slaves of the Polyan, Waloovan, and Parayen races must stand at a distance of seventy-two paces from the Brahman and Nair: the Kunnakuns may approach within sixty-four, and other servile castes within forty-eight paces of the priestly and military orders.

CHAPTER XIII.

THE MOSLEM AND OTHER NATIVES OF MALABAR.

We are informed by the Moslem historians that their faith spread wide and took deep root in the southern parts of Western India, principally in consequence of the extensive immigration of Arabs. It may be observed that the same cause which provided the Hindoos with serfs, supplied the stranger with proselytes: a Rajah would often, when in want of money, dispose of his outcastes to the Faithful, who, in such cases, seldom failed to make converts of their purchasers.

The Moplahs, or Mapillahs,*—the Moslem inhabitants of Malabar—are a mixed breed, sprung

* There are three different derivations of this word. Some deduce it from the pure Hindostani and corrupted Sanscrit word ma (a mother), and the Tamul pilla (a son), "sons of their mothers," the male progenitor being unknown. Others suppose it to be a compound of mukkul (a daughter) and pilla (a son), "a daughter's son," also an allusion to their origin.

from the promiscuous intercourse that took place between the first Arab settlers and the women of the country. Even to the present day they display in mind and body no small traces of their mongrel origin. They are a light coloured and good looking* race of men, with the high features, the proud expression, and the wiry forms of the descendants of Ishmael: their delicate hands and feet, and their long bushy beards,† show that not a little Hindoo blood flows in their veins. They shave the hair, trim the mostachios according to the Sunnat,‡ and, instead of a turban, wear a small silk or cloth cap of peculiar shape upon their heads. The chest and shoulders are left exposed, and a white or dyed piece of linen, resembling in cut

The third is a rather fanciful derivation from Mokhai-pilla "sons of, or emigrants from, Mocha," in Arabia.

* This description applies exclusively to the higher orders; the labouring classes are dark and ill-favoured.

† The genuine Arab, especially in Yemen and Tehamah, is, generally speaking, a Kusaj, or scant-bearded man; and his envy when regarding the flowing honours of a Persian chin, is only equalled by the lasting regret with which he laments his own deficiency in that semi-religious appurtenance to the human face.

‡ The practice of the Prophet, whom every good Moslem is bound to imitate, even in the most trivial and every-day occasions.

and colour the "lung" or bathing cloth of Central Asia, is tied round the loins. The garment, if we may so call it, worn by the males, does not reach below the calves of the legs, whereas the fair sex prolongs it to the ankles. Unlike the Hindoo inhabitants of Malabar, the upper portion of the female figure is modestly concealed by a shift buttoned round the neck, with large sleeves, and the opening in front: according to the custom of the Faithful a veil is always thrown over the head.

The only peculiarity in the Moplah lady's costume is the horrible ornamenting of the ear. At an early age the lobe is pierced, and a bit of lead, or a piece of Shola wood * is inserted in order to enlarge the orifice. After a time the lobe becomes about the size of a crown piece, and a circle of gold, silver, or palm-leaf, dyed red, white, or yellow, is inserted into it—the distended skin of the lobe containing and surrounding the ring. There is something peculiarly revolting to a stranger's eye in the appearance of the two long strips of flesh instead of ears, which hang down on each side of

* The *Æschynomene paludosa*, a wood of porous texture, which swells when water is poured upon it. Lead is sometimes used to distend the flap of the ear by its weight.

the head in old age, when ornaments are no longer worn.

The countenance of the Moplah, especially when it assumes the expression with which he usually regards infidels and heretics, is strongly indicative of his ferocious and fanatic disposition. His deep undying hatred for the Kafir * is nurtured and strengthened by the priests and religious instructors. Like the hierarchy of the Moslem world in general, they have only to hold out a promise of Paradise to their disciples as a reward, and the most flagrant crimes will be committed. In Malabar they lie under the suspicion of having often suggested and countenanced many a frightful deed of violence. The Moplah is an obstinate ruffian. Cases are quoted of a culprit spitting in the face of a judge when the warrant of execution was being read out to him. Sometimes half a dozen desperadoes will arm themselves, seize upon a substantial house, and send a message of defiance to the collector of the district. Their favourite weapon on such occasions is the long knife that usually hangs from the waist: when entering battle they generally carry two, one in the hand, and the other

* A name, by no means complimentary, applied to all who are not Moslems.

between the teeth. They invariably prepare themselves for combat by a powerful dose of hemp or opium, fight to the last with frenzied obstinacy, despise the most dreadful wounds, and continue to exert themselves when a European would be quite disabled—a peculiarity which they probably inherit from their Arab * ancestors. Like the Malay when he runs a-muck, these men never think of asking for, or giving quarter, they make up their minds to become martyrs, and only try to attain high rank in that glorious body by slaying as many infidels as they can. At times they have been eminently successful. On one occasion we heard of a rencontre in which about a dozen desperate robbers, dropping from the window of a house into the centre of a square, inopportunely formed by a company of seapoys, used their knives with such effect upon the helpless red-coats' backs, that they ran away with all possible precipitation. The result of a few such accidents is, that the native soldier cannot always be trusted to act against them, for, with the usual Hindoo superstition and love of the marvellous, he considers their bravery

* The descendants of the Wild Man have at all times been celebrated for obstinate individual valour, and enduring an amount of "punishment" which seems quite incredible.

something preternatural, and connected with certain fiendish influences.

In former days, the Moplas played a conspicuous part among the pirates who infested the Malabar coast. Marco Polo mentions that there issued annually "a body of upwards of one hundred vessels,* who captured other ships and plundered the merchants." He alludes to their forming what they called a ladder on the sea, by stationing themselves in squadrons of twenty, about five miles from each other, so as to command as great an extent of water as possible. But in the old Venetian's day, the corsairs appear to have been by no means so sanguinary as they afterwards became. He expressly states, that when the pirates took a ship, they did no injury to the crew, but merely said to them, "Go and collect another cargo, that we may have a chance of getting it too." In later times, Tavernier describes them as blood-thirsty in the extreme. "The Malavares are violent Mahometans and very cruel to the Christians.† I saw a barefoot

* Manned in those days by Hindoos. Marco Polo tells us that the people of Malabar are idolaters, and subject to no foreigner.

† Who retorted by hanging them upon the spot, or throwing them overboard. This style of warfare was productive of great barbarities. There is a pile of stone rising above the sea, about

Carmelite friar, who had been taken by the pirates, and so tortured, in order to obtain his ransom,* that his right arm and one leg were shorter by one half than the other." He alludes to their audacity in attacking large armed vessels with squadrons composed of ten or fifteen barques, each carrying from two hundred to two hundred and fifty men, and describes their practice of boarding suddenly and setting fire to the ship with pots of artificial fire. The style of defence usually adopted was to prepare for them by closing the scuttles, and swamping the deck with water, to hinder the fire-pots from doing execution.

The Moplahs being now deprived of their old occupation, have addicted themselves, in some places, to gang-robbery and smuggling. The principal contraband articles are tobacco and salt, both of which are government monopolies.† To

seven leagues north-west of Calicut, called the Sacrifice Rock, from the slaughter of the crew of a Portuguese vessel which was captured by the Cottica cruisers shortly after the settlement of the Christians in India.

* The sum usually paid was from eight to ten shillings, a portion of which went to the Rajah, part to the women who had lost their husbands in these predatory encounters, and the remainder was "prize-money."

† Few would be disposed to consider the salt-duty a practi-

strengthen their bands, they will associate to themselves small bodies of Nairs and villains of the lowest Hindoo castes, who shrink from no species of cruelty and outrage. But, generally speaking, especially in the quieter districts of Malabar, the Moplahs and the Nairs are on terms of deadly enmity. The idolaters, who have been taught to hate the Faithful by many a deed of blood, would always act willingly against them, provided that our rulers would ensure subsistence to their families, according to the ancient custom of the country.* Both are equally bigoted, violent, and fond of the knife. In few parts of the world there are more deadly feuds than in this province; and whenever a Nair is killed by a Moplah, or *vice versâ*, the relations will steep a cloth in the dead man's blood, and vow never to lose sight of it till they have taken revenge upon the murderer.

cal proof of the enlightened nature of our rule in the East, and there is no one, we believe, except a "crack collector," who would not rejoice to see it done away with, or at least much reduced.

* The rajah was expected to grant lands to the families of those who heroically bound themselves by solemn vow to fight till death against the enemy. If the self-devoted escaped destruction, he became an outcaste, and was compelled to leave the country.

Near the coast, the Moplahs are a thriving race of traders, crafty, industrious, and somewhat refined by the influence of wealth. Those of the interior cultivate rice and garden lands. Some few of the latter traffic, but as they do not possess the opportunities of commerce enjoyed by their maritime brethren, their habitations and warehouses are not so comfortable, substantial, and spacious. Both of them have a widely diffused bad name. Among the people of Southern India generally, the word Moplah is synonymous with thief and rascal. All are equally celebrated for parsimony, a Hindoo, as well as an Arab, quality, and for rigid observance of their religious rites and ceremonies. The desire of gaining proselytes is one of their ruling passions; consequently Islam is steadily extending itself. The zeal of its followers is well supported by their means, and the willingness with which they admit new converts, even of the lowest and most despised classes, to perfect social equality with themselves, offers irresistible attractions to many wretched outcastes of Hinduism. They transgress the more laudable ordinances of their faith, and yet cling fondly to its worse spirit. They will indulge to excess in the forbidden pleasures of distilled waters and intoxicating drugs, in immorality and depravity; at the same time they never hesitate to protect a criminal of their own creed, and, to save him, would gladly perjure themselves, in the belief that, under such circumstances, false oaths and testimony are not only justifiable, but meritorious in a religious point of view.*

The faith professed by the Moplahs is the Shafei form of Islam. All their priests and teachers are of the same persuasion; and such is their besotted bigotry, that they would as willingly persecute a Hanafi† Moslem as the Sunni of most Mussulman countries would martyr a heretic or schismatic. No Sheah dare own his tenets in Malabar. We doubt whether the mighty hand of British law would avail to save from destruction any one who had the audacity to curse Omar or Usman at Calicut. They carefully cultivate the classical and religious branches of study, such as Sarf o Nahv,

* This is the universal belief and practice of the more bigoted parts of the Moslem world, and so deep-rooted is the feeling, that it acquires a degree of power and influence truly formidable, and difficult to deal with.

† The natives of India generally belong to the Hanafi: the Arabs are the principal followers of the Shafei sect. Both are Sunnis, or orthodox Moslems, and there is little difference between them, except in such trifling points as the eating or rejecting fish without scales, &c.

grammar, and syntax; Mantik, or logic; Hadis, the traditions of the Prophet; and Karaat, or the chaunting of the Koran. They seldom know Persian; but as they begin the Arabic language almost as soon as they can speak, and often enjoy the advantage of Arab instructors, their critical knowledge of it is extensive, and their pronunciation good. The vernacular dialect of the Moplah is the Malayalim, into which, for the benefit of the unlearned, many sacred books have been translated. The higher classes are instructed by private tutors, and appear to be unusually well educated. The priest has charge of the lower orders, and little can be said in praise of the schoolmaster or the scholar.

As regards testaments and the law of inheritance, the Moplahs have generally adhered to the Koran; in some families, however, the succession is by nephews, as amongst the Nairs.* This custom is palpably of Pagan origin, like many of the heterogeneous practices grafted by the Mussulmans of India upon the purer faith of their forefathers. Of course they excuse it by tradition. When Cheroo-man Rajah, they say, became a convert to Islam,

* Except that a Moslem father may always allot a portion of property during his lifetime to his children.

and was summoned by Allah in a vision to Mecca, he asked his wife's permission to take his only son with him. She refused. The ruler's sister then offered to send her child under his charge. The Rajah adopted the youth, and upon his return from the Holy City he instituted the custom of murroo-muka-tayum, in order to commemorate the introduction of Islam into the land of the Infidel.

The Mokawars, Mokurs, or as we call them, the Mucwars, are an amphibious race of beings, half fishermen, half labourers:* generally speaking Moslems, sometimes Hindoos. Very slight is the line of demarcation drawn between them, and they display little or no fanaticism. It is common for one or two individuals in a family to become Poothoo Islam, or converts to the faith of Mohammed, and yet to eat, sleep, and associate with the other members of the household as before.†

In appearance these fishermen are an uncommonly ill-favoured race; dark, with ugly features, and forms which a developist would pronounce to

* Usually they prefer the occupation of carrying the palanquin to any other bodily labour.

† Intermarriage, however, is not permitted.

be little removed from the original orang-outang. Their characters, in some points, show to advantage, when contrasted with those of their superiors—the Nairs and Moplahs. They are said to be industrious, peaceful, and as honest as can be expected. A Mucwa village is usually built close to the sea; the material of its domiciles consisting of wattle or matting, roofed over with thatch; the whole burned to blackness by the joint influence of sun, rain, wind, and spray.

Servitude amongst the Moslems partook more of the nature of social fraternity, and was dissimilar in very essential points, to that of the Hindoos. The slaves were always domestic, never prædial: instead of inhabiting miserable huts built in the centre of the paddy fields, they lived in the houses of their proprietors. They were efficiently protected by law, for in case of ill-treatment, duly proved before the Kazee, the complainant was either manumitted or sold to some other master, and so far from being considered impure outcastes, they often rose to confidential stations in the family. This is the case generally throughout the Moslem world.

The native Christians do not constitute a large or influential portion of the community in this part of India, although the Nestorians in very early times settled and planted their faith on the western coast of the peninsula. About the towns of Cannanore and Tellichery, there are a few fishermen and palanquin bearers, called Kolakar and Pandee, said to have migrated from the Travancore country. The other "Nussuranee (Nazarene) Moplahs," as the Christians are styled by the Heathen, are almost all Catholics, either the descendants of the Portuguese, or converted by them to Romanism. They reside principally in the large towns upon the coast: unlike their brethren in Canara, they imitate the European costume, and occupy themselves either with trade, or in the government courts and cutcherries. They are notorious for dishonesty and habitual intoxication.*

Amongst the many social usages and customs peculiar to the natives of Malabar, the two follow-

* The races above described are those settled in the country. The fluctuating portion of the community is composed of the Europeans, the soldiery and camp followers, Arabs and foreign Mussulmans, Banyans from Guzerat, a few Parsees, and some boat loads of the half-starved wretches that leave the Maldives and Laccadives in search of employment during the cold season

ing deserve some mention. There is a kind of general meeting, called Chengathee koree, or the "Society of friends," established for the purposes of discussing particular subjects, and for inquiring into the conduct of individuals. It is supported by the monthly subscriptions of the members, and all must in regular turn—the order being settled by lots—give an entertainment of rice, flesh, and fruit to the whole party. As the entertainer is entitled to the amount of money in deposit for the month, and the feast does not cost half that sum, each member is anxious to draw the ticket with his name upon it as soon as possible. In some places these convivial meetings are heterogeneously composed of Nairs, Moplahs, and Tiyars; when such is the case, the master of the house provides those of the other faith with raw food, which they cook and serve up for and by themselves.

The way in which "dinner parties" are given show some talent in the combination of hospitality with economy. A feast is prepared, and all the guests are expected to present a small sum of money, and a certain number of cocoa-nuts, plantains, betel-nuts or pepper-vine leaves to the master of the house. An account of each offering is regularly kept, and a return of the invitation is considered *de rigueur*. Should any member of society betray an unwillingness to make the expected requital, or to neglect the gifts with which he ought to come provided, they despatch a little potful of arrack, and the bone of a fowl, desiring the recusant in derision to make merry upon such small cheer. The taunt is, generally speaking, severe enough to ensure compliance with the established usages of society.

CHAPTER XIV.

THE LAND JOURNEY.

Being desirous of seeing as much as possible of the country we preferred the route which winds along the sea-shore to Poonanee, and then striking westward ascends the Blue Hills, to the short mountain-cut up the Koondah Range. Our curiosity, however, more than doubled the length of the march.*

No detailed account of the ten stages† will be inflicted upon the peruser of these pages. The journey as far as Poonanee was a most uninteresting one: we have literally nothing to record, except the ever-recurring annoyances of being ferried over backwaters, riding through hot sand fetlock deep,

* The Koondah road is about seventy, that *viâ* Poonanee, one hundred and sixty miles in length.

† The pages of the Madras directories and road-books give ample accounts of all the chief routes in the presidency.

enduring an amount of glare enough to blind anything but a Mucwa or a wild beast ; and at the end of our long rides almost invariably missing the halting place. Arrived at the head-quarter village of Paulghaut, the victims of its deceptive nomenclature,* we instituted a diligent inquiry for any objects of curiosity the neighbourhood might offer ; and having courted deceit we were deceived accordingly. A " native gentleman" informed us that the Yemoor Malay Hills, a long range lying about ten miles to the north of the town, contains a variety of splendid *points de vue*, and a magnificent cataract, which every traveller is in duty bound to visit. Moreover, said the Hindoo, all those peaks are sacred to Parwati, the mountain deity, who visited them in person, and directed a number of small shrines to be erected there in honour of her goddesship.

So after engaging a mancheel we set out in quest of the sublime and beautiful. After winding for about three quarters of the total distance through a parched-up plain, the road reaches the foot of a

* Judging from the name, a stranger would suppose that the place was called after some neighbouring Ghaut, or pass, in the hills. The uncorrupted native appellation, however, is Palakad, from Kadu, a jungle, and Pala, a tree used in dyeing.

steep and rugged hill overgrown with bamboos, and studded with lofty trees, whose names and natures are—

> —— To ancient song unknown,
> The noble sons of potent heat and floods.

As we advanced, the jungle became denser and denser: there were evident signs of hog and deer in the earths of those animals which strewed the ground. Tigers and elephants, bisons and leopards, are said to haunt the remoter depths, and the dry grass smouldering on our path proved the presence of charcoal burners—beings quite as wild as the other denizens of the forest.

The difficulty of the ascent being duly overcome we arrived at the cascade, and stood for a while gazing with astonishment at the prospect of —— a diminutive stream of water, trickling gently down the sloping surface of a dwarf rock. Remembering Terni and Tivoli, we turned our bearers' heads homewards, not however forgetting solemnly to enjoin them never to let a tourist pass by that way without introducing him to the Prince of all the Cataracts.

We were curious to see the fort of Paulghaut, once the key of Malabar, the scene of so many bloody conflicts between the power of Mysore and British

India in the olden time.* A square building, with straight curtains, and a round tower at each angle, with the usual intricate gateway, the uselessly deep fosse, and the perniciously high glacis that characterize native fortifications—such was the artless form that met our sight. In the present day it would be untenable for an hour before a battery of half-a-dozen mortars.

Passing through the magnificent and most unhealthy Wulliyar jungle,† celebrated at all times for teak and sport, and during the monsoon for fever and ague, and dangerous torrents even more

* For a detailed description of the sieges and captures of Paulghaut, we beg to refer to a work entitled, "Historical Record of the H. E. I. Company's First European Regiment; Madras. By a Staff Officer."

† Anciently an excellent forest. The trees were felled, hewn into rough planks, and floated down the Poonanee river at very little expense. This valuable article has, however, been sadly mismanaged by us in more ways than one. All the timber growing near the streams has been cleared away, and as the local government will not lay out a few lacs of rupees in cutting roads through the forests, its expense has been raised almost beyond its value. Considerable losses in the dockyards have been incurred in consequence of the old erroneous belief that "teak is the only wood in India which the white ants will not touch." The timber should be stacked for at least eight years, three of which would enable it to dry, and the remaining five to become properly seasoned.

dangerously bridged, we arrived by a rough and rugged road at Coimbatore, a place which every cotton student and constant reader of the Indian Mail familiarly knows. A most unpromising looking locality it is—a straggling line of scattered houses, long bazaars, and bungalows, separated from each other by wide and desert "compounds." The country around presented a most unfavourable contrast to the fertile region we had just quitted, and the high fierce wind raising clouds of gravelly dust from the sun-parched plain, reminded us forcibly of similar horrors experienced in Scinde and Bhawalpore.

A ride of twenty miles along a dry and hard highway, skirted with numerous and, generally speaking, ruinous villages, led us to Matypolliam at the foot of the Neilgherry Hills—our destination. And now as we are likely to be detained here for some time by that old offender the Bhawany River, who has again chosen to assault and batter down part of her bridge, we will deliberately digress a little and attempt a short description of land travelling in the "land of the sun."

For the conveyance of your person, India supplies you with three several contrivances. You may, if an invalid, or if you wish to be expeditious, engage a palanquin, station bearers on the road, and travel either with or without halts, at the rate of three or four miles an hour: we cannot promise you much pleasure in the enjoyment of this celebrated Oriental luxury. Between your head and the glowing sun, there is scarcely half an inch of plank, covered with a thin mat, which ought to be, but never is, watered. After a day or two you will hesitate which to hate the most, your bearers' monotonous, melancholy, grunting, groaning chaunt, when fresh, or their jolting, jerking, shambling, staggering gait, when tired. In a perpetual state of low fever you cannot eat, drink, or sleep; your mouth burns, your head throbs, your back aches, and your temper borders upon the ferocious. At night, when sinking into a temporary oblivion of your ills, the wretches are sure to awaken you for the purpose of begging a few pice, to swear that they dare not proceed because there is no oil for the torch, or to let you and your vehicle fall heavily upon the ground, because the foremost bearer very nearly trod upon a snake. Of course you scramble as well as you can out of your cage, and administer discipline to the offenders. And what is the result? They all run away and leave you to pass the night, not in solitude, for probably a hungry tiger circumambulates your box, and is only prevented by a somewhat superstitious awe of its general appearance, from pulling you out of it with claw and jaw, and all the action of a cat preparing to break her fast upon some trapped mouse.

All we have said of the palanquin is applicable to its humble modification. The mancheel in this part of the world consists merely of a pole, a canvas sheet hung like a hammock beneath it, and above it a square moveable curtain, which you may draw down on the sunny or windy side. In this conveyance you will progress somewhat more rapidly than you did in the heavy wooden chest, but your miseries will be augmented in undue proportion. As it requires a little practice to balance oneself in these machines, you will infallibly be precipitated to the ground when you venture upon your maiden attempt. After that a sense of security, acquired by dint of many falls, leaves your mind free to exercise its powers of observation, you will remark how admirably you are situated for combining the enjoyments of ophthalmic glare, febrile reflected heat, a wind like a Sirocco, and dews chilling as the hand of the Destroyer. You feel that your back is bent at the most inconvenient angle, and that the pillows which should support your head invariably find their way down between your shoulders, that you have no spare place, as in the palanquin, for carrying about a variety of small comforts, no, not even the room to shift your position—in a word, that you are a miserable being.

If in good health, your best plan of all is to mount one of your horses, and to canter him from stage to stage, that is to say, between twelve and fifteen miles a day. In the core of the nineteenth century you may think this style of locomotion resembles a trifle too closely that of the ninth, but, trust to our experience, you have no better. We will suppose, then, that you have followed our advice, engaged bandies * for your luggage, and started them off overnight, accompanied by your herd of domestics on foot. The latter are all armed with sticks, swords, and knives, for the country is not a safe one, and if it were, your people are endowed with a considerable development of cautiousness. At day-break, your horse-keeper brings up your nag saddled, and neighing his impatience to set

* The common country carts, called garees in other parts of India. Here they are covered with matting, for the same reason that compels the people to thatch their heads.

out: you mount the beast, and leave the man to follow with a coolie or two, bearing on their shoulders the little camp-bed, on which you are wont to pass your nights. There is no danger of missing the road: you have only to observe the wheel-ruts, which will certainly lead you to the nearest and largest, perhaps the only town within a day's march. As you canter along, you remark with wonder the demeanour of the peasantry, and the sensation your appearance creates. The women veil their faces, and dash into the nearest place of refuge, the children scamper away as if your countenance, like Mokanna's, were capable of annihilating a gazer, the very donkeys and bullocks halt, start, and shy, as you pass them.* In some places the men will muster courage enough to stand and gaze upon you, but they do so with an expression of countenance, half-startled, half-scowling, which by no means impresses you with a sense of your individual popularity.

Between nine and ten A.M. you draw in sight of some large village, which instinct suggests is to be the terminus of that day's wandering. You

* In Malabar the horse is perhaps as great an object of horror as the rider, the natives are so little accustomed to see such quadrupeds.

had better inquire where the travellers' bungalow is. Sign-posts are unknown in these barbarous regions, and if you trust overmuch to your own sagacity, your perspiring self and panting steed may wander about for half an hour before you find the caravanserai.

At length you dismount. A horse-keeper rising grumbling from his morning slumbers, comes forward to hold your nag, and, whilst you are discussing a cup of tea in the verandah, parades the animal slowly up and down before you, as a precautionary measure previous to tethering him in the open air. Presently the "butler" informs you that your breakfast, a spatchcock, or a curry with eggs, and a plateful of unleavened wafers, called aps — bread being unprocurable hereabouts — is awaiting you. You find a few guavas or plantains, intended to act as butter, and when you demand the reason, your domestic replies at once, that he searched every house in the village, but could procure none. You might as well adopt some line of conduct likely to discourage him from further attempts upon your credulity, otherwise you will starve before the journey's end. The fact is, he was too lazy to take the trouble of even inquiring for that same butter.

We must call upon you to admire the appearance of the travellers' bungalows in this part of the country. You will see in them much to appreciate if you are well acquainted with Bombay India. Here they are cleanly looking, substantially built, tiled or thatched tenements, with accommodation sufficient for two families, good furniture, at least as far as a table, a couch, and a chair, go, outhouses for your servants, and an excellent verandah for yourself. There you may remember, with a touch of the true *meminisse juvat* feeling, certain dirty ill-built ruinous roadside erections, tenanted by wasps and hornets, with broken seats, tottering tables, and populous bedsteads, for the use of which, moreover, you were mulcted at the rate of a rupee a day. The result of the comparison will be that the "Benighted Land,"* in this point at least, rises prodigiously in your estimation.

A siesta after breakfast, and a book, or any such *passe-temps,* when you awake, bring you on towards sunset. You may now, if so inclined, start for an hour's constitutional, followed by a servant carrying your gun, and keep your hand in by knocking down a few of the old kites that are fighting with the Pariah dogs for their scanty meal of offals,

* The pet name for the Madras Presidency.

or you may try to bag one or two of the jungle cocks, whose crowing resounds from the neighbouring brakes.

Dinner! lovely word in English ears, unlovely thing—hereabouts—for English palate. The beer is sure to be lukewarm, your vegetables deficient, and your meat tough, in consequence of its having lost vitality so very lately.

You must take the trouble, if you please, of personally superintending the departure of your domestics. And this you will find no easy task. The men who have charge of the carts never return with their cattle at the hour appointed, and, when at last they do, there is not a box packed, and probably half your people are wandering about the bazaar. At length, with much labour, you manage to get things somewhat in order, witness with heartfelt satisfaction the first movement of the unwieldy train, and retire to the bungalow for the purpose of getting through the evening, with the assistance of tea, and any other little "distractions" your imagination may suggest.

Before retiring to rest you might as well look to the priming and position of your pistols. Otherwise you may chance to be visited by certain animals, even more troublesome than sand-flies and white ants. A little accident of the kind happened to us at Waniacollum, a village belonging to some Nair Rajah, whose subjects are celebrated for their thievish propensities. About midnight, the soundness of our slumbers was disturbed by the uninvited presence of some half-a-dozen black gentry, who were gliding about the room with the stealthy tread of so many wild cats *in purissimis naturalibus*, with the exception of an outside coating of cocoa-nut oil. One individual had taken up a position close to our bedside, with so very long a knife so very near our jugular region, that we judged it inexpedient in the extreme to excite him by any display of activity; so, closing our eyes, we slept heavily till our visitors thought proper to depart.

Our only loss was the glass shade of a candlestick, which the thieves, supposing to be silver, had carried into the verandah, where, we presume, after discovering that it was only plated, they had thrown it upon the ground and abandoned it as a useless article. We had, it is true, pistols in the room, but as the least movement might have produced uncomfortable results; and, moreover, we felt uncommonly like Juvenal's poor traveller, quite reckless of consequences as regarded goods and chattels, we resolved not to be blood-thirsty. At the same time we confess that such conduct was by no means heroic. But an officer of our own corps, only a few weeks before, was severely wounded, and narrowly escaped being murdered, not fifty miles from the scene of our night's adventure, and we had little desire to figure among the list of casualties recorded in the bimonthly summaries of Indian news.

You would scarcely believe the extent of benefit in a sanitary point of view, derived from riding about the country in the way we have described. Every discomfort seems to do one good: an amount of broiling and wetting, which, in a cantonment, would lead directly to the cemetery, on the road seems only to add to one's ever-increasing stock of health. The greatest annoyance, perhaps, is the way in which the servants and effects suffer; a long journey almost invariably knocks up the former for an unconscionable time, and permanently ruins the latter.

We are still at Matypolliam, but our stay will be short, as the bridge is now nearly repaired. By weighty and influential arguments we must persuade the Kotwal*—a powerful native functionary—to collect a dozen baggage-bullocks and a score of naked savages, destined to act as beasts of burden: no moderate inducement will make the proprietors of the carts drive their jaded cattle up the steep acclivities of the hills. A ridiculous sight it is—the lading of bullocks untrained to carry weight; each animal requires at least half-a-dozen men to keep him quiet; he kicks, he butts, he prances, he shies: he is sure to break from them at the critical moment, and, by an opportune plunge, to dash your unhappy boxes on the ground, scattering their contents in all directions. What a scene of human and bestial viciousness, of plunging and bellowing, of goading of sides, punching of stomachs, and twisting of tails! We must, however, patiently sit by and witness it; otherwise the fellows will not start till late in the afternoon.

You would scarcely believe that the inmates of that little bungalow which just peeps over the

* It is curious to see the different way in which the kotwals, peons, and other such official characters behave towards the Bombay and the Madras traveller. The latter escapes their importunity, whereas the former, by keeping up his presidency's bad practice of feeing government servants, teaches them incivility to all who either refuse or neglect to pay this kind of "black mail."

brow of the mountain, are enjoying an Alpine and almost European climate, whilst we are still in all the discomforts of the tropics. The distance between us is about three miles, as the crow flies—eleven along the winding road. We must prepare for the change by strapping thick coats to our saddle-bows, and see that our servants are properly clothed in cloths and flannels. Otherwise, we render ourselves liable to the *peine forte et dure* of a catarrh of three months' probable duration, and our domestics will certainly be floored by fever and ague, cholera or rheumatism.

It is just nine o'clock A.M., rather an unusual time for a start in these latitudes. But the eddying and roaring of Bhawany's muddy stream warns us that there has been rain amongst the hills. The torrents are passable now; they may not be so a few hours later. So we will mount our nags, and gallop over the five miles of level country, partially cleared of the thick jungle which once invested it, to the foot of the Neilgherry hills.

We now enter the ravine which separates the Oolacul from the Coonoor range. A vast chasm it is, looking as if Nature, by a terrible effort, had split the giant mountain in twain, and left its two halves standing separated opposite each other. A rapid and angry little torrent brawls down the centre of the gap towards the Bhawany river, and the sides are clothed with thick underwood, dotted with tall wide-spreading trees. After the dusty flats of Mysore, and even the green undulations of Malabar, you admire the view with a sensation somewhat resembling that with which you first gazed upon the "castled crag of Drachenfels," when you visited it *en route* from monotonous France, uninteresting Holland, or unpicturesque Belgium. Probably, like certain enthusiastic individuals who have indited high-flown eulogies of Neilgherry beauty, you will mentally compare the scenery with that of the Alps, Apennines, or Pyrenees. We cannot, however, go quite so far with you: with a few exceptions the views generally—and this particularly—want grandeur and a certain *nescio quid* to make them really imposing.

Slowly our panting nags toil along the narrow parapetless road up the steep ascent of the Coonoor Pass. The consequence of the storm is that our pathway appears plentifully besprinkled with earth, stones, and trunks of trees, which have slipped from the inner side. In some places it has been worn by the rain down to the bare rock, and the gutters or channels of rough stone, built at an average distance of fifty yards apart to carry off the water, are slippery for horses, and must be uncommonly troublesome to wheeled conveyances. That cart which on the plains requires a single team, will not move here without eight pair of oxen; and yonder carriage demands the united energies of three dozen coolies, at the very least. As, however, its too-confiding owner has left it to a careless servant's charge, it will most probably reach its destination in a state picturesque, if not useful — its springs and light gear hanging in graceful festoons about the wheels.

And now, after crossing certain torrents and things intended for bridges — during which, to confess the truth, we did feel a little nervous — our nags stand snorting at the side of the stream which forms the Coonoor Falls. Its bottom is a mass of sheet rock, agreeably diversified with occasional jagged points and narrow clefts: moreover, the water is rushing by with uncomfortable rapidity, and there is no visible obstacle to your being swept down a most unpleasant slope. In fact it is the kind of place usually described as growing uglier the more you look at it, so you had better try your luck as soon as possible. Wheel the nag round, "cram" him at the place, and just when he is meditating a sudden halt, apply your spurs to his sides and your heavy horsewhip to his flanks, trusting to Providence for his and your reaching the other side undamaged.

The Burleyar bungalow — a kind of half-way house, or rather an unfinished shed, built on an eminence to the right of the road,—informs us that we are now within six miles of our journey's end. The air becomes sensibly cooler, and we begin to look down upon the sultry steaming plain below with a sensation of acute enjoyment.

We might as well spend a day or two at Coonoor. Ootacamund is at least ten miles off, and it is perfectly useless to hurry on, as our baggage will certainly not arrive before the week is half over, even if it does then. Not, however, at the government bungalow — that long rambling thing perched on the hill above the little bazaar, and renowned for broken windows, fireless rooms, and dirty comfortless meals, prepared by a native of "heathen caste." We will patronize the hotel kept, in true English style, by Mr. Davidson, where we may enjoy the luxuries of an excellent dinner, a comfortable sitting-room, and a clean bed.

A survey of the scenery in this part of the

A. Burton, del.

Printed by Hullmandel & Walton.

COONOOR.
FROM THE TRAVELLER'S BUNGALOW.
London. Richard Bentley, New Burlington Street 1851

Neilgherries takes in an extensive range of swelling waving hill, looking at a distance as if a green gulf had suddenly become fixed for ever. On the horizon are lofty steeps, crowned with remnants of forests, studded with patches of cultivation, and seamed with paths, tracks, and narrow roads. There is little or no table-land: the only level road in the vicinity is scarcely a mile long. At the bottom of the hollow lies the bazaar, and upon the rising knolls around are the nine or ten houses which compose the first European settlement you have seen on the Blue Hills.

Coonoor occupies the summit of the Matypolliam Pass, about five thousand eight hundred and eighty feet above the level of the sea. The climate is warmer than that of the other stations, and the attractions of an occasional fine day even during the three odious months of June, July, and August, fill it with invalids flying from the horrors of Ootacamund. The situation, however, is not considered a good one: its proximity to the edge of the hills, renders it liable to mists, fogs, and a suspicion of the malaria which haunts the jungly forests belting the foot of the hills. Those who have suffered from the obstinate fevers of the plains do well to avoid Coonoor.

The day is fine and bright—a *sine quâ non* in Neilgherry excursions,—if the least cloud or mist be observed hanging about the mountain tops, avoid trips!—so we will start off towards that scarcely-distinguishable object, half peak, half castle, that ends the rocky wall which lay on our left when we rode up the Pass.

You look at Oolacul * Droog, as the fort is called, and wonder what could have been the use of it. And you are justified in your amazement. But native powers delight in cooping up soldiery where they may be as useless as possible; they naturally connect the idea of a strong place with isolated and almost inaccessible positions, and cannot, for the life of them conceive, what Europeans mean by building their fortifications on level ground. Hyder Ali and his crafty son well knew that the unruly chieftains of the plains would never behave themselves, unless overawed and overlooked by some military post which might serve equally well for a

* Etymologists write the word "Hullicul," deriving it from cul, a rock, and hulli, a tiger, as formerly a stone figure of one of those animals that had been slain by a chief single-handed, stood thereabouts. There are several forts in other parts of the hills similar to Oolacul Droog: some suppose them to have been built by Hyder Ali, others assign an earlier date to them.

watch-tower and a dungeon. We think and act otherwise, so such erections go to ruin.

Starting, we pursue a road that runs by the travellers' bungalow, descends a steep, rough, and tedious hill—where we should prefer a mule to a horse—crosses two or three detestable watercourses, and then skirting the western end of the Oolacul chasm shows us a sudden ascent. Here we dismount for convenience as well as exercise. The path narrows; it becomes precipitous and slippery, owing to the decomposed vegetation that covers it, and presently plunges into a mass of noble trees. You cannot see a vestige of underwood: the leaves are crisp under your feet; the tall trunks rise singly in all their sylvan glory, and the murmurs of the wind over the leafy dome above, inform you that

> This is the forest primæval—

as opposed to a rank bushy jungle. You enjoy the walk amazingly. The foot-track is bounded on both sides by dizzy steeps: through the intervals between the trees you can see the light mist-clouds and white vapours sailing on the zephyr far beneath your feet. After about an hour's hard work, we suddenly come upon the Droog, and clambering over the ruined parapet of stone—the only part of it that remains — stand up to catch a glimpse of scenery which even a jaded lionizer would admire.

The rock upon which we tread falls with an almost perpendicular drop of four thousand feet into the plains. From this eyrie we descry the houses of Coimbatore, the windings of the Bhawany, and the straight lines of road stretching like ribbons over the glaring yellow surface of the low land. A bluish mist clothes the distant hills of Malabar, dimly seen upon the horizon in front. Behind, on the far side of the mighty chasm, the white bungalows of Coonoor glitter through the green trees, or disappear behind the veil of fleecy vapour which floats along the sunny mountain tops. However hypercritically disposed, you can find no fault with this view; it has beauty, variety, and sublimity to recommend it.

If an inveterate sight-seer, you will be persuaded by the usual arguments to visit Castle Hill, an eminence about three miles to the east of Coonoor, for the purpose of enjoying a very second rate prospect. Perhaps you will also be curious to inspect a village inhabited by a villanous specimen of the Toda race, close to Mr. Davidson's hotel. We shall not accompany you.

CHAPTER XV.

FIRST GLIMPSE OF "OOTY."

THE distance from Coonoor to the capital of the Neilgherries is about ten miles, over a good road. We propose, however, to forsake the uninteresting main line, and, turning leftwards, to strike into the bye way which leads to the Khaity Falls.

Khaity is a collection of huts tenanted by the hill people, and in no ways remarkable, except that it has given a name to a cascade which "everybody goes," &c.

After six miles of mountain and valley in rapid and unbroken succession, we stand upon the natural terrace which supports the little missionary settlement, and looking over the deep ravine that yawns at our feet, wonder why the "everybody" above alluded to, takes the trouble of visiting the Khaity falls. They are formed by a thin stream which dashes over a gap in the rock, and disperses into spray before it has time to reach the basin below. As usual with Neilgherry cascades they only want water.

Now as our disappointment has brought on rather a depressed and prosy state of mind, we will wile away the tedium of the eight long miles which still separate us from our destination, with a little useful discourse upon subjects historical and geographical connected with the Neilgherries.

The purely European reader will consider it extraordinary that this beautiful range of lofty hills should not have suggested to all men at first sight the idea of a cool, healthy summer abode. But we demi-Orientals, who know by experience the dangers of mountain air in India, only wonder at the daring of the man who first planted a roof-tree upon the Neilgherries.

From the year 1799 to 1819 these mountains were in the daily view of all the authorities from the plains of Coimbatore; revenue was collected from them for the company by a native renter; but, excepting Dr. Ford and Capt. Bevan, who in 1809 traversed the hill with a party of pioneers, and certain deputy surveyors under Colonel Monson, who partially mapped the tract, no strangers had ventured to explore the all but unknown region.

In 1814, Mr. Keys, a sub-assistant, and Mr. McMahon, then an apprentice in the survey department, ascended the hills by the Danaynkeucottah Pass, penetrated into the remotest parts and made plans, and sent in reports of their discoveries. In consequence of their accounts, Messrs. Whish and Kindersley, two young Madras civilians, availing themselves of the opportunity presented by some criminal's taking refuge amongst the mountains, ventured up in pursuit of him, and proceeded to reconnoitre the interior. They soon saw and felt enough to excite their own curiosity and that of others. Mr. Sullivan, collector of Coimbatore, built the first house upon the Neilgherries. He chose a hillock to the east of the hollow, where the lake now lies, and after some difficulty in persuading the superstitious natives to work—on many occasions he was obliged personally to set them the example—he succeeded in erecting a tenement large enough to accommodate his family.

In the month of May, 1819, the same tourists from Coimbatore, accompanied by Mons. Leschnault de la Tour, naturalist to the King of France, repeated their excursion, and published the result of their observations in one of the Madras newspapers. They asserted the maximum height of the thermometer in the shade to be 74° at a time when the temperature of the plains varied from 90° to 100°. Such a climate within the tropics was considered so great an anomaly that few would believe in its existence. At length the Madras Government determined to open one of the passes, and the pioneer officer employed on this service deriving immediate and remarkable benefit from the mountain air—he had been suffering from fever and ague—hastened to corroborate the accounts of it already published. The road was opened in 1821; some families then took up their abode on the hills; the inveterate prejudice against them began to disappear, and such numbers presently flocked to the region of health, that the difficulty was to find sufficient accommodation. As late as 1826, Bishop Heber complained that for want of lodgings he was unable to send his family to the sanitarium. Incredulity received its *coup de grace* from the hand of the Rev. Mr. Hough, a chaplain in the Madras establishment, who in July, 1826, published in the Bengal Hurkaru, under the *nom de guerre* of Philanthropos, a series of eight letters,* de-

* See Chapter XIX. for a further account of the work.

scribing the climate, inhabitants, and productions of the Neilgherries, with the benevolent intention of inducing the Government of India to patronize the place as a retreat for invalids.

Having "done" the history, we will now attempt a short geographical account of the Blue Mountains. *En passant* we may remark, that the native name Nilagiri,* limited by the Hindoos to a hill sacred to Parwati, has been extended by us to the whole range.

The region commonly known by the name of the Neilgherries, or Blue Mountains of Coimbatore, is situated at the point where the Eastern and Western Ghauts† unite, between the parallels of 11° and 12° N. lat., and 76° and 77° E. lon. Its shape is a trapezoid, for though quadrilateral, none

* The "blue hill:" it lies near the Danaynkeucottah Pass, one of the first ascended by Europeans. The visitors would naturally ask the natives what name they gave to the spot, and when answered Nilagiri, would apply the word to the whole range. The sacred mount is still a place of pilgrimage, although its pagoda has long been in ruins.

† The Eastern Ghauts begin south of the Cavery river, and extend almost in a straight line to the banks of the Krishna. The western range commences near Cape Comorin, and after running along the western coast as far north as Surat, diverges towards the north-east, and is lost in the valley of the Tapti.

of its sides are equal or even: it is bounded on the north by the table-land of Mysore, on the south and east by the provinces that stretch towards the Arabian Sea; another range of hills forms its western frontier. Its base covers a surface of about two hundred miles; the greatest length from east to west at an elevation of five thousand feet, is nearly forty-three, and the medium breadth at the same height, is little less than fifteen, miles. The major part of the mass presents a superficies of parallel and irregular hill and knoll, intersected by deep valleys and precipitous ravines; a loftier chain, throwing off a number of minor ridges, runs north-east and south-west, and almost bisects the tract. In the loftier parts many small streams, such as the Pykarry, the Porthy, and the Avalanche take their rise, and, after winding over the surface, sweep down the rocky sides of the mountains, and fall into the Moyar,* or swell the Bhawany River.

The Neilgherries are divided into four Nads, or provinces: Perunga Nad, the most populous, occu-

* The Pykarry becomes the Moyar river, and under that name flows round the north and north-west base of the hills: it falls into the Bhawany, which bounds the south and east slopes, and acts as the common drain of every little brook and torrent in the Neilgherries.

pies the eastern portion; Malka lies towards the south; Koondah is on the west and south-west margin; and Toda Nad, the most fertile and extensive,* includes the northern regions and the crest of the hills. Many lines of roads have been run up the easier acclivities; the most travelled upon at present are the Seegoor Ghaut,† which enters from the Mysore side, and the Coonoor, or Coimbatore Pass, by which, if you recollect, we ascended.

Our Government asserts no right to this bit of territory, although the hills belonged to Hyder, and what was Hyder's now belongs to us. The peculiar tribe called the Todas,‡ lay claim to the land, and though they consent to receive a yearly rent, they firmly refuse to alienate their right to the soil, considering such measure "nae canny" for both seller and buyer. Chance events have established this superstition on a firm footing. When Europeans first settled in the Neilgherries, a murrain broke out among the Toda cattle, and the savages naturally

* Its extent is about twenty miles from east to west, and seven from north to south.

† The Seegoor Ghaut, which was almost impassable in Captain Harknes and Dr. Baikie's time, is now one of the easiest and best ascents.

‡ See Chapter XVIII.

attributed their misfortune to the presence of the new comers. Sir W. Rumbold lost his wife, and died prematurely soon after purchasing the ground upon which his house stood—of course, in consequence of the earth-god's ire.

In August, 1847, there were a hundred and four officers on sick leave, besides visitors and those residing on the Neilgherries. The total number of Europeans, children included, was between five and six hundred. It is extremely difficult to estimate the number of the hill people. Some authorities give as many as fifteen thousand; others as few as six thousand.

Now we fall into the main road at the foot of the zigzag, which climbs the steep skirt of Giant Dodabetta.* Our nags, snorting and panting, breast

* Dodabetta, or the "Great Mountain," called by the Todas, Pet-, or Het-marz. The summit is eight thousand seven hundred and sixty feet above the level of the sea, and forms the apex of the Neilgherry range. The vicinity of the giant has its advantages and disadvantages. It is certainly a beautiful place for pic-nics, and the view from the observatory on the top is grand and extensive. But as a counterpoise, the lofty peak attracting and detaining every cloud that rolls up from the coast during the rainy season, makes one wish most fervently that the Great Mountain were anywhere but in its present position.

the hill—we reach the summit—we descend a few hundred yards—catch sight of some detached bungalows — a lake — a church — a bazaar — a station.

The cantonment of Ootacamund,* or, as it is familiarly and affectionately termed by the abbreviating Saxon, "Ooty," is built in a punch bowl, formed by the range of hills which composes the central crest of the Neilgherries. But first for the "Windermere."

The long narrow winding tarn which occupies the bottom of Ooty's happy vale, is an artificial affair, intended, saith an enthusiastic describer, "like that of Como, to combine utility with beauty." It was made by means of a dam, which, uniting the converging extremities of two hills, intercepted the waters of a mountain rivulet, and formed an "expansive and delightful serpentine lake," about two miles in length, upon an average six hundred yards broad, in many places forty feet deep, generally

* Ootacamund, Wootaycamund, or Wotay. "Mund" means a village in the language of the hill people. Ootac is a corruption of the Toda vocable Hootkh, a word unpronounceable to the Indians of the plain. The original hamlet still nestles against the towering side of Dodabetta, but its pristine inhabitants, the Todas, have given it up to another race, and migrated to the wood which lies behind the public gardens.

very muddy, and about as far from Windermere or Como as a London Colosseum or a Parisian Tivoli might be from its Italian prototype. Two roads, the upper and the lower, wind round the piece of water, and it is crossed by three embankments; the Willow Bund, as the central one is called, with its thick trees and apologies for arches, is rather a pretty and picturesque object. The best houses, you may remark, are built as close to the margin of the lake as possible. Turn your eyes away from the northern bank; that dirty, irregular bazaar is the very reverse of romantic. The beauties of the view lie dispersed above and afar. On both sides of the water, turfy peaks and woody eminences, here sinking into shallow valleys, there falling into steep ravines, the whole covered with a tapestry of brilliant green, delight your eye, after the card-table plains of Guzerat, the bleak and barren Maharatta hills, or the howling wastes of sun-burnt Scinde. The back-ground of distant hill and mountain, borrowing from the intervening atmosphere the blue and hazy tint for which these regions are celebrated, contrasts well with the emerald hue around. In a word, there is a rich variety of form and colour, and a graceful blending of the different features that combine to make a beautiful *coup d'œil,* which, when the gloss of novelty is still upon them, are infinitely attractive.

The sun is sinking in the splendour of an Indian May, behind the high horizon, and yet, marvellous to relate, the air feels cool and comfortable. The monotonous gruntings of the frequent palanquin-bearers—a sound which, like the swift's scream, is harsh and grating enough, yet teems in this region with pleasant associations—inform us that the fair ones of Ootacamund are actually engaged in taking exercise. We will follow their example, beginning at "Charing Cross,"—the unappropriate name conferred upon those few square yards of level and gravelled ground, with the stunted tree boxed up in the centre. Our path traverses the half-drained swamp that bounds this end of the Neilgherry Windermere, and you observe with pain that those authors who assert the hills to be "entirely free from the morasses and the vast collection of decayed vegetables that generate miasma," have notably deceived you. In 1847, there is a small swamp, formed by the soaking of some arrested stream, at the bottom of almost every declivity. We presume the same was the case in 1826. Indeed, were the Neilgherries seven or eight hundred feet, instead of as many thousands, above the level of the sea, even the Pontine marshes would not be better adapted for the accommodation of Quartana and Malaria. Before you have been long on the hills, you will witness many amusing accidents occurring to new comers, who attempt to urge their steeds through the shaking bogs of black mud, treacherously lurking under a glossy green coating of grassy turf.

"Probably it is to the local predilections for such diversion that I must attribute the unwillingness of the authorities to remedy the nuisance?"

We cannot take upon ourselves to reply, yes or no. The cantonment is by no means scrupulously clean. The bazaar is at all times unpleasant, and, during the rains, dirty in the extreme. Making all due allowance for the difficulty of keeping any place where natives abound, undefiled, still we opine, that the authorities might be much more active, in promoting the cause of cleanliness, than they are. But, if report speak true, the local government is somewhat out of temper with her hill *protégée*, for spending her rupees a little too freely.

There go the promenaders—stout pedestrians—keeping step in parties and pairs. Equestrians ride the fashionable animals—a kind of horse cut down to a pony, called the Pegu, Arabs being rare and little valued here. And invalids, especially ladies, "eat the air," as the natives say, in palanquins and tonjons. The latter article merits some description. It is a light conveyance, open and airy, exactly resembling the seat of a Bath chair, spitted upon a long pole, which rests on the shoulders of four hammals, or porters. Much barbaric splendour is displayed in the equipments of the "gang." Your first thought, on observing their long scarlet coats, broad yellow bands round the waist, and the green turban, or some other curiously and wonderfully made head-gear, which surmounts their sooty faces, is a sensation of wonder that the tonjon and its accompaniments have not yet been exhibited in London and Paris. Much hardness of heart is occasionally shown by the fair sex to their unhappy negroes. See those four lean wretches staggering under the joint weights of the vehicle that contains the stout daughter and stouter mama, or the huge Ayah who is sent out to guard those five or six ponderous children, whose constitutional delicacy renders "carriage exercise" absolutely necessary for them.

Two things here strike your eye as novel, in India.

There is a freshness in the complexion of the Sanitarians that shows wonderfully to advantage when compared with the cadaverous waxy hue which the European epidermis loves to assume in the tropics. Most brilliant look the ladies; the gentlemen are sunburnt and robust; and the juveniles appear fresh and chubby, quite a different creation from the pallid, puny, meagre, sickly, irritable little wretches that do nothing but cry and perspire in the plains. Another mighty pleasant thing, after a few years of purely camp existence, is the non-military appearance and sound of Ootacamund. Uniform has been banished by one consent from society, except at balls and parties. The cotton and linen jackets, the turbaned felt "wide-awake," and the white jockey's cap, with its diminutive apron, intended to protect the back of the head from the broiling sun, are here exchanged for cloth coats and black hats. Morning bugles and mid-day guns, orderlies, and order-books, the "Officers' call" and "No parade to-day," are things unknown. Vestiges of the "shop" will, it is true, occasionally peep out in the shape of a regimental cap, brass spurs, and black pantaloons, denuded of the red stripe. But such traces rather add to our gratification than otherwise, by reminding us of

A.M. drills, meridian sword exercises, and P.M. reviews in days gone by.

And now, advancing along the gravelled walk that borders the lake, we pass beneath a thatched cottage, once a masonic lodge,* but now, *proh pudor!* converted into a dwelling-house. Near it, we remark a large building—Bombay House. It was formerly appropriated to officers of that presidency. At present they have no such luxury.† Taking up a position above the south end of the Willow-Bund, we have a good front view of the principal buildings in the cantonment. On the left hand is the Protestant church of St. Stephens, an unpraisable erection, in the Saxo-Gothic style, standing out from a grave-yard, so extensive, so well stocked, that it makes one shudder to look at it. Close by the church are the Ootacamund Free School, the Post-office, the Pay-office, and the bungalow where the Commanding officer of the station transacts his

* It was established at Ootacamund under a warrant of constitution from the Provincial Grand Lodge on the coast of Coromandel.

† The Bombayites had, moreover, their own medical attendant, with a hospital and the usual number of subalterns attached to it. There are now but three surgeons on the hills, attending on one hundred and four invalids, who are scattered over many miles of country.

multifarious business. Below, near the lake, you see the Library, the Victoria hotel—a large and conspicuous building—the Dispensary, the subordinate's courts, and the Bazaar. Beyond the church a few hundred yards of level road leads to the "palace," built by Sir W. Rumbold, which, after enduring many vicissitudes of fortune, has settled down into the social position of a club-house and place for periodical balls. Around it, the mass of houses thickens, and paths branch off in all directions. In the distance appears the wretched bazaar of Kaundlemund—the haunt of coblers and thieves; —a little nearer is the old Roman Catholic chapel; closer still, the Union hotel—a huge white house, which was once the Neilgherry Church Missionary grammar school,—bungalows by the dozen, and several extensive establishments, where youth, male and female, is lodged, boarded, and instructed. On the southern side of a hill, separated from the Kaundle bazaar, stands Woodcock Hall, the locality selected for Government House, and, in 1847 at least, a most unimportant place, interiorly as well as exteriorly.

We will conclude our ciceronic task with calling your attention to one fact, namely, that the capital of the Neilgherries is growing up with maizelike rapidity. Houses are rising in all directions; and if fickle fortune only favour it, Ooty promises fair to become in a few years one of the largest European settlements in India. But its fate is at present precarious. Should the Court of Directors be induced to revise the old Furlough and Sick-leave Regulations, then will poor Ooty speedily revert to the Todas and jackals — its old inhabitants. On the contrary, if the *status quo* endure, and European regiments are regularly stationed on the hills,* officers will flock to Ootacamund, the settlers, retired servants of Government, not Eurasian colonists, will increase in number, schools † will flourish

* The measure was advocated by Mr. Sullivan as early as 1828, but financial, not common-sensical or medical, considerations have long delayed its being carried into execution.

† The principal schools now (1847) to be found at Ootacamund are four in number, viz.:—

1. The Ooty free school, established for the purpose of giving education gratis to the children of the poor: it is supported by voluntary contributions, and superintended by the chaplain of the station. The number of scholars on the rolls is generally about thirty.

2. Fern Hill, the Rev. Mr. Rigg's boarding-school for young gentlemen. It contains twenty-six pupils, varying in age from five to fifteen. Of these, fourteen are the sons of officers in the service, and the rest are youths of respectable families. Terms for boarders, 4*l.* *per mensem*, the usual charges on the Neilgherries.

and prosperity steadily progress. The "to be or not to be" thus depends upon the turn of a die.

The chilly shades of evening are closing rapidly upon us, and we know by experience that some care is necessary, especially for the newly arrived health-hunter. So we wend our way homewards, remarking, as night advances, the unusual brilliancy of the heavenly bodies. Venus shines almost as brightly as an average English moon in winter: her light with that of the lesser stars is quite sufficient to point out to us the direction of "Subaltern Hall."

3. An establishment for young ladies, conducted by Miss Hale and Miss Millard.

4. Ditto for young ladies and young gentlemen under ten years of age, conducted by Mrs. James and Miss Ottley.

Besides those above mentioned, several ladies receive a limited number of pupils.

The schools for natives at Ootacamund are—

1. The Hindostani school } Conducted by the Rev. Bernard
2. The Tamul school } Schmidt, D.D.

There are many other similar establishments for native children in different parts of the hills.

So that the pedagogue has not neglected to visit this remote corner of his wide domains.

CHAPTER XVI.

LIFE AT OOTY.

If a bachelor, you generally begin by depositing your household gods in the club buildings, or one of the two hotels *—there is no travellers' bungalow at Ootacamund—if a married man, you have secured lodgings by means of a friend.

The Neilgherry house merits description prin-

* The Union and the Victoria. For bed and board the prices usually charged are—

For a lady or gentleman, 22*l.* *per mens.*

Ditto for any broken period in a month, 16*s.* *per diem.*

For children under ten years of age and European servants, 2*s.* *per diem.*

Native ayah or nurse, 1*s.* *per diem.*

The expense of housekeeping is not great at Ootacamund. A single man may manage to live for 20*l.* *per mensem*, comfortably for 30*l.* It is common for two or more bachelors to take a house together, and the plan suits the nature of the place well.

Only be careful who your monsoon "chum" is!

cipally because it is a type of the life usually led in it. The walls are made of coarse bad bricks—the roof of thatch or wretched tiles, which act admirably as filters, and occasionally cause the downfall of part, or the whole of the erection. The foundation usually selected is a kind of platform, a gigantic step, cut out of some hill-side, and levelled by manual labour. The best houses occupy the summits of the little eminences around the lake. As regards architecture the style bungalow—a modification of the cow-house—is preferred: few tenements have upper stories, whilst almost all are surrounded by a long low verandah, perfectly useless in such a climate, and only calculated to render the interior of the domiciles as dim and gloomy as can be conceived. The furniture is decidedly scant, being usually limited to a few feet of drugget, a chair or two, a table, and a bedstead. The typical part of the matter is this. If the diminutive rooms, with their fire-places, curtained beds, and boarded floors, faintly remind you of Europe, the bare walls, puttyless windows and doors that admit draughts of air small yet cutting as lancets, forcibly impress you with the conviction that you have ventured into one of those uncomfortable localities—a cold place in a hot country.

So it is with life on the Nielgherries—a perfect anomaly. You dress like an Englishman, and lead a quiet gentlemanly life — doing nothing. Not being a determined health-hunter, you lie in bed because it passes the hours rationally and agreeably, and you really can enjoy a midday doze on the mountain-tops. You sit up half the night because those around you are not shaking the head of melancholy, in consequence of the dispiriting announcement that "the Regiment will parade, &c., at four o'clock next morning" (A.M. remember!). At the same time your monthly bills for pale ale and hot curries, heavy tiffins, and numerous cheroots, tell you, as plainly as such mute inanimate things can, that you have not quite cast the slough of Anglo-Indian life.

We will suppose that your first month in the Nielgherry Hills with all its succession of small events has glided rapidly enough away. You reported your arrival in person to the commanding officer, who politely desired your signature to a certain document,* threatening you as well as others

* The most stringent measures have been found necessary to prevent gentlemen from committing suicide by means of elephant shooting in the pestilential jungles below the hills.

with all the penalties of the law if you ventured to quit Ootacamund without leave. The Auditor-General's bill, which you received from the Pay-master, Bombay, authorizing you to draw your salary from him of the southern division of the Madras army, was not forwarded before the first of the month, or it was forwarded but not in duplicate —something of the kind must happen—so you were most probably thrown for a while upon your wits, rather a hard case, we will suppose. Then you tried to "raise the wind" from some Parsee, but the way in which he received you conclusively proved that he has, perhaps for the best of reasons, long since ceased to "do bijness" in that line. You began to feel uncomfortable, and consequently to abuse the "authorities."

During your first fortnight all was excitement, joy, delight. You luxuriated in the cool air. Your appetite improved. The mutton had a flavour which you did not recollect in India. Strange, yet true, the beef was tender, and even the "unclean" was not too much for your robust digestion. You

Besides, there is some little duty to be done by the Madrassees on the Neilgherries: a convalescent list is daily forwarded to the Commanding officer, reporting those who are equal to such labours as committees and courts of inquest.

praised the vegetables, and fell into ecstasy at the sight of peaches, apples, strawberries, and raspberries, after years of plantains, guavas, and sweet limes. From the exhilarating influence of a rare and elastic atmosphere you, who could scarcely walk a mile in the low country, induced by the variety of scenery and road, wandered for hours over hill and dale without being fatigued. With what strange sensations of pleasure you threw yourself upon the soft turf bank, and plucked the first daisy which you ever saw out of England! And how you enjoyed the untropical occupation of sitting over a fire in June! —that very day last year you were in a state of semi-existence, only "kept going" by the power of punkahs * and quasi-nudity.

The end of the month found you in a state of mind bordering upon the critical. You began to opine that the scenery has its deficiencies — Can its diminutive ravines compare with glaciers and seas of ice — the greenness of its mountain-tops compensate for the want of snow-clad summits, and "virgin heights which the foot of man never trod?" You decided that the Neilgherries are, after all, a tame copy of the Alps and the Pyrenees. You came to the conclusion that grandeur on a small

* Large fans, suspended from the ceiling.

scale is very unsatisfactory, and turned away from the prospect with the contempt engendered by satiety. As for the climate, you discovered that it is either too hot in the sun or too cold in the shade, too damp or too dry, too sultry or too raw. After a few days spent before the fire you waxed weary of the occupation, remarked that the Neilgherry wood is always green, and the Neilgherry grate a very abominable contrivance. At last the mutton and pork, peaches and strawberries, palled upon your pampered palate, you devoured vegetables so voraciously that pernicious consequences ensued, and you smoked to such an extent that —perhaps tobacco alone did not do it—your head became seriously affected.

And now, sated with the joys of the eye and mouth, you turn round upon Ootacamund and inquire blatantly what amusement it has to offer you.

Is there a hunt? No, of course not!

A race-course? Ditto, ditto!

Is there a cricket-club? Yes. If you wish to become a member you will be admitted readily enough; you will pay four shillings *per mensem* for the honour, but you will not play at cricket.

A library? There are two: one in the Club,

the other kept by a Mr. Warren : the former deals in the modern, the latter in the antiquated style of light—extremely light—literature. Both reading-rooms take in the newspapers and magazines, but the periodical publications are a very exclusive kind of study, that is to say, never at home to you.. By some peculiar fatality the book you want is always missing. And the absence of a catalogue instead of exciting your industry, seems rather to depress it than otherwise.

Public gardens, with the usual "scandal point," where you meet the ladies and exchange the latest news? We reply yes, in a modifying tone. The sum of about 200*l.*, besides monthly subscriptions, was expended upon the side of a hill to the east of Ooty, formerly overrun with low jungle, now bearing evidences of the fostering hand of the gardener in the shape of many cabbages and a few cauliflowers.

Is there a theatre, a concert-room, a tennis, a racket, or a fives-court? No, and again no!

Then pray what is there?

We will presently inform you. But you must first rein in your impatience whilst we enlarge a little upon the constitution and components of Neilgherry society.

Two presidencies—the Madras and Bombay—meet here without mingling. Officers belonging to the former establishment visit the hills for two objects, pleasure and health; those of the latter service are always votaries of Hygeia. If you ask the Madrassee how he accounts for the dearth of amusements, he replies that no one cares how he gets through his few weeks of leave. The Bombayite, on the contrary, complains loudly and bitterly enough of the dull two years he is doomed to pass at Ooty, but modesty, a consciousness of inability to remedy the evil, or most likely that love of a grievance, and lust of grumbling which nature has implanted in the soldier's breast, prevents his doing anything more. Some public-spirited individuals endeavoured, for the benefit of poor Ooty, to raise general subscriptions from the Madras Service, every member of which has visited, is visiting, or expects to visit, the region of health. The result of their laudable endeavours—a complete failure—instanced the truth of the ancient adage, that "everybody's business is nobody's business." Besides the sanitarians and the pleasure-seekers, there are a few retired and invalid officers, who have selected the hills as a permanent residence, some coffee-planters, speculators in silk and mulberry-trees, a stray mercantile or two from Madras, and several professionals, settled at Ootacamund.

With all the material above alluded to, our circle of society, as you may suppose, is sufficiently extensive and varied. Among the ladies, we have elderlies who enjoy tea and delight in scandal: grass widows—excuse the term, being very much wanted, it is *comme il faut* in this region—and spinsters of every kind, from the little girl in bib and tucker, to the full blown Anglo-Indian young lady, who discourses of her papa the Colonel, and disdains to look at anything below the rank of a field-officer. The gentlemen supply us with many an *originale.* There are *ci-devant* young men that pride themselves upon giving ostentatious feeds which youthful gastronomes make a point of eating, misanthropes and hermits who inhabit out-of-the-way abodes, civilians on the shelf, authors, linguists, oriental students, amateur divines who periodically convert their drawing-rooms into chapels of ease rather than go to church, sportsmen, worshippers of Bacchus in numbers, juniors whose glory it is to escort fair dames during evening rides, and seniors who would rather face his Satanic Majesty himself than stand in the dread presence of a "woman." We have clergymen, priests, missionaries, tavern-keepers, school-masters, and scholars, with *précieux* and *précieuses ridicules* of all descriptions.

But, unhappily, the said circle is divided into several segments, which do not willingly or neatly unite. In the first place, there is a line of demarcation occasionally broken through, but pretty clearly drawn between the two Presidencies. The Mulls * again split into three main bodies, 1, the very serious; 2, the *petit-sérieux;* and, 3, the unsanctified. So do the Ducks, but these being upon strange ground are not so exclusive as they otherwise would be. Subdivision does not end here. For instance, the genus serious will contain two distinct species, the orthodox and the heterodox serious. The unsanctified also form numerous little knots, whose bond of union is some such accidental matters as an acquaintance previous to meeting on the hills, or a striking conformity of tastes and pursuits.

---

* As the Madrassees are familiarly called. The cunning in language derive the term from mulligatawny soup, the quantity of which imbibed in South India strikes the stranger with a painful sense of novelty.

A brief account of the Neilgherry day will answer your inquiry about the existence of amusement. We premise that there are two formulas, one for the sanitarian, the other for the pleasure-hunter.

And first, of Il Penseroso, or the invalid. He rises with the sun, clothes himself according to Dr. Baikie,* and either mounts his pony, or more probably starts stick in hand for a four mile walk. He returns in time to avoid the sun's effects upon an empty stomach, bathes, breakfasts, and hurries once more into the open air. Possibly, between the hours of twelve and four, his dinner-time, he may allow himself to rest awhile in the library, to play a game at billiards, or to call upon a friend, but upon principle he avoids tainted atmospheres as much as possible. At 5 P.M. he recommences walking or riding, persevering laudably in the exercise selected, till the falling dew drives him home. A cup of tea, and a book or newspaper, finish the day. This even tenor of his existence is occasionally varied by some such excitement as a pic-nic, or a shooting-party, but late dinners, balls, and parties, know him not.

Secondly of L'Allegro, as the man who obtains

* See Chapter XIX.

two months' leave of "absence on urgent private affairs" to the Neilgherries, and the Penseroso become a robust convalescent, may classically and accurately be termed. L'Allegro, dresses at mid-day, he has spent the forenoon either in bed or *en deshabille,* in dozing, tea-drinking, and smoking, or, if of a literary turn of mind, in perusing the pages of "The Devoted," or, "Demented One." He dilates breakfast to spite old Time, and asks himself the frequent question What shall I do to-day? The ladies are generally at home between twelve and two, but L'Allegro, considering the occupation rather a "slow" one, votes it a "bore." But there is the club, and a couple of hours may be spent profitably enough over the newspapers, or pleasantly enough with the assistance of billiards and whist. At three o'clock our Joyful returns home, or accompanies a party of friends to a hot and substantial meal, termed tiffin, followed by many gigantic Trichinopoly cigars, and glasses of pale ale in proportion.

A walk or a ride round the lake, is now deemed necessary to recruit exhausted Appetite, who is expected to be ready at seven for another hot and substantial meal, called dinner. And now, the labours of the day being happily over, L'Allegro concludes it with prodigious facility by means of cards or billiards, with whiskey and weeds.

This routine of life is broken only by such interruptions, as a shooting-party, an excursion, a pic-nic, a grand dinner, *soirée*, or a ball. Short notices of these amusements may not be unacceptable to the reader.

There are many places in the neighbourhood of Ooty—such as Dodabetta, Fair Lawn, and others—where, during the fine season, the votaries of Terpsichore display very fantastic toes indeed, particularly if they wear Neilgherry-made boots, between the hours of ten A.M. and five P.M. Much innocent mirth prevails on these social occasions, the only remarkable characteristic of their nature being, that the gentlemen generally ride out slowly and deliberately, but ride in, racing, or steeple-chasing, or enacting Johnny Gilpin.

A more serious affair is a grand dinner. This truly British form which hospitality assumes, may be divided into two kinds, the pure and the mixed. The former is the general favourite, as, consisting of bachelors only, it admits of an *abandon* in the style of conversation, and a general want of ceremoniousness truly grateful to the Anglo-Indian mind. A dinner where ladies are admitted is, by

L'Allegro, considered an unmitigated pest; and those who dislike formality and restraint, scant potations, and the impossibility of smoking, will readily enter into his feelings.

The Ootacamund *soirée* happens about once every two months to the man of pleasure, who exerts all the powers of his mind to ward off the blow of an invitation. When he can no longer escape the misfortune, he resigns himself to his fate, dresses and repairs to the scene of unfestivity, with much of the same feeling he remembers experiencing when "nailed" for a Bath musical reunion, or a Cheltenham tea-party. He will have to endure many similar horrors. He must present Congo to the ladies, walk about with cakes and muffins, listen to unmelodious melody, and talk small—he whose body is sinking under the want of stimulants and narcotics, whose spirit is fainting under the *peine forte et dure* of endeavouring to curb an unruly tongue, which in spite of all efforts will occasionally give vent to half or three-quarters of some word utterly unfit for ears feminine or polite. If, as the Allegri sometimes are, the wretch be nervous upon the subject of being "talked about in connexion with some woman," another misery will be added to the list above detailed. He has certainly passed the evening by the side of the young lady whom he first addressed—his reasons being that he had not courage to break away from her—and he may rest assured that all Ooty on the morrow will have wooed and won her for him. Finally, he observes that several of his married friends look coldly upon him, beginning the morning after the *soirée*. Probably he endeavoured to compensate for his want of vivacity, by a little of what he considered brilliancy, in the form of satire,—quizzing, as it is generally called. The person for whose benefit he ventured to

> Tamper with such dangerous art,

looked amused by his facetiousness, encouraged him to proceed by

> —— The smile from partial beauty won,

and lost no time in repeating the substance of his remarks, decked, for the sake of excitement, in a richly imaginative garb, to the sensitive quizzee.

There are about half-a-dozen balls a year on the Neilgherries, the cause of their infrequency being the expense, and the unpopularity of the amusement amongst all manner and description of men, save and except the "squire of dames" only. This un-English style of festivity is also of two kinds, the subscription and the bachelors': the former thinly attended, because 1*l.* is the price of a ticket, the latter much more numerously, because invitations are issued gratis. The amusement commences with the notes which the ladies indite in reply to their future entertainers, who scrutinize all such productions with a severity of censure and a rigidity of rule which might gratify a Johnson, or a Lindley Murray. And woe, woe, to her who slips in her syntax, or trips in her syllabication! Then the members of the club carve out for themselves a grievance, all swear that it is a "confounded shame to turn the place into a hop-shop," and one surlier individual than the rest declares that "it shan't be done again." At the same time you observe they endure the indignity patiently enough, as it is a magnificent opportunity for disposing of their condemnable though not condemned gooseberry.

And here we pause for a moment in indignation at such a proceeding. May that man never be our friend who heedlessly sets a bottle of bad champagne before a fellow-creature at a ball! Heated and excited by the dancing atmosphere around, the victim's palate becomes undiscerning, he drinks a tumbler when at other times a wine-glass full would have been too much, and in the morning—aroynt thee, Description! Well do we remember the bitter feelings with which we heard on one of these occasions, two gentlemen felicitating each other upon the quantity of sour gooseberry disposed of unobserved. Unobserved! we were enduring tortures from the too observable effects of it.

At eleven or twelve the ladies muster. The band—a trio of fiddlers, and a pianist, who performs on an instrument which suggests reminiscences of Tubal Cain—strikes up. The dancing begins—one eternal round of quadrilles, lancers, polkas, and waltzes. There is no difficulty in finding partners: the "wall-flower," an ornament to the ball-room unknown in India generally, here blooms and flourishes luxuriantly as in our beloved fatherland. But if you are not a bald-headed colonel, a staff-officer in a gingerbread uniform, or a flash sub. in one of Her Majesty's corps, you will prefer contemplating the festal scene from the modest young man's great stand-by—the doorway. About one o'clock there is a break for supper—a hot substantial meal of course:—the dancing that follows is strikingly of a more spirited nature than that which preceded it. The general exhilaration infects, perhaps, even you. You screw up your courage to the point of asking some smiling spinster if she "may have the pleasure of dancing with you?" and by her good aid in action as well as advice, you find out, with no small exultation, that you have not quite forgotten your quadrille.

At three P.M. the ladies retire, apparently to the regret, really to the delight of the bachelors, who, with gait and gestures expressive of the profoundest satisfaction, repair to the supper-room for another hot and substantial meal. The conversation is lively: the toilettes, manners, conversation and dancing of the fair sex are blamed or extolled *selon*; the absence of the Bombay ladies and the scarcity of the Bombay gentlemen are commented upon with a *naïveté* which, if you happen to consider yourself one of them, is apt to be rather unpleasant. Before, however, you can make up your mind what to do, the cigars are lighted, spirits mixed, and the singing commences. This performance is usually of the style called at messes the "sentimental," wherein a long chorus is a *sine quâ non*, the usual accompaniments a little horse-play in different parts of the room, and the conclusion a hammering of tables or rattling of glasses and a drumming with the heels, which, when well combined, produce truly an imposing effect. At length Aurora comes slowly in, elbowing her way, and sidling through the dense waves of rolling smoke, which would oppose her entrance, but failing therein, content themselves with communicating to her well known saffron-coloured morning wrapper a rather dull and dingy hue. Phœbus looks red and lowering at the prospect of the dozen gentlemen, who, in very pallid complexions, black garments, and patent leather boots, wind, with frequent halts, along a common road, leading, as each conceives, directly to his own abode. And the Muses thus preside over the conclusion, as they ushered in the beginning of the eventful *fête*.

"On the — of —— the gay and gallant bachelors of Ootacamund entertained all the beauty and fashion of the station in the magnificent ball-room of the club. The scene was a perfect galaxy of light and loveliness, etc."

You have now, we will suppose, almost exhausted the short list of public amusements, balls and parties; you have boated on the lake; you have ridden and walked round the lake till every nodule of gravel is deadly familiar to your eye; you have contemplated the lake from every possible point, and can no longer look at it, or hear it named, without a sensation of nausea. You have probably wandered "over the hills and far away" in search of game; your sport was not worth speaking of, but its consequences, the headache, or the attack of liver which resulted from over-exertion, *was* —. Perhaps you have been induced to ride an untrained Arab at a steeple-chase, and, curious to say, you have not broken an arm or even your collar-bone. What are you to do now? You wish to goodness that you could obtain leave to visit the different stations in the low country, but, unhappily, you forgot to have your sick certificate worded, "For the Neilgherries and the Western Coast." You find yourself cooped up in the mountains as securely as within the lofty walls of your playground in by-gone days, and if you venture to play truant, you will certainly be dismissed the establishment, which is undesirable:—you are not yet over anxious to return to "duty," although you are by no means happy away from it.

Suddenly a little occurrence in your household affords you a temporary diversion. You dismissed your Bombay servants, first and foremost the Portuguese, a fortnight after your arrival at Ootacamund, because the fellows grumbled at the climate and the expense:—they could not afford to get drunk half as often as in the plains:—demanded exorbitant wages, and required almost as many comforts and luxuries as you yourself do. So you paid their passage back to their homes, and secured the usual number of Madras domestics, men of the best character, according to their own account, and provided with the highest, though more than dubious testimonials. You found that the change was for the better. Your new blacks worked like horses, and did not refuse to make themselves generally useful. Presently, they, seeing your "softness," began to presume upon it. You found it necessary to dismiss one of them, summarily, for exaggerated insolence. The man left your presence, and stepped over to the edifice where sits in state the "Officer Commanding the Neilgherries." About half an hour afterwards you received a note, couched in terms quite the reverse of courteous, ordering you to pay your dismissed servant his wages, and peremptorily forbidding you to take the law into your own hands by kicking him. But should you object to obey, as you probably will do, you are allowed the alternative of appearing at the office the next day.

At the hour specified you prepare to keep your appointment, regretting that you are not a civilian:—you might then have tossed the note into the fire:—but somewhat consoled by a discovery, made in the course of the evening, that the complainant has stolen several articles of clothing from you. You walk into the room, ceremoniously bow and are bowed to, pull a chair towards you unceremoniously, because you are not asked to sit down, wait impatiently enough, — you have promised to ride out with Miss A——, who will assuredly confer the honour of her company upon your enemy Mr. B—— if you keep her waiting five minutes,—a mortal hour and a half. When the last case has been dismissed, the Commanding officer, after some little time spent in arranging his papers, nibbing his pens and conversationizing with a native clerk about matters more than indifferent to you, turns towards you a countenance in which the severity of justice is somewhat tempered by the hard stereotyped smile of polite inquiry. Stimulated by the look, you forget that you are the defendant, till reminded of your position in a way which makes you feel all its awkwardness. The Commanding officer is a great "stickler for abstract rights," and is known to be high-principled upon the subjects of black skins and British law. So you, who expected, as a matter of course, that the "word of an officer and gentleman" would be taken against that of a "native rascal," find yourself notably in the wrong box. Indignant, you send for your butler. And now Pariah meets Pariah with a terrible tussle of tongue. Complainant swears that he was not paid ; witness oathes by the score that he was. The former strengthens his position by cursing himself to Patal * if he has not been swindled by the "Buttrel" and his Sahib out of two months' wages. The head servant, not to be outdone, devotes the persons of his Brahman, his wife, and his eldest son, to a very terrible doom indeed, if he did not with his own hands advance complainant three months' pay, — and so on. At length the Commanding officer, who has carefully and laboriously been taking down the evidence, bids the affidavits cease, and reluctantly dismisses the complaint.

And now for your turn, as you fondly imagine. You also have a charge to make. You do so emphatically. You summon your witnesses, who are standing outside. You prove your assertion triumphantly, conclusively. You inform the Commanding officer, with determination, that you are resolved to do your best to get the thief punished.

The Commanding officer hears you out most patiently, urges you to follow up the case, and remarks, that the prosecution of the affair will be productive

* The region of eternal punishment.

of great advantage to the European residents on the Hills. You are puzzled transiently: the words involve an enigma, and the sarcastic smile of the criminal smacks of a mystery. But your mental darkness is soon cleared up; the Commanding officer hints that you will find no difficulty in procuring a fortnight's leave to Coimbatore, the nearest Civil station, for the purpose of carrying out your public-spirited resolution. As this would involve a land journey of one hundred miles—in India equal to one thousand in Europe—with all the annoyances of law-proceedings, and all the discomforts of a strange station, your determination suddenly melts away, and gentle Pity takes the place of stern Prosecution; you forget your injury, you forgive your enemy.

You must not, however, lay any blame upon the Commanding officer; his hands are tied as well as yours. He is a justice of the peace, but his authority is reduced to nothing in consequence of his being subject to the civil power at Coimbatore. A more uncomfortable position for a military man to be placed in you cannot conceive.

This little bit of excitement concludes your list of public amusements. And now, again, you ask What shall you do? You put the question, wishing to heaven that Echo—Arabian or Hibernian—would but respond with her usual wonted categoricality; but she, poor maid! has quite lost her voice, in consequence of the hard-talking she has had of late years. So you must even reply to and for yourself—no easy matter, we can assure you.

Goethe, it is said, on the death of his son, took up a new study. You have no precise ideas about Goethe or his proceedings, but your mind spontaneously grows the principle that actuated the great German. You are almost persuaded to become a student. You borrow some friend's Akhlak i Hindi,* rummage your trunks till you discover the remnant of a Shakespeare's Grammar, and purchase, at the first auction, a second-hand copy of Forbes's Dictionary. You then inquire for a Moonshee—a language-master — and find that there is not a decent one in the place. The local government, in the plenitude of its sagacity, has been pleased to issue an order forbidding examination committees being held at the Sanitarium; so good teachers will not remain at a station where their services are but little required. Your ardour, however, is only damped, not extinguished. You find some clerk in

* "The ethics of India;" the Cornelius Nepos of Hindostani.

one of the offices who can read Hindostani ; you set to—you rub up your acquaintance with certain old friends, called Parts of Speech—you master the Verb, and stand in astonishment to see that you have read through a whole chapter of the interesting ethical composition above alluded to. That pause has ruined you. Like the stiff joints of a wearied pedestrian, who allows himself rest at an inopportune time, your mind refuses to rise again to its task. You find out that Ootacamund is no place for study ; that the houses are dark, the rooms cold, and the air so exciting that it is all but impossible to sit down quietly for an hour. Finally, remembering that you are here for health, you send back the Akhlak, restore Shakespeare to his own trunk, and, after coquetting about the conversational part of the language with your Moonshee for a week or two—dismiss him.

CHAPTER XVII.

LIFE OUTSIDE OOTY.

SPEAKING seriously, the dearth of diversion or even occupation at Oòtacamund, considerably diminishes its value as a sanitary station. It is generally remarked, that a man who in other places drinks a little too freely, here seldom fails to bring on an attack of delirium tremens. After the first excitement passes away, it is apt to be succeeded by a sense of dreariness and ennui more debilitating to the system than even the perpetual perspirations of the plains.

The chief occupations for a visitor outside of Ooty are curiosity-hunting, field-sports, and excursionizing.

Of late years, the Neilgherries have been so exposed to the pickaxes of indefatigable archæologists, that their huge store of curiosities has been almost exhausted. Little now remains but the fixtures. In many parts almost every hill is crowned by single and double cairns, enclosing open areas, which, when opened, were found to contain numerous pottery* figures of men and animals. There are some remarkable remains which remind us of the Cromlechs † and Kistvaens ‡ of Druidism; all, however, have been rifled of the funeral urns and the other relics which they contained. Vases holding burnt bones and charcoal, brass vessels, spear heads, clay images of female warriors on horseback, stone pestles, pots and covers ornamented with human figures and curious animals, have been taken from the barrows that abound in different parts of the Neilgherries. The ruins of forts and pagodas, traces of buildings and manual labour, may be discovered in the darkest recesses of ancient forests.

* No inscriptions have as yet been discovered. The only coin we have heard of was a Roman aureus, whereas in the cairns that stud the plains, medals, of the Lower Empire especially, are commonly met with.

† Consecrated stones.

‡ The kistvaens, or closed cromlechs of the Neilgherries, are tumuli about five feet high. The internal chamber is composed of four walls, each consisting of an entire stone seven feet long and five broad, floored and roofed with similar slabs. In the monolithe, constituting the eastern wall, is a circular aperture large enough to admit the body of a child.

Long and deep fosses, the use of which cannot be explained, and diminutive labyrinths still remain the monuments of ancient civilization. At St. Catherine's Falls, near Kotagherry, the natives show marks in the rock which they attribute to a certain hill Rajah who urged his horse over the precipice to escape the pursuit of his foes. The land is rich in such traditions. There is a name for every hill;* to every remarkable one is attached some cherished legend. Here we are shown the favourite seats of the Rishi, or saintly race, who, in hoary eld, honoured the green tops of the Blue Mountains with their holy presence. There, we are told, abode the foul Rakhshasa (demon) tribe, that loved to work man's mortal woe; and there, dwarfish beings, somewhat like our fairies, long since passed away, lived in the dancing and singing style of existence usually attributed by barbarians to those pretty creatures of their imaginations.

The Toda family—the grand depository of Neilgherry tradition—has supplied our curiosity-hunters

* The colonists have followed the example of the aborigines. Little, however, can be said in favour of our nomenclature. There is a Snowdon, without snow; a Saddle-back Hill, whose *dorsum* resembles anything as much as a saddle; an Avalanche Hill, without avalanches, and so on.

with many a marvel. But, let the young beginner beware how he trusts to their information. The fellows can enjoy a hoax. Moreover, with the instinctive cunning of the wild man, they are inveterate liars, concealing truth because they perceive that their betters attach some importance to extracting it, and yet cannot understand the reason why they should take the trouble to do so. For instance — we heard of a gentleman who, when walking near one of the villages, saw some roughly-rounded stones lying upon the ground, and asked a Toda what their use might be. The savage replied extempore, that the biggest piece was, according to his creed, the grandfather of the gods; another was the grandmother, and so on to a great length. He received a rupee for the intelligence given; and well he won it. The stones were those used by the young men of the hamlet for "putting" in their leisure hours—a slender foundation, indeed, to support so grand a superstructure of traditional lore!

Antiquarians are everywhere a simple race: in India, "con tutto rispetto parlando," we are almost tempted to describe them as simpletons. Who does not recollect the Athenæum sauce-jar which some wag buried in the ruins of a fort, said to have been founded by Alexander the Great at Sehwan in Scinde, and the strange theories which the Etruscan images upon that article elicited from grave and learned heads?

Game is still plentiful in the Neilgherries. The little woods about Ootacamund abound in woodcock, leopard,* and ibex. Near Coonoor, elk and wild hog are to be met with, and to the east of Kotagherry there is excellent bison-shooting. Elephants occasionally ascend the Koondah hills to escape the fiery heat of the luxuriant jungles below the mountains. Tigers are rare in these parts, and no one takes the trouble to attack them: the cold climate ruins them for sport by diminishing their ferocity and the chance of one's being clawed. The wolf is not an aboriginal of the hills: he sometimes, however, favours us with a visit, in packs, gaunt with hunger and sufficiently fierce, for the purpose of dining on the dogs. The small black bear, or rather ant-eater of the plains, affords tolerable sport; but

* Dr. Baikie (in 1834) mentions that one of these animals had held possession of a thick wood close to the cantonment for some years. The same spot is still tenanted, it is said, by a cheeta, but whether it be the original occupant, his ghost, or one of his descendants, men know not.

this Alpine region does not produce the large and powerful brown animal of the Pyrenees and Central Asia.

The peculiarity of Neilgherry hunting is, that nothing can be done by means of beaters only —the plan adopted in India generally. Cocks cannot be flushed without spaniels, and foxhounds are necessary for tracking large game. The canine species thrives prodigiously on the hills, and seems to derive even more benefit from the climate than the human dogs. The crack sportsman from the plains must here abandon his favourite pig-sticking, or exchange it for what he always considered the illicit practice of hog-shooting. *En revanche*, he has the elk, the bison, and the ibex.

The Neilgherry Sambur, or elk,* is the giant of the cervine race—often fourteen hands high, with antlers upwards of three feet long, spanning thirty-two or thirty-three inches between the extremities. In spite of this beast's size and unwieldiness—some of them weigh seven hundred pounds—they are sufficiently speedy to distance any but a good horse. They

* Not Buffon's elk. It is the *Cervus Aristotelis*, or black rusa of Cuvier; the "Shambara" of classical India; the Gavazn of Persia; and the Gav i Gavazn of Affghanistan and Central Asia.

divide their time between the mountain-woods and the lower jungles, resorting to the former for the sake of the water, and descending to the latter to get at the "salt-licks," in which they abound. Elk are usually met with in pairs, or in greater numbers, and when once sighted are easily shot. The neck and the hollow behind the shoulder are the parts aimed at, for these animals are extraordinarily tenacious of life, and will carry off a most unreasonable number of balls, unless hit in a vital region. The flesh is coarse, but makes excellent mulligatawny, the shin-bones afford good marrow, the hoofs are convertible into jelly, the tongue is eatable, and the skin useful for saddle-covers, gaiters, and hunting boots. The head, stuffed with straw and provided with eyes, skilfully made out of the bottom of a black bottle, is a favourite ornament for the verandah or the mantelpiece. Samburs are easily tamed: several of them may be seen about Ootacamund, grazing with halters round their necks, almost as tame as cows. There are several ways of hunting elk. On the hills skirting the Pykarry river, where there is little swamp or bog, attempts have been made to run and spear them. Some sportsmen stalk them; but the usual mode is to post the guns, and then to make the beast break cover. Dogs are preferred to beaters for this purpose, as their giving tongue warns one when the game is coming, and the animal will almost always fly from his fourfooted, whereas it often succeeds in charging and breaking through the line of biped foes. Samburs, when wounded and closely pursued, will sometimes stand and defend themselves desperately with tooth and antler; the "game thing" then is to "walk into them" with a hunting-knife.

Bison-hunting upon the hills is a most exciting sport, requiring thews and sinews, a cool head and a steady hand. A charge of one of these animals is quite the reverse of a joke: Venator had better make sure of his nerve before he goes forth to stand before such a rush. The bison is a noble animal. We have seen heads* which a strong man was scarcely able to lift, and horns that measured twenty inches in circumference. They are usually shot with ounce or two ounce iron or brass balls, and plugs made by the hill-people, who cut a bar of metal and file it down to the size required with the

* Upon this part Nature has provided the animal with a bony mass, impenetrable to anything lighter than a grapeshot, occupying the whole space between the horns, and useful, we should suppose, in forcing a way through dense and thorny jungle.

rudest tools and remarkable neatness. The Hindoos, however, do not patronise bison-hunting, as they consider the beast a wild species of their sacred animal.

The word "ibex," like the "jungle sheep"* of the Neilgherries, is a misnomer: the denominated being the Capra Caucasica, not the Capra ibex of Cuvier. It is to these hills what the chamois is to the Alps, and the izzard to the Pyrenees. If you are sportsman enough to like difficulty and danger, incurred for nothing's sake, you will think well of ibex-hunting. In the first place you have to find your game, and to find it also in some place where it can be approached when alive, and secured when dead. The senses of these wild goats are extraordinarily acute, and often, after many hours of toil, the disappointed pursuer is informed by the peculiar whistling noise which they make when alarmed, that, warned of his proximity — probably by the wind — they have moved off to safer quarters. Secondly, you must hit them—hard, too; otherwise

* This "jungle sheep" is the *Cervus porcinus*, the hog-deer or barking-deer of Upper India, which abounds in every shikargah of delectable Scinde. In Sanscrit it is called the Preushat ("sprinkling," in allusion to its spotted hide); in Hindostani, Parha; and in Persian, the Kotah-pacheb, or "short hoof."

you will never bring about a dead stop. And, lastly, as they are addicted to scrambling down and rolling over tremendous precipices—especially after they have felt lead—you must either lose the beast or risk your neck to bag the body. Not for the pot. The flesh is never eaten, but the stuffed head is preserved as a trophy of venatic prowess.

The hill people, when not employed in spearing and netting game on their own account, will generally act as lookers-out and beaters. We are apt, however, to be too generous with our money: the effect of the liberality proving it to be ill-advised. Often it will happen to you—especially during your first month's sporting—that some black scoundrel rushes up in a frantic hurry to report game trove, in the hope that you will, upon the spur of the moment, present him with a rupee. And suppose you do so, what is the result? It is sad weather; the clouds rain cats and dogs—to use an old phrase —the wind is raw as a south-easter off the Cape; the ground one mass of slippery mud. Do you look out of the window, roll your head, dismiss the "nigger," return to your fire, the "Demented," and your cigar. No! emphatically no!! You rush into your room, pull on shoes and gaiters, don your hunting-garb with astonishing rapidity, catch up your guns, roar for the favourite servant that carries them, and start in the middle of the howling storm. Your eagerness to "get a slap at a bison" incites you to cruelty: you think nothing of dashing into the first village, and compelling a troop of half-naked wretches to accompany you. Now mark the consequence of giving away that rupee in a hurry. The head beater leads you up and down the steepest, the most rugged, stony, and slippery hills he can hit upon, with the benevolent view of preventing your making a fool of yourself to any greater extent. But when your stout English legs have completely "taken the shine" out of those baboon-like shanks which support his body, then he conducts you to some Shola,* places you and your servant upon the top of an elevated rock commanding a thorough enjoyment of the weather, and an extensive view of the ravine through which the beast is to break cover, and retires with his comrades to the snug cavern, which he held all along in mental view. There he sits before a cosy bit of fire, occasionally indulging you with a view-halloo, proving how actively the gang is engaged in dis-

* A shola is a thick mass of low wood, which may be measured by yards or miles, clothing the sides, the bottoms, and the ravines of the hills and mountains.

covering the game. Half an hour has passed; you are wet through, "*jusqu'aux os*," and the chill blasts feel as if they were cutting their way into your vitals: still your ardour endures. Another twenty minutes—your fingers refuse to uphold the cocked rifle.

"We really must go if they can't find this beast in another quarter of an hour, Baloo!"

"Han, Sahib!—yes, sir,"—quavers forth your unhappy domestic, in a frozen treble—"if the Sahib were to—to go, just now—would it not be good? It is very cold—and—perhaps—they have been telling the Sahib lies."

Baloo is right. The head beater appears, followed by his attendant train. He swears that it is a case of "stole away."

You feel that there is something wrong about that bison, by the way in which the man's eye avoided you. But probably a sense of justice prevents your having recourse to the baculine discipline which, on any other occasion, we should have advised you to administer with no niggardly hand.

Sounders of hog are commonly found at certain seasons about Coonoor especially. They are often shot, and more often missed, as their gaunt forms boring through the high grass afford a very uncertain mark. If Diana favour you, you may have the luck to come upon that beautiful variety of the leopard tribe, the black cheeta, and wreak upon him the revenge which his brethren's ravages amongst your "bobbery-pack"* has roused in your bosom. If you are proud of your poultry yard you will never allow a jungle cat to pass without rolling her over: the large fierce beasts are so uncommonly fond of ducks and fowls. The jackals† on the hills are even more daring and impudent than they are in the plains. Hares are so numerous and voracious that they will destroy any garden, flower or kitchen, unless it is defended by a dwarf-fencing of split bamboos. Your careful Malee‡ takes, moreover, the precaution of surrounding your cabbages with a deep ditch in order to keep out the huge porcupines that abound here. *En passant* we advise every one who has not tasted a

* *I.e.* ten or twenty dogs and curs, young and old, of high and low degree, terriers, pointers, spaniels, setters, pariahs, and mongrels, headed by a staunch old hound or two.

† There is a large kind of solitary jackal whose cry is never answered by the other animals of the same species: the sound somewhat resembles the hyæna's laugh, and has been mistaken for it by many.

‡ Gardener.

rôti of one of those animals to do so *sine morâ*, not, however, forgetting to roll up the flesh in a layer of mutton fat, and thus to remedy its only defect — dryness. Martins, polecats, mongooses, and the little grey gilahri * of Hindostan, flourish on the hills; there is also a large dark brown squirrel, with a huge bushy tail, but the flying species, so common on the western coast, is not an inhabitant of the Neilgherries. The woods are tenanted by several kinds of monkeys, black and red, large and small: the otter is occasionally met with in the fords of the Pykary river.

There are two varieties of the wild dog, one a large nondescript, with a canine head, the body of a wolf, and a brush instead of a tail: the other is a smaller beast of similar appearance. They generally hunt in large packs, and the skill with which they follow up the game is admirable. When pressed by hunger they are very ferocious. It is at no time a pleasant sight to see fifty or a hundred of their ill-omened faces glaring at you and your horse as you ride by them: especially after you have heard certain well-authenticated anecdotes of their cannibal propensities. When such rencontre does occur, the best way is to put a bold face upon

* A species of squirrel.

the matter, ride up to them, and use your heavy horsewhip as well as you can: if you endeavour to get away they will generally feel inclined to follow you, and as for escaping from them on horseback, it is morally impossible.

Another animal—though not a wild one—of which we bid you beware, is the Neilgherry buffalo, especially the fine fawn-coloured beasts, belonging to the Todas. Occasionally, as you are passing along the base of some remote hill, you will be unpleasantly surprised by a sudden and impetuous charge of a whole herd. Unless you have a gun with you, you must ride for it. And *how* you must ride will probably surprise you. We well recollect a kind of adventure which once occurred to ourselves, when quietly excursionizing in the vicinity of Ooty. Excited by the appearance of our nag's red saddle-cloth, some twenty huge beasts resolved to dispute with us the right of passage through one of the long smooth lawns, which run down the centre of the woodlands. At first they looked up curiously, then fiercely. Presently they advanced, snorting rabidly, in a rude line, a huge black bull the leader of the movement. The walk soon broke into a trot, the trot became a gallop, the intention of the gallop, was clearly a charge, and the consequences of a charge might have been serious. We found little difficulty in escaping the general rush of our assailants, by means of a sharp touch with the spur: one by one they tailed off, stood looking at our decreasing form in angry disgust, and returned to their normal occupation. But Taurus, the ringleader, seemed determined upon mischief. He pursued us with the dogged determination of a lyme hound: he had speed as well as bottom. Whenever we attempted to breathe the pony, the rapidity with which our friend gained ground upon us, was a warning not to try that trick too long. Close upon our quarters followed the big beast with his curved horns duly prepared: his eyes flashing fire, and his grunting snorts indicative of extreme rage. We could scarcely help laughing at the agility with which the monstrous body, on its four little legs, bowled away over the level turf, or at the same time wishing that our holsters contained the means of chastising his impudence.

How long the recreation might have lasted, or how it might have ended had not a long mud wall got between Taurus and ourselves, we cannot say. He followed us for at least a mile, and seemed by no means tired of the occupation. We were beginning to anticipate the pleasure of entering Ootacamund at the top of our nag's speed, with a huge buffalo at his heels, and though we might have enjoyed seeing a friend in such novel predicament, the thing lost all its charms, when we ourselves expected to afford such spectacle to our friends.

We should strongly advise all public spirited individuals immediately after suffering from such a nuisance to find out the herdsman, and persuade him by a judicious application of the cravache, to teach his cattle better manners. He will be much more careful the next time he sees a stranger ride by.

Among the feathered tribes, the woodcock, probably on account of its comparative rarity, is the favourite sport. Three or four brace are considered an excellent bag, even with the assistance of good dogs, and a thorough knowledge of their covers. Cock shooting lasts from November to March. Partridges are rare, not being natives of the hills. Snipe, and solitary snipe, abound in the swamps. Quails of both species, red and grey,—the former especially — are found in the warmer localities, and when properly tamed and trained, they are as game birds as those of the low country. Our list concludes with peacocks, jungle * and spur fowl.

After perusing our brief sketch of Neilgherry sport, you will easily understand that to some ardent minds it offers irresistible attractions. Officers have been known to quit the service, or to invalid solely with the view of devoting themselves wholly to the *pleasures* of the chase. They separate themselves from their kind, inhabit the jungles for weeks together, and never enter a station except for the purpose of laying in a fresh store of powder and shot, calomel and quinine. Attended by a servant or two, they wander about, rifle in hand, shooting their meals—some curried bird—sleeping away the rabid hours of noontide heat under some thick brake, and starting with renewed vigour as soon as the slanting rays of the sun diffuse a little activity throughout the animal creation. Sometimes breakfast is rudely interrupted by an angry old tusker, who, in spite of his race's proverbial purblindness, detects the

* We have heard much about the difficulty of taming these birds. Some go so far as to assert that they pine away and die when deprived of their liberty. The Affghans seem to find nothing hard in the operation, as they use the birds for fighting. They show excellent pluck, and never fail to fight till death, although steel and silver are things unknown.

presence of an enemy, and rushes on trumpeting to do a deed of violence. A "striped skin" will occasionally invite himself to partake of the dinner, and when not treated with all possible ceremony walks off with a raw joint in the shape of some unhappy black. There is little to be gained by such a life. Government gives, it is true, a reward of 7*l.** for every slaughtered elephant, and tiger-skins, as well as ivory, find a ready sale: but no one can become a Crœsus by the favour of Diana. Not much, however, do our adventurous sportsmen think of lucre: they go on shooting through existence, only pausing at times when the bites of the tree-leeches,† scorpions, centipedes, and musquitoes, or a low fever, which they have vainly endeavoured to master by means of quinine administered in doses sufficient to turn an average head, imperiously compel them to lay up, till assailed by a Foe against whom the dose and the rifle

* Seven pounds for a full grown, 5*l.* for a young animal. When the reward is claimed the tusks must be given up. Tuskers, however, are not often met with in these days.

† Every swamp on and about the hills is full of small leeches,—the lake also abounds in them,—which assail your legs, and swarming up the trees, drop down your shirt collar to your extreme annoyance. They are quite useless for medical purposes, as the bite is highly inflammatory.

are equally unefficacious. Many are almost blinded by the terrible glare and damp heat of the jungles: the fetid swamps breed brain fevers as well as snipe, bisons have horns, and cheetahs claws: so that such career, though bright enough in its own way, is generally speaking at least as brief as it is brilliant.

Before the monsoon sets in, we will "get through," as our Irish cousin expressed himself at the Vatican, "the sight-seeing" in the neighbourhood of Ooty.

Maleemund, or, as others write it, Meyni, a favourite spot for pic-nics, is a Toda village lying about three miles north of the grand station: it affords you a pleasant ride through pretty woodlands, and a very inferior view. Beyond it is Billicul, a little Berger settlement surrounded by cultivation: here a resident on the hills has built a bungalow, and the locality is often visited for the pleasure of contemplating the reeking flats of Mysore. Striking across country into the Seegoor Pass, you may, if you have any curiosity, inspect the Kulhutty Falls, certain cataracts upon a very diminutive scale indeed. You must see the Pykarry river, a deep and irregular stream flowing down a winding bed full of rocks, rapids, and sand-banks : it supplies your curries with a shrunken specimen of the finny tribe—alas ! how different from certain fishes which you may connect in memory with certain mountain streams in the old country. The surrounding hills are celebrated for containing abundance of game. An indefatigable excursionist would ride seven miles further on the Goodalore road for the sake of the *coups-d'œil*, and to be able to say that he has seen Neddi-wuttun. All the pleasure he derives from this extra stage along a vile path, is a sense of intense satisfaction that he is not compelled to pass a night in the damp, dreary, moss-clad bungalow, where unhappy travellers must at times perforce abide. Three miles from Ooty, in the direction of the Koondah hills, you pass Fair Lawn, the bit of turf which Terpsichore loves. Finally, after a long and dreary stretch over a tiresome series of little eminences, after fording the Porthy river, and crossing its sister stream, the Avalanche, by an unsafe bridge, you arrive at the Wooden House,* whence sportsmen issue to disturb the innocent enjoyments of elk and ibex, bison and elephant.

* The Maroo Bungla, or log-house, as the natives call the Avalanche bungalow.

CHAPTER XVIII.

THE INHABITANTS OF THE NEILGHERRIES.

THERE are five different races now settled upon the Blue Mountains :—

1. *Bergers*, the mass of the population ; supposed to be about ten thousand.

2. *Erulars*,
3. *Cooroombars*, } The wild men dwelling on the woody sides of the hills ; about two thousand.

4. *Kothurs*,
5. *Todas*, } The old inhabitants and owners of the land ; about three thousand.

The Bergers, Vaddacars,* or, as the Todas call them, the Marves, are an uninteresting race of Shudra Hindoos, that immigrated from the plains in the days of Hyder or Tippoo. They attempt to

* The first name is a corruption of the second, which is derived from Vadacu, "the north," these people having migrated from that direction.

invest their expatriation with the dignity of antiquity by asserting that upwards of four centuries ago they fled to the hills from the persecutions of Moslem tyrants. This caste affects the Lingait or Shaivya * form of Hinduism, contains a variety of sub-families, speaks a debased dialect of modern Canarese, and still retains, in the fine climate of the Neilgherries, the dark skin, the degraded expression of countenance, and the puny figure, that characterise the low caste native of Southern India. They consider the wild men of the hills as magicians, and have subjected themselves to the Todas, in a social as well as a religious point of view, by paying a tax for permission to occupy their lands. They have been initiated in some of the mysterious practices of the mountaineers, and have succeeded in infecting the minds of their instructors with all the rigid exclusiveness and silly secrecy of their own faith. It redounds, however, to their credit that they have not imitated the debauched and immoral habits which their lords have learned by intercourse with strangers. There is nothing remarkable in their dress, their manners, or their habitations; they employ themselves in

* The worship of the terrible and destructive incarnation of the Deity.

cultivating the soil and acting as porters, beater s labourers, and gardeners.

The Erulars * and Cooroombars † are utter savages, very much resembling the Rankaris of Maharatta Land and the Bheels of Candeish. Their language, a kind of Malayalim, proves that they were originally inhabitants of the plains, but nothing more is known about them. They dwell in caves, clefts in the rocks, and miserable huts, built upon the slopes of the mountains, and they support themselves by cultivation and selling wax and honey. In appearance they are diminutive, dark men, distinguishable from the highest order of Quadrumana by the absence of pile upon their bodies, and a knack of walking on their hind legs. Their dress is limited to about a palm's breadth of coarse cotton cloth, and their only weapon a little knife, which hangs from a bit of string to the side. They are rarely seen. When riding about the wild parts of the hills you occasionally meet one of these

* Signifying the "unenlightened or barbarous," from the Tamul word Erul, darkness.

† "Cooroombar," or "Curumbar," literally means "wilful, or self-willed." Sometimes the word mulu, a "thorn," is prefixed to the genuine name by way of epithet, alluding to the nature of the race.

savages, who starts and stands for a moment, staring at you through his bush of matted hair, in wonder, or rather awe, and then plunges headlong into the nearest thicket. Man is the only enemy the poor wretches have reason to fear. By the Todas, as well as the Bergers, they are looked upon as vicious magicians, who have power of life and death over men and beasts, of causing disease, and conjuring tigers from the woods to assist them; they are propitiated by being cruelly beaten and murdered, whenever a suitable opportunity presents itself. The way in which this people will glide through the wildest woods, haunted by all manner of ferocious foes, proves how fine and acute the human senses are capable of becoming when sharpened by necessity and habit.

In investigating the origin of the Kothurs, Cohatars,* or Cuvs, the usual obstacles,—a comparatively unknown language, and the want of a written character,— oppose the efforts of inquirers. The palpable affinity, however, between the Toda and Kothur

* So Captain Harkness writes the word, remarking, that "as this tribe kill and eat a great deal of beef, it was no doubt intended by their Hindu neighbours that they should be called 'Gohatars,' from go, a cow, and hata, slaying." "Cuv," in the Toda dialect, means a "mechanic."

dialects, proves that both the races were originally connected, and the great change* that has taken place in the languages, shows that this connection was by no means recently dissolved. Why or how the separation took place, even tradition † does not inform us; but the degraded customs, as well as the appearance, dress, and ornaments of the Kothurs point most probably to a loss of caste, in consequence of some unlawful and polluting action.

The Kothurs show great outward respect to the Todas, and the latter return the compliment more substantially by allowing their dependants a part of the tax which they receive from the Bergers. They are an industrious and hard-working race; at once cultivators and musicians, carpenters and potters, bricklayers, and artizans in metal as well as in wood. Their villages composed of little huts, built with rough wattling, are almost as uncleanly as their persons. Every considerable settlement contains two places of worship, for the men do not

* Many of the words have been corrupted, and the pronunciation has become nasal, not guttural, like that of the Todas. The Kothurs can, however, express themselves imperfectly in Canarese.

† All that we can gather from their songs and tales is, that anciently they were the zemindars, or landed proprietors of the hills.

TODA FAMILY AND VILLAGE.
Londan Bichard Bentiey New Burlingto Street 1851

pray with the women ; in some hamlets they have set up curiously carved stones, which they consider sacred, and attribute to them the power of curing diseases, if the member affected be only rubbed against the talisman. They will devour any carrion, even when in a semi-putrid state : the men are fond of opium, and intoxicating drinks ; they do not, however, imitate the Todas in their illicit way of gaining money wherewith to purchase their favourite luxuries.

As the Toda* race is, in every way, the most remarkable of the Neilgherry inhabitants, so it has been its fate to be the most remarked. Abundant observation has been showered down upon it ; from observation sprang theories, theories grew into systems. The earliest observer remarking the Roman noses, fine eyes, and stalwart frames of the savages, drew their origin from Italy,—not a bad beginning! Another gentleman argued from their high Arab features, that they are probably immigrants from the Shat el Arab,† but it is apparent that he used the subject only to inform the world of

* Todawars, Tudas, or Toders. Captain Harkness derives the word from the Tamul, Torawar, a herdsman, and this is probably the true name of the race.

† The north-west parts of the Persian Gulf.

the length and breadth of his wanderings. Captain Harkness discovered that they were aborigines. Captain Congreve determined to prove that the Todas are the remnants of the Celto-Scythian race, which *selon lui*, inhabited the plains, and were driven up to the hills before the invading Hindoo; he even spelt the word "Thautawars," to sound more Scythic. He has treated the subject with remarkable acuteness, and displayed much curious antiquarian lore; by systematically magnifying every mote of resemblance,* and, by pertinaciously

* *E. g.* The peaks of the Todas are venerated by the Todas, as they were by the Celto-Scythians. The single stone in the sacred lactarium of the former, was the most conspicuous instrument of superstition in the Druidical or Scythic religion. Captain Congreve asserts that the Toda faith is Scythicism, *because* they sacrifice female children, bulls, calves, and buffaloes, as the Scythians did horses; that they adore the sun (what old barbarians did not?), revere fire, respect certain trees and bunches of leaves, worship the Deity in groves of the profoundest gloom, and have some knowledge of a future state. He proves that the hills are covered with vestiges of Scythicism, as cairns, barrows, and monolithic altars, and believes them to have belonged to the early Todas, inasmuch as "the religion of the Todas is Scythicism, and these are monuments of Scythicism." He concludes the exposition of his theory with the following recapitulation of his reasons for considering the Todas of Scythian descent:—1. Identity of religion (not proved). 2. Physiological position of the Todas in the great family race

neglecting or despising each beam of dissimilitude,* together with a little of the freedom in assertion allowed to system-spinners, he has succeeded in erecting a noble edifice, which lacks nothing but a foundation. The metaphysical German traced in the irreverent traditions† of the barbarians con-

(we are not told how it resembles that of the Scythians). 3. The pastoral mode of life among the Todas. 4. The food of the Todas, which consisted originally of milk and butter (we "doubt the fact"). 5. Their architecture, religious, military, and domestic, the yards of the Toda houses, their temples, their sacred enclosures, their kraals for cattle, are circular, as were those of the Celts, and, indeed, of most ancient people whose divinity was Sun, Light, Fire, Apollo, Mithra, &c. 6. Their marriage customs and funeral rites are nearly identical (an assertion). 7. Their ornaments and dress closely approximate (ditto). 8. Their customs are generally similar (ditto). 9. The authority of Sir W. Jones that the ancient Scythians did people a mountainous district of India (*quasi* irrelevant). 10. History mentions that India has been invaded by Scythian hordes from the remotest times (ditto). 11. Their utter separation in every respect from the races around them.

* Such as want of weapons, difference of colour, dissimilarity of language. With respect to the latter point Captain Congreve remarks, that "a comparison with the Gothic, Celtic, and other ancient dialects of Europe is a great desideratum; but should no affinity be found to prevail, I should not consider the absence detrimental to my views, for this reason, that the people of Celto-Scythic origin having various languages, have been widely dispersed." After this, *Quid facias illi?*

† In many parts of the Neilgherries there is a large species

cerning the Deity, a metaphorical allusion to the creature's rebellion against his Creator; the enthusiastic Freemason warped their savage mystifications into a semblance of his pet mysteries. And the grammar-composing Anglo-Indian discovered unknown niceties in their language, by desiring any two Todas to do a particular thing, then by asking them how they expressed such action, and, lastly, by recording the random answer as a dual form of the verb.

When every one theorises so will we. The Todas are merely a remnant of the old Tamulian tribes originally inhabiting the plains, and subsequently driven up to the mountains by some event,* re-

of solitary bee which the Todas declared incurred the displeasure of the Great Spirit by stinging him, and was therefore condemned to eternal separation from its kind. But as huge combs and excellent honey abound on these hills, their savage inhabitants of course superstitionize upon the subject of the bee. The Creator, they say, desirous of knowing how honey is made, caught the animal, and she proving obstinate and refractory, confined her by means of a string tied round the middle; hence her peculiar shape! Is not this clearly a psychological allusion to the powerful volition for which the fair sex is proverbially famous?

* Not, however, by the victory of Brahmanism over Buddhism, as some have supposed. The leading tenet of Buddha's faith was the sin of shedding blood, whereas the Todas practise

specting which history is silent. Our opinion is built upon the rock of language.

It has been proved* that the Toda tongue is an old and obsolete dialect of the Tamul, containing many vocables directly derived from Sanscrit,† but corrupted into

> Words so debased and hard, no stone
> Is hard enough to touch them on.

Thus, for a single instance, the mellifluous Arkas a-pakshi—the winged animal of the firmament,—becomes Ha*kh*'sh-pa*kh*'sh, a bird. In grammar it is essentially Indian, as the cases of the noun and pronoun, and the tenses of the verb demonstrate;

infanticide and eat meat. Moreover, there is a bond of union between them and those Anti-Buddhists the Lingaits, who adhere to the religion of Shiva pure and undefiled.

This Buddhistic theory rests upon the slender foundation that the Todas call Wednesday, Buddhi-aum (Buddh's day). But the celebrated Eastern reformer's name has extended as far as the good old island in the West. It became Fo-e and Xa-ca (Shakya) in China; But in Cochin-China, Pout in Siam; Pott or Poti, in Thibet; perhaps the Wadd of Pagan Arabia; Toth in Egypt; Woden in Scandinavia; and thus reaching our remote shores, left its traces in "Wednesday." So say the etymologists.

* By the Rev. Mr. Schmidt's vocabulary of the Toda tongue.

† Captain Harkness is egregiously mistaken when he asserts that the dialect of his aborigines "has not the least affinity in roots, construction, or sound, with the Sanscrit."

the days of the week, and the numerals, are all of native, not foreign growth. The pronunciation is essentially un-Indian,* true; but with grammar and vocabulary on our side, we can afford to set aside, even if we could not explain away, the objection. A great change of articulation would naturally result from a long residence upon elevated tracts of land; the habit of conversing in the open air, and of calling aloud to those standing at a distance, would induce the speaker to make his sounds as rough and rugged as possible. This we believe to be the cause of the Bedouin-like gutturalism, which distinguishes the Toda dialect. We may observe that the Kothurs, who work in tents, have exchanged their original guttural for a nasal articulation; and the Bergers, who originally spoke

* In some points. Thus we find the Ain, Ghain, Fa and *Kh*a of the Arabs, together with the Zha of the Persians. But the step from the Indian अ to the Arabic ع, from घ (g'h) to غ, and from फ (p'h) to ف, is easily made; and the kha and zha belong to some Indian dialects as well as to Arabic and Persian.

It is supposed that the Toda language is still divided, like the Tamul, into two distinct dialects, one the popular, the other the sacred; the former admitting foreign words, derived from the Canarese, the latter a pure form generally used by the priesthood.

Most Todas can speak a few words of corrupted Canarese.

pure Canarese, have materially altered their pronunciation during the last century.

The main objection to our theory is the utter dissimilarity of the Toda, in all respects, physical as well as moral, to the races that now inhabit the plains. This argument would be a strong one, could the objector prove that such difference existed in the remote times, when our supposed separation took place. It is, we may remind him, the direct tendency of Hinduism to degenerate, not to improve, in consequence of early nuptials, the number of outcastes, perpetual intermarriage, and other customs peculiar to it. The superiority of the Toda, in form and features, to the inhabitants of the lowlands may also partially be owing to the improvement in bodily strength, stature, and general appearance that would be effected by a lengthened sojourn in the pure climate of the Blue Mountains.

The Todas, as we have said before, assert a right to the soil of the Neilgherries, and exact a kind of tax * from the Bergers. Their lordly position was

* A share of the land-produce varying from one-third to one-sixth of the whole, settled by the eye, and generally paid in kind. The Toda has made himself necessary to the Berger; he must sow the first handful of grain, and reap the first fruits

most probably the originator of their polyandry and infanticide:* disdaining agriculture, it is their object to limit the number of the tribe. According to their own accounts, they were, before the date of the Berger immigration, living in a very wild state, wearing the leaves of trees, and devouring the flesh of the elk, when they could get it, and the wild fruits of the hills; this they exchanged for a milk diet; they are now acquiring a taste for rice, sweetmeats, and buffalo meat.

The appearance of this extraordinary race is peculiarly striking to the eye accustomed to the smooth delicate limbs of India. The colour is a light chocolate, like that of a Beeloch mountaineer. The features are often extraordinarily regular and handsome; the figure is muscular, straight, manly, and well-knit, without any of that fineness of hand and wrist, foot and ankle, which now distinguishes the Hindoo family, and the stature is remarkably tall. They wear the

of the harvest, otherwise the land would be allowed to lie fallow, and the crop to rot upon the ground.

* The polyandry practised of yore seems at present on the decline. Infanticide, though said to have been abolished, probably holds its ground in the remote parts of the hills. Near the stations the lives of female children are spared with the view of making money by their immorality. Old women are still by no means common.

beard long, and allow their bushy, curly locks to lie clustering over the forehead—a custom which communicates to the countenance a wild and fierce expression, which by no means belongs to it. The women may be described as very fine large animals; we never saw a pretty one amongst them. Both sexes anoint the hair and skin with butter, probably as a protection against the external air; a blanket wound loosely round their body being their only garment. Ablution is religiously avoided.

There is nothing that is not peculiar in the manners and customs* of the Todas. Ladies are not allowed to become mothers in the huts: they are taken to the nearest wood, and a few bushes are heaped up around them, as a protection against rain and wind. Female children are either drowned in milk, or placed at the entrance of the cattle-pen to be trampled to death by the buffaloes. The few preserved to perpetuate the breed, are married to all the brothers of a family; besides their three or four husbands, they are allowed the privilege of a cicisbeo. The religion of the Toda is still *sub judice*, the general opinion being that they are imperfect Monotheists, who respect, but do not

* For a more detailed account of them, we refer the reader to the amusing pages of Captain Harkness.

adore, the sun and fire that warm them, the rocks and hills over which they roam, and the trees and spots which they connect with their various superstitions. When a Toda dies, a number of buffaloes are collected, and barbarously beaten to death with huge pointed clubs, by the young men of the tribe. The custom, it is said, arose from the importunate demands of a Toda ghost; most probably, from the usual savage idea that the animal which is useful in this world will be equally so in the next.

The Toda spends life in grazing his cattle, snoring in his cottage, and churning butter. The villages belonging to this people consist of, generally speaking, three huts, made with rough planking and thatch; a fourth, surrounded by a low wall, stands a little apart from, and forms a right angle with the others. This is the celebrated Lactarium, or dairy, a most uninteresting structure, but ennobled and dignified by the variety of assertions that have been made about it, and the mystery with which the savages have been taught to invest it. Some suppose it to be a species of temple, where the Deity is worshipped in the shape of a black stone, and a black stone, we all know, tells a very long tale, when interpreted by even a second-rate antiquary. Others declare that it is a masonic lodge,* the strong ground for such opinion being, that females are never allowed to enter it, and that sundry mystic symbols, such as circles, squares, and others of the same kind, are roughly cut into the side wall where the monolith stands. We entered several of these huts when in a half-ruinous state, but were not fortunate or imaginative enough to find either stone or symbols. The former might have been removed, the latter could not; so we must believe that many of our wonder-loving compatriots have been deceived by the artistic attempts made by some tasteful savage, to decorate his dairy in an unusual style of splendour. Near each village is a kraal, or cattle-pen, a low line of rough stones, as often oval as circular, and as often polygonal as oval. The different settlements are inhabited, deserted, and reinhabited, according as the neighbouring lands afford scant or plentiful pasturage.

---

* A brother mason informs us, that "the Todas use a sign of recognition similar to ours, and they have discovered that Europeans have an institution corresponding with their own." Hence, he remarks, "a Toda initiated will bow to a gentleman, never to a lady."

But in our humble opinion, next to the Antiquary in simplicity of mind, capacity of belief, and capability of assertion, ranks the Freemason.

Ye who would realise the vision of the wise, respecting savage happiness and nomadic innocence —a sweet hallucination, which hitherto you have considered the wildest dream that ever issued from the Ivory Gate—go, find it in the remote corners of Toda land, the fertile, the salubrious. See Hylobius, that burly barbarian—robust in frame, blessed with the best of health, and gifted with a mind that knows but one idea—how to be happy —sunning himself, whilst his buffaloes graze upon the hill side, or wandering listlessly through the mazy forest, or enjoying his rude meal of milk and rice, or affording himself the lazy luxury of squatting away the rainy hours round his primitive hearth. What care has he for to-day: what thought of to-morrow? He has food in abundance: his and his brothers' common spouse and dubious children, make up, strange yet true, a united family; he is conscious of his own superiority, he claims and enjoys the respect of all around him. The use of arms he knows not: his convenient superstition tends only to increase his comforts here below, and finally, when Hylobius departs this transitory life, whatever others may think of his prospects, he steps fearlessly into the spirit-world, persuaded that he and his buffaloes are about to find a better climate, brighter scenes, and broader grass lands — in a word, to enjoy the fullest felicity. Contrast with this same Toda in his rude log hut amidst the giant trees, the European *pater-familias*, in his luxurious, artificial, unhappy civilized home!

But has not your picture of savage felicity its reverse?

Yes, especially when uncivilized comes into contact with semi-civilized or civilized life. Our poor barbarians led the life of hunted beasts, when Tippoo Sultan, incensed with them for being magicians and anxious to secure their brass bracelets, which he supposed were gold, sent his myrmidons into their peaceful hills. They are now in even a worse state.* The "noble unsophisticated Todas," as they were once called, have been morally ruined by collision with Europeans and their dissolute attendants. They have lost their honesty: truth is become almost unknown to them; chastity, sobriety, and temperance, fell flat before the strong temptations of rupees, foreign luxuries, and ardent spirits. Covetousness is now the mountaineer's ruling passion: the Toda is an inveterate, indefatigable beggar, whose cry, Eenam Kuroo, "give me a

* What follows alludes particularly to the Todas living in the vicinity of Ooty, Coonoor, and Kotagherry.

present!" no matter what,—money, brandy, cigars, or snuff—will follow you for miles over hill and dale: as a pickpocket, he displays considerable ingenuity; and no Moses or Levi was ever a more confirmed, determined, grasping, usurer. His wife and daughters have become vile as the very refuse of the bazaar. And what can he show in return for the loss of his innocence and happiness? True, he is no longer pursued by Tippoo, or the neighbouring Polygars: but he is persecuted by growing wants, and a covetousness which knows no bounds. He will not derive any benefit from education, nor will he give ear to a stranger's creed. From the slow but sure effects of strange diseases, the race is rapidly deteriorating*—few of the giant figures that abound in the remote hills, are to be found near our cantonments—and it is more than probable that, like other wild tribes, which the progress of civilization has swept away from the face of the earth, the Toda will, ere long, cease to have "a local habitation and a name" among the people of the East.

* The habit of intoxication is now so fatally common amongst the rising generation, that their fathers will not, it is said, initiate them into their mysteries, for fear that the secret should be divulged over the cup.

CHAPTER XIX.

KOTAGHERRY.—ADIEU TO THE BLUE MOUNTAINS.

What a detestable place this Ootacamund is during the rains!

From morning to night, and from night to morning, gigantic piles of heavy wet clouds, which look as if the aerial sprites were amusing themselves by heaping misty black Pelions upon thundering purple Ossas, rise up slowly from the direction of the much-vexed Koondahs; each, as it impinges against the west flank of the giant Dodatetta, drenching us with one of those outpourings that resemble nothing but a vast aggregation of the biggest and highest Douche baths. In the interim, a gentle drizzle, now deepening into a shower, now driven into sleet, descends with vexatious perseverance. When there is no drizzle there is a Scotch mist: when the mist clears away, it is succeeded by a London fog. The sun, "shorn of his rays," spitefully diffuses throughout the atmosphere a muggy warmth, the very reverse of genial. Conceive the effects of such weather upon the land in general, and the mind of man in particular! The surface of the mountains, for the most part, is a rich and reddish mould, easily and yet permanently affected by the least possible quantity of water. Thus the country becomes impassable, the cantonment dirty, every place wretched, every one miserable.

All the visitors have returned to the plains, all the invalids that can afford themselves the luxury, have escaped to Coonoor or Kotagherry. You feel that if you remain at Ootacamund—the affectionate "Ooty" somehow or other now sticks in your throat — you must be contented to sit between the horns of a fierce dilemma. If you stay at home you lose all the pleasure of life: if you do not, still you lose all the pleasure of life. In the former case your eyes* will suffer, your digestion become impaired, your imagination

* The faculty unanimously assert that the air of the hills is not prejudicial to those suffering from ophthalmic disease. We observed, however, that a large proportion of invalids complained of sore eyes and weakness of sight, produced, probably, by the glare of the fine season and the piercing winds of the monsoon.

fall into a hypochondriacal state, and thus you expose yourself to that earthly pandemonium, the Anglo-Indian sick bed. But should you, on the contrary, quit the house, what is the result? The roads and paths not being covered with gravel, are as slippery as a *mât de cocagne* at a French fair; at every one hundred yards your nag kneels down, or diverts himself by reclining upon his side, with your leg between him and the mud. If you walk you are equally miserable. When you cannot find a companion you sigh for one; when you can, you probably discover that he is haunted by a legion of blue devils even more furious than those that have assailed you.

It is impossible! Let us make up a party—a bachelor party—and hire a bungalow for a month or two at Kotagherry. We do not belong to the tribe of "delicate invalids," nor are our "complaints liable to be aggravated by internal congestions;" therefore we will go there as visitors, not valetudinarians.

Kotagherry, or more correctly, Kothurgherry,* stands about six thousand six hundred feet above the level of the sea, on the top of the Sreemoorga

* The "hill of the Kothurs."

Pass, upon a range of hills which may be called the commencement of the Neilgherries. The station contains twelve houses, most of them occupied by the proprietors: at this season of the year lodgings cannot always be found.

The air of Kotagherry is moister than that of Ootacamund, and the nights and mornings are not so cool. We see it to great advantage during the prevalence of the south-west monsoon. The atmosphere feels soft and balmy, teeming with a pleasant warmth, which reminds you of a Neapolitan spring, or an autumn at amene Sorrento. The roads are clean, the country is comparatively dry, and the people look comfortable. For the first few days you enjoy yourself much: now watching the heavy rain-clouds that veil the summit of Dodabetta, and thinking with pleasure of what is going on behind the mountain: now sitting in the cool verandah, with spy-glass directed towards Coimbatore, and thanking your good star that you are not one of the little body of unhappy perspirers, its inhabitants.

But is not man born with a love of change—an Englishman to be discontented—an Anglo-Indian to grumble? After a week spent at Kotagherry, you find out that it has literally nothing but climate to recommend it. The bazaar is small and bad, provisions of all kinds, except beef and mutton, must come from Ootacamund. Rich, you complain that you cannot spend your money; poor, you declaim against the ruinous rate of house-rent and living. You observe that, excepting about half a mile of level road, there is no table-land whatever in the place, and that the hill-paths are cruelly precipitous. The houses are built at considerable distances from one another—a circumstance which you testily remark, is anything but conducive to general sociability. You have neglected to call upon old Mrs. A——, who supplies the station with milk and butter from her own dairy, consequently that milk and butter are cut off, and therefore the Kotagherryites conclude and pronounce that you are a very bad young man. Finally, you are *sans* books, *sans* club, *sans* balls, *sans* everything,—except the will and the way, of getting away from Kotagherry, which you do without delay.

The determined economist, nothing daunted by the miseries of solitude and fleas, finds Dimhutty *

* The termination "hutty," so common in the names of the hill villages, is used to denote a Berger settlement, as "mund" means a Toda hamlet.

afford him ample opportunities for exercising his craft. The little cluster of huts, from which the place derives its name, lies in a deep hollow about a mile north of Kotagherry; it is sheltered from the cold southerly winds by a steep hill, and consequently the climate is at least three degrees warmer than that of its neighbour. Originally it was a small station, consisting of five or six thatched cottages belonging to a missionary society: they were afterwards bought by Mr. Lushington, then Governor of Madras. That gentleman also built a large substantial house, with an upper floor, and spared no expense to make it comfortable, as the rafters which once belonged to Tippoo Sultan's palace testify. When he left the hills, he generously placed all these tenements at the disposal of government, for the use of "persons who really stand in need of lodging on their first arrival." The climate of Dimhutty has been pronounced highly beneficial to hepatic patients, and those who suffer from mercurial rheumatism. Dr. Baikie, a great authority, recommends it for the purpose of a "Subordinate Sanitarium for European soldiers." The unhappy cottages, however, after having been made the subject of many a lengthy Rule and Regulation, have at last been suffered to sink into artistic masses of broken wall and torn thatch, and the large bungalow now belongs to some Parsee firm established at Ootacamund.

Three miles beyond and below Dimhutty stretches a long wide ravine, called the Orange Valley, from the wild trees which formerly flourished there. The climate is a mixture between the cold of the hills and the heat of the plains : and the staple produce of the place appears to be white ants.

St. Katherine's Falls, the market village of Jackanary, Kodanad or the Seven Mile Tope,* and beyond it the sacred Neilgherry Hill are the only spots near Kotagherry, with whose nomenclature Fame is at all acquainted. But as one and all of them are equally uninteresting, we are disposed to be merciful and to waive description.

The present appears as good as any other time and place for a few remarks upon the climate of the Neilgherries, and a list of the travellers whose footsteps and pens preceded ours.

The mean annual temperature of Ootacamund is 58° 68′, about 30° lower than that of the low country on the Coimbatore and Mysore sides.

* Or tuft : it is so called from a clump of trees which crowns the ridge of a high hill.

The average fall of water is forty-five inches in the year; there are nineteen days of heavy rain; of showers with fair intervals, eighty-seven; cloudy, twenty-one; and two hundred and thirty-eight perfectly fair and bright.* Frost generally appears about the beginning of November, and ends with February; in the higher ranges of the hills ice an inch and a-half thick is commonly seen.

The first and most obvious effect of the Neilgherry climate on invalids is to repel the blood from the surface, and to throw it on the internal organs, by constricting the vessels of the skin and decidedly checking perspiration and transpiration. The liver, viscera, head and lungs are affected by this unequal distribution of the circulation, the effect being increased in the case of the respiratory organs by the rarefaction of the mountain air. The digestive powers seldom keep pace with the increase of appetite which generally manifests itself, and unless the laws of diet are obeyed to the very letter, dyspepsia, colic, and other more obstinate complaints, will be the retributive punishment for the infraction. Strangers frequently

* The Neilgherries are exposed to the violence of both monsoons, the south-west and the north-east. The fall of rain during the latter is, however, comparatively trifling.

suffer from sleeplessness, cold feet, and violent headaches.

When no actual organic disease exists, and when the constitutional powers are not permanently debilitated, Nature soon restores the balance by means of slight reaction. Invalids are strongly advised on first arrival to be particularly cautious about their hours, their diet, their clothing, and their exercise. They should avoid exposure to the night air, and never, indeed, be out after sunset: the reduction of temperature which follows the disappearance of the sun must be felt to be understood, and no one residing here for the sake of health would expose himself to the risk of catching an obstinate cold by quitting a crowded room to return home through the nocturnal chills. Medical men advise the very delicate to wait till the sun has driven away the cold and moisture of the dawn before they venture out, and to return from their morning walks or drives in time to avoid the effects of the direct rays, which are most powerful about 9 A.M. But in regulating hours regard must of course be had to previous modes of life, and the obstinate early riser of the plains should gradually, not suddenly, alter his Indian for English habits. The diet of valetudinarians on the first ascent ought in a great degree to be regulated by circumstances depending on the nature of each individual's complaint. In general, they are told to prefer light animal and farinaceous food, eschewing pastry, vegetables, and cheese, and to diminish the quantity of such stimulants as wine, spirits, and beer, till the constitution has become acclimatized. In all cases, of whatever description they may be, warm clothing is a *sine quâ non:* every valetudinarian should, as he values his life, be provided with a stock of good flannels, worsted socks, stout shoes, and thick, solid boots. Exercise is another essential part of regimen at the Sanitarium. Riding is considered more wholesome than walking, especially on first arrival, as less liable to accelerate the circulation, to produce a feeling of constriction in the chest, and to expose the body to chills. The quantum of exercise should be increased by slow degrees, and when convalescence has fairly set in, the invalid is advised to pass as much of his time in the open air, during daylight, as his strength will permit him to do.

To conclude the subject of climate. It cannot be too strongly impressed upon the minds of our fellow-countrymen in Southern and Western India, that in cases of actual organic disease, or when the debility of the constitution is very great, serious and permanent mischief is to be dreaded from the climate of these mountains. Many an officer has lost his life by preferring the half measure of a medical certificate to the Neilgherries to a home furlough on sick leave. The true use of the Sanitarium is to recruit a constitution that has been weakened to some extent by a long residence in the plains, or to afford a change of air and scene when the mind, as frequently happens in morbific India, requires some stimulus to restore its normal vigour.

The Rev. Mr. Hough was, as we said before, the first pen that called the serious attention of the Anglo-Indian community to the value of the Neilgherry Hills. His letters to the Hurkaru newspaper were published in a collected form in 1829. Five years afterwards Captain Mignan, of the Bombay army, sent forth a little volume, entitled "Notes extracted from a Private Journal written during a Tour through a part of Malabar and among the Neilgherries." The style appears to be slightly tinged with bile, as if the perusal of Mr. Hough's flowery descriptions of the mountain scenery had formed splendid anticipations which were by no means realised. The *brochure* is now quite out of date: the bazaar, rates, roads, postage, rent, and number of houses — all are changed, only remain the wretched state of the police therein chronicled, and the "fatal facility" of finding bad servants. In the same year (1834) Dr. Baikie's well known book,* entitled "Observations on the Neilgherries, including an Account of their Topography, Climate, Soil, and Productions," issued from the Calcutta press. The original edition consisted, we believe, of only five hundred copies, and we cannot but wonder that the book has not yet enjoyed the honour of a reprint. Lieut. H. Jervis, of H. M. 62nd regiment, published by subscription, also in 1834, and dedicated to Mr. Lushington, the governor, a "Narrative of a Journey to the Falls of Cavery, with an Historical and Descriptive Account

* It commences with a *résumé* of the peculiarities of the hills, and accounts of the three great stations; proceeds to a description of the geography and geology, soil and productions, botany, zoology, and the inhabitants of the Neilgherries, and discusses at some length the effects of the climate upon the European constitution, sound as well as impaired. The Appendix presents a mass of information valuable enough when the work was published, but now, with the exception of the meteorological and other tables, too old to be useful. Thirteen or fourteen years work mighty changes, moral and physical, in an Anglo-India settlement.

of the Neilgherry Hills."* The book contains a curious letter from Mr. Bannister, who states that, after a careful analysis of the Neilgherry water, he was surprised to find no trace whatever of saline, earthy, or metallic substance in it.

In 1844-5, Captain H. Congreve, an officer in the Madras Artillery, wrote in the "Madras Spectator," the Letters upon the subject of the Hills and their inhabitants, to which we alluded in our last chapter. His pages are, in our humble opinion, disfigured by a richness of theory which palls upon the practical palate, but the amount of observation and curious lore which they contain makes us regret that the talented author has left his labours to lie *perdus* in the columns of a newspaper. Also, in 1844, a valuable Report on the Medical Topography and Statistics of the Neilgherry Hills, with notices of the geology, botany, climate and population, tables of diseases amongst officers, ladies, children, native convicts, etc., and maps of the country compiled from the records of the Medical Board Office, were published, by order of Government, at Madras.

* The book contains one hundred and forty-four pages, enlivened with a dozen lithographed sketches, and NOT enlivened by descriptions of Poonamalee, Vellore, Laulpett, Bangalore, and Closepett.

In 1847, when we left the Hills, a Mr. Lowry, who had charge of the Ootacamund English Free School, was preparing to print a "Guide to, and Handbook of, the Neilgherries, containing brief and succinct accounts of the same, with statements of the accommodations there to be found, rents of houses, expense of living, and other particulars useful to visitors and residents." We were favoured with a sight of the MS., and found that it did what it professed to do—no small feat for a Handbook, by the bye.

There is a great variety of papers and reports upon particular topics connected with the Neilgherries, published in the different literary journals and transactions of learned societies. The principal works which elucidate minor details, are those of the Rev. Mr. Schmidt, upon the Botany of the Hills, and the language of its inhabitants; the "Description* of a singular aboriginal race, inhabiting the summit of the Neilgherries, or the Blue Mountains of Coimbatore," by Captain Henry Hark-

* A little volume of one hundred and seventy-five pages, containing graphic sketches of the scenery, excellent accounts of the different tribes of hill people, a weather-table from July to December, 1829, the height of the principal mountains, and a short and meagre vocabulary of the Toda language.

ness, of the Madras Army; and Notices upon the Ornithology of this interesting region, by T. C. Jerdon, Esq., of the Madras medical establishment.

And now for our valediction.

We found little difficulty in persuading the officer to whose care and skill the charge of our precious health was committed, to report that we were fit for duty long before the expiration of the term of leave granted at Bombay; so we prepared at once for a return-trip per steamer—it would require *æs triplex* indeed about the cardiac region to dare the dangers and endure the discomforts of a coasting voyage, in a sailing vessel, northwards, in the month of September—"over the water to Charley," as the hero of Scinde was familiarly designated by those serving under him.

We started our luggage yesterday on bullock and coolie back. The morning is muggy, damp, and showery: as we put our foot in stirrup, a huge wet cloud obscures the light of day, and hastens to oblige us with a farewell deluging. Irritated by the pertinacious viciousness of Pluvian Jove, we ride slowly along the slippery road which bounds the east confines of the lake, and strike off to the right hand, just in time to meet, face to face, the drift of rain which sails on the wings of the wind along the skirt of that—Dodabetta. Gradually we lose sight of the bazaar, the church, the Windermere, the mass of bungalows. Turning round upon the saddle, we cast one last scowl upon Ootacamund, not, however, without a grim smile of joy at the prospect of escaping from it.

Adieu . . . . .! Farewell . . . . land of . . . . .! May every . . . .! May . . . .! And when . . . . . ., so may . . . . as thou hast . . . . . ourselves!

To the industry of an imaginative reader we leave the doubtlessly agreeable task of filling up the hiatus in whatever manner the perusal of our modest pages may suggest to his acuteness and discernment. As some clue to the mazy wanderings of our own ideas, we may mention that we were, during the solemn moment of valediction, exposed to such weather as has rarely been the fate of man, with the exception of Deucalion and other diluvian celebrities, to experience in this stormy world.

THE END.

A FIGURATIVE PLAN OF THE CITY OF GOA.

Taken on the Spot, comprehending a Space of Ground of about one mile and a half from East to West and three quarters of a mile from North to South

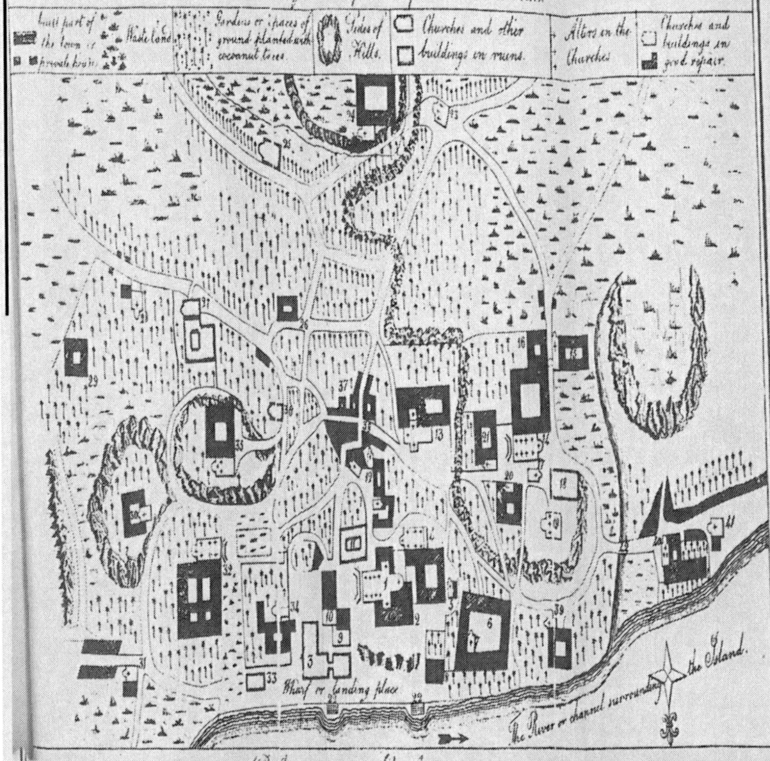

References and Explanations

1 Cathedral.
2 Archiepiscopal palace.
3 Palace of the Viceroy in ruins
4 Church and Convent of St. Francis.
5 Chapel of St. Catherine
6 Arsenal.
7 Chapel of the 5 wounds in the Arsenal.
8 Archbishops Prison or Aljuvar.
9 Senate house.
10 Old Senate house, now an hospital.
11 Inquisition in ruins.
12 3 Churches & houses of Misericordia
13 Church and house of Bom Jesus with the shrine of St. Francis Xavier.
14 Church & convent of St. Augustine.
15 College of the Augustinians.
16 Noviciate of the same.
17 Chapel of St. Antony of Padua.
18 College of St. Roc in ruins.
19 Collegiate and parochial church of the Rosary.
20 Nunnery of St. Monica.
21 Convent & church of St. John of God.
22 Landing Stairs.
23 Collegiate & parochial church of Luz belonging to & adjoining the convent of the priests of the congregation
25 parochl. church of the Bd. Trinity in ruins
26 Old city Hospital almost abandoned.
27 Ch. & college of St. Paul in ruins
28 parochial ch. of St. Thomas Ap.
29 Hospital of St. Lazarus.
30 Church & house of N. Senhora Lelmonte
31 parochial church of St. Lucia.
32 Church & convent of St. Dominic
33 Old Custom house in ruins
34 Church & convent of St. Cayetan.
35 and ch. & convent of the Carmelites now college of the priests of the congregation
36 parroch. ch. of St. Alexius in ruins.
37 Slaughter house.
38 Bazaar.
39 College of St. Bonaventure bel. to the order of the Franciscans.
40 College of St. Thomas Aquinas belonging to the Dominicans in the suburb of Pannely.
41 parochial Church of St. Peter in the suburb of Pannely.
42 Bridge over the ditch the waters of which flow from the Hills.

W. Jones Sculpt. Madras